Jamaat-e-Islami Women in Pakistan

Gender and Globalization
Susan S. Wadley, *Series Editor*

Other titles in the Gender and Globalization series

*Bodies That Remember: Women's Indigenous Knowledge
and Cosmopolitanism in South Asian Poetry*
Anita Anantharam

Family, Gender, and Law in a Globalizing Middle East and South Asia
Kenneth M. Cuno and Manisha Desai, eds.

*From Patriarchy to Empowerment: Women's Participation, Movements,
and Rights in the Middle East, North Africa, and South Asia*
Valentine M. Moghadam, ed.

Hijab and the Republic: Uncovering the French Headscarf Debate
Bronwyn Winter

*Imperial Citizen: Marriage and Citizenship
in the Ottoman Frontier Provinces of Iraq*
Karen M. Kern

Lines in Water: Religious Boundaries in South Asia
Eliza F. Kent and Tazim R. Kassam, eds.

Policing Egyptian Women: Sex, Law, and Medicine in Khedival Egypt
Liat Kozma

*Super Girls, Gangstas, Freeters, and Xenomaniacs:
Gender and Modernity in Global Youth Cultures*
Susan Dewey and Karen J. Brison, eds.

*Transforming Faith: The Story of Al-Huda
and Islamic Revivalism among Urban Pakistani Women*
Sadaf Ahmad

Jamaat-e-Islami Women in Pakistan

VANGUARD OF A NEW MODERNITY?

Amina Jamal

Syracuse University Press

For a listing of books published and distributed by Syracuse University Press,
visit our website at SyracuseUniversityPress.syr.edu.

ISBN: 978-0-8156-3327-3 (cloth)   978-0-8156-5237-3 (e-book)

Library of Congress Cataloging-in-Publication Data

Jamal, Amina.
Jamaat-e-Islami women in Pakistan : vanguard of a new modernity? /
Amina Jamal. — First edition.
pages cm. — (Gender and globalization)
Includes bibliographical references and index.
ISBN 978-0-8156-3327-3 (cloth : alk. paper) 1. Muslim women—
Political activity—Pakistan   2. Feminism—Religous aspects—Islam.
3. Jama'at-i Islami-yi Pakistan.   I. Title.
HQ1170.J355 2013
305.48'697—dc23   2013029674

Manufactured in the United States of America

To my parents,
Maulana Jamal Mian
of Firangi Mahal (d. November 2012)
and Kaniz Fatima Asar
of Rudauli Sharif (d. December 2009),
and their spiritual ancestors in gratitude
for their interminable prayers
and unconditional blessings.

Amina Jamal is associate professor of sociology at Ryerson University, Toronto, Canada. Claiming social, political, cultural, and affective ties to Canada, India, Bangladesh, and Pakistan, her work straddles the domains of contemporary transnational feminist social and political theories and the rich spiritual, philosophical, and political heritage of Islam and Muslims in South Asia.

Contents

Acknowledgments ❀ *ix*

Introduction
Transnational Identities and Religious-Political Modernities ❀ *1*

1. Newly Emerging Subjects
Feminism, Islamic Feminism, and Post-Islamic Feminism ❀ *46*

2. The Spaces of the Public-Religious ❀ *70*

3. Politics of Morality ❀ *113*

4. Vanguard of a New Modernity?
Cultural Politics in a Postcolonial State ❀ *136*

5. Gender and Development and Its Discontents
Jamaat Women and the "Woman Question" in Pakistan ❀ *170*

6. To Forbid Evil and Enjoin Virtue
Creating Moral Citizens ❀ *208*

7. Conclusion
Gendered Selves, Modernist Trajectories, and Community Building ❀ *250*

Appendix ❀ *267*

Glossary ❀ *271*

Bibliography ❀ *277*

Index ❀ *291*

Acknowledgments

I am grateful to many friends, relatives, and research assistants for helping me complete this book. Although I take responsibility for the content and ideas, I owe my insights to several mentors: Professor Kari Dehli, OISE-University of Toronto, Professor Sherene Razack, OISE-University of Toronto, and Professor Homa Hoodfar, Concordia University Montreal, contributed to the development of my ideas, arguments, and claims; my brothers Bari Mian and Mahmood Jamal guided me in the dense terrain of Islamic mystical thought and poetry; and my friends Sheryl Nestel, Jane Ku, and Almas Zakiuddin provided lively debate and discussion.

I am grateful for a generous postdoctoral fellowship from the Social Sciences and Humanities Research Council of Canada and support from Concordia University, which enabled me to conduct research for this project. I benefited immensely from the funding provided by Ryerson University for research assistants, editing, and numerous important tasks related to compiling a manuscript. I take this opportunity to once again express my appreciation to my research assistants, Hanan Harb and Melissa Chung, for their meticulous work. A special thanks is due to Jehan Shibli for many hours of volunteer support with editing and proofreading.

I am intellectually indebted to Professor Vali Reza Nasr, Dean and Professor of International Relations at Johns Hopkins University, for his groundbreaking work on the Jamaat-e-Islami. It is from him that I have borrowed the concept of the Vanguard and its implications for Jamaat-e-Islami women. I am grateful to Professor Nasr and to the University of California Press for permission to use material from S. V. R. Nasr, *The Vanguard of the Islamic Revolution: The Jama'at-I Islami of Pakistan* (Berkeley and Los Angeles: Univ. of California Press, 1994).

I am also indebted to Mary Selden Evans, executive editor of Syracuse University Press, for her support of my work. I also acknowledge the insightful comments of those anonymous reviewers of my manuscript who were able to recognize and appreciate the worth of my analysis at a critical moment in the interrelationship of Islam, the West, gender, and modernity.

Some of the chapters in this book include material and ideas that were previously published in journal articles or book chapters. For these reprints/adaptations I would like to acknowledge: Taylor & Francis, UK, www.tandonline.com for "Just between Us: Identity and Representation among Muslim Women," *Inter Asia Cultural Studies Journal* 12, no. 2 (2010): 202–12; and "To Enjoin Virtue and Restrain Vice: Modernizing Discourses and Engendered Traditions in Pakistan's Jamaat-e-Islami," *Totalitarian Movements and Political Religions* 11, nos. 3/4 (2010): 327–40. Palgrave Macmillan for "Gendered Islam and Modernity in the Nation-Space," *Feminist Review*, no. 91 (February 2009): 9–28; and "Feminist 'Selves' and Feminism's 'Others': Feminist Representations of Jamaat-e-Islami Women in Pakistan," *Feminist Review*, no. 81 (November 2005): 52–73. Indiana University Press for my Book Review Essay of three works: "Politics of Piety: The Islamic Revival and the Feminist Subject," "An Enchanted Modern: Gender and Public Piety in Shi'i Lebanon," and "Performing Islam: Gender and Ritual in Iran," *Journal of Middle East Women's Studies* 4, no. 3 (2008): 121–28. Duke University Press for "Global Discourses, Situated Traditions, and Women's Agency in Pakistan," in *South Asian Feminisms: Feminisms for the Present Theory and Activism in South Asia*, ed. Ania Loomba and Ritty Lukose (Durham: Duke Univ. Press, 2012). Koninklijke Brill NV for "Overview: Women, Gender, Islam and Modernities," in *Encyclopedia of Women and Islamic Cultures*, vol. 5, ed. Suad Joseph (Leiden: Koninklijke Brill NV, 2007), 209–15.

I owe profuse thanks to the women leaders of the Jamaat-e-Islami in Pakistan for sharing with me their valuable time, their ideas and resources, and their kind hospitality.

Finally, I thank those who have sustained me affectively and socially in Canada, Pakistan, and Abu Dhabi, including many whom I have not been able to name here, and some whom I must mention: Mahrukh Hashim,

Sadia Ali, Humo Jamal, Allu Jamal, Farida Jamal, Shaheena Hafeez, Raana Rahim, Nusrat Jameel, Shahana Agha, Ayesha Shibli, and Fatima Majid. And of course I could not have survived without the emotional and intellectual support of my nested family: Ahmed, Zaid, and Mariam.

Jamaat-e-Islami Women in Pakistan

Introduction

Transnational Identities and Religious-Political Modernities

Growing up in Pakistan in the 1960s and 1970s, many of us from purdah-observing families (those practicing women's seclusion), spent our girlhood energies challenging our parents' attempts to impose the burqa (the head and/or face-covering veil now popularly known as hijab).[1] We considered the burqa particularly unacceptable in the modern public space of the English medium school that some of us attended.[2]

Our imaginations were rich with what I might now call "purdah narratives," which are similar to harem narratives and some, more recently produced by Muslim women, escape-from-Islam narratives.[3] These purdah narratives are accounts, often written in English but also in local

1. Purdah as practiced in South Asia refers to a variety of rituals related to women's seclusion, which include forms of veiling such as the burqa or chadar, but cannot be reduced to notions of veiling or hijab or even modesty.

2. "English medium" refers to the language in which instruction is imparted; this term is also an important marker of class and cultural affiliation in Pakistan. A legacy of British colonial rule, Pakistan's education system is a two-tiered one; private schools provide education in English and "Urdu medium" schools, mostly state-run, provide education in Urdu.

3. The term "harem narratives" have been used by feminists to refer to modernist stories by women about their lives in the harem, and I draw on this topology to use the term "escape-from-Islam" to define the spate of narratives by Muslim women such as Irshad Manji, Ayan Hirsi Ali, Azer Nafisi, and others. In using this term I suggest that these narratives are mainly written to titillate a primarily Western audience with an

1

languages such as Urdu, of the intrepid travels of elite women from the private sphere of seclusion in an aristocratic Muslim family to the public space of nationalist politics in pre- and post-independence South Asia (Ikramullah 1963; Shahnawaz 1971; Jung 1987). Like the journeys we imagined and all journeys launched at the intersection of Islam, gender, and modernity, most of these biographies, autobiographies, and memoirs need to be read as not simply spatial but also temporal, since they invariably signify the gendered subject's change in location from a zone of tradition and culture to "modernity." Through revisiting these school days with my sisters and cousins, I became aware of another layer of complexity as I came to understand the raucous alterity signified by the burqa in our school, which prided itself on being one of the modern national institutions for the education of girls in the developing nation-state. We were rebelling against the potential of the burqa to instantly lower us in social class and relegate us to the culturally left behind.

Beginning the research for this book, I had a general sense of curiosity, shared with many other Muslim feminist scholars, as to why contemporary Muslim women would opt for practices that I considered to be constraining of freedom and autonomy, especially veiling and purdah. And like some other Muslim feminists writing about veiled Muslim women (Mahmood 2005; Shehabuddin 2008; Ahmad 2009), my interest in publicly religious women such as those of the Jamaat-e-Islami (Party of Islam) began from a space that is seen to be the domain of secular feminism in South Asia. Even though, unlike some other feminists, I was familiar with and able to understand the strong emotional and spiritual force of religious devotion, I was intrigued as to why Muslim women in South Asia would seek out what appeared to me to be unfamiliar and overly prescriptive discourses of Islam rather than other, more easily available, understandings of scriptural texts. Traditional or classical Sunni Islam in South Asia, sometimes referred to as "Barelvi" and/or "Sufi" Islam today, is heavily influenced by Islamic mysticism, tends to be tolerant of diverse

---

adventure story about the protagonist's imprisonment in the cultural premodernity of Islam and subsequent escape to Western modernity and its freedoms.

devotional practices and cultural influences, and is more flexible about notions of gendered modesty. The Barelvi form of faith and practice was given institutional status through the efforts of Ahmed Reza Barelvi, who started a movement in the 1880s to safeguard classical Islam against attacks from reformist and modernist movements like the Ahl-e-Hadith of Deoband. It had followed a largely quietist path in Pakistan until the 1980s, when Barelvis started organizing to counter the rising influence and sectarian violence of their main Sunni opponents, the Deobandis and Saudi-backed Wahabis. While the women I discuss in this book are associated with the Jamaat-e-Islami, a party that does not affiliate itself with any of these groups, they share an ideology closely aligned with the puritanical and reformist elements of both Deobandis and Wahabis.[4]

A variety of religiously based women's groups with widely differing constituencies are presently noticeable at different levels in contemporary urban societies in Pakistan. In this book I focus on the political and cultural activism of women in the Jamaat-e-Islami, which is one of the most significant politico-religious groups in Pakistan. The Jamaat-e-Islami is a movement for moral reform of Muslims that was set up by Maulana Abul Ala Maududi in 1941 in British colonial India. Maududi wanted to reconstruct faith or piety as a system that could resist colonial cultural dominance and also distinguish Muslims from an emergent Hindu nation (Reza Nasr 1996; Jalal 2002). The Jamaat-e-Islami has a wide appeal among Muslim men and women not only in South Asia, East Asia, and the Middle East, but also Europe, especially the United Kingdom, and North America (Reza Nasr 1996; Grare 2001). In Pakistan the Jamaat-e-Islami gained ascendance

---

4. For a good discussion of classical Islam in South Asia and the emergence of the Barelvi movement, see: Usha Sanyal, *Ahmad Riza Khan Barelwi: In the Path of the Prophet: Makers of the Muslim World* (Oxford: Oneworld, 2005). Also see: Gregory C. Doxlowski, "Devotional Islam and Politics in British India: Ahmad Riza Khan Barelwi and His Movement, 1870–1920," *The Journal of the American Oriental Society* 119, no. 4 (1999): 707–9. "Wahabism" is the popular term for an austere mode of Islam imposed on Arab society and later on other Muslims through an ideological alliance in the eighteenth century between the reformer Mohammed Ibn Abdul Wahab and the Al Saud family that rules the kingdom of Saudi Arabia.

in politics after 1977 amid the backdrop of the US-Soviet proxy war in Afghanistan. During that period the military dictatorship of Pakistani President General Zia-ul-Haq enlisted the help of Jamaat leaders in promoting the war, at home and in other Muslim societies, as a form of jihad or moral struggle (Rashid 2001; Jalal 2008). General Zia also incorporated Jamaat leaders into his nominated parliament, where they provided legitimacy for his sweeping political and legal measures aimed at imposing a puritanical version of Islam on Pakistani society. With the help of its influence in the military, and those it considers to be true Islamic political forces, the Jamaat seeks to institutionalize a mode of Islamic life that is closer to the Wahabi-inspired legalistic tradition that prevails in Saudi Arabia and some other Middle Eastern societies. In this process it tends to undermine the devotional and mystical traditions of Islam, associated with the teachings of Sufi masters and saints that have thrived in South Asian societies for centuries. In Pakistan's large urban centers, the Jamaat-e-Islami has acquired a following among women, mostly of the middle classes, who are inspired by modern Islamic revivalism, but who seek a moderate way between what they consider to be overly restrictive practices of many Muslim groups and what they reject as the ultra-modern culture of the elite classes. Although its membership is limited and it does not draw significant electoral support, the political-cultural project of the Jamaat permeates many of the symbolic moves and formal measures toward official Islamization undertaken at significant moments by various governments in Pakistan in an attempt to placate the so-called religious forces. It is in recognition of this influence that I decided to focus on the Jamaat-e-Islami in my quest to understand the seeming resurgence of "Islam" among Pakistani women.

I understood the strength and value of religious and community ties and did not want my project to replicate a dichotomy, prevalent in feminist literature on Islamist women, of "pious Muslim women" and "nonpious women"/"sinful" feminists.[5] Furthermore, I considered it important to

5. Here I invoke the poignant use of *gunahgaar* (sinful) subjectivity as a common strategy by Muslim poets, writers, and mystics seeking to underline the ethical egoism and intolerance that upholds constructions of "the pious self."

go beyond recent attempts by secular/critical scholarship that approaches Islam as a "discursive tradition" to explain the seemingly incomprehensible bodily practices of Muslims to mostly Western scholarly audiences (e.g., Mahmood 2005; Deeb 2006; Iqtidar 2011). Talal Asad's arguments for studying Islam as a discursive tradition problematize methodologies that approach Islam as a static, homogenous, and ahistorical entity (Asad 1986). Asad also invokes the idea of Islam as a discursive tradition to refute the argument that contemporary Islamism is a modern formation and a mode of cultural nationalism whose emergence is directly linked to the histories of colonialism and ideas of Western modernist social and political thought. Indeed Asad and, following him, other scholars such as Mahmood and Deeb suggest that secular concepts of agency and subjectivity related to modern social realities of state and nation are ineffective for understanding agentive actions of Islamists (Asad 2003; Mahmood 2005; Deeb 2006). While acknowledging the motivation of these scholars to challenge hegemonic modes of representation, it is important to point out that approaching Islam as a discursive tradition precludes important Islamic subjectivities related to pre-discursive, affective, and intuitive modes of self-formation.[6] It disregards the faith and experiences of millions of Muslims, possibly the majority of the world's Muslims, whose self-construction and religious practices hinge on precognitive, nondiscursively transmitted and affective knowledge. In this tradition it is not discourses, practices, or dispositions, but rather affective and intuitive conditions and states in which knowing/being are inseparable, that are important for comprehending how Muslims become Muslims. As I discuss in chapter 6, this is the experience of the vast majority of Muslims of different social classes and in diverse regions of South Asia; these mystical dimensions of Islam involving intercessionary practices, shrine veneration, mystical poetry and music, and radiated affects are frequently

6. The concept of "nontransmitted knowledge" or "knowledge of the heart" was expounded in different ways by Abu Ghazzali (1058–1111) and Muhiuddin Ibn Arabi (1165–1240). For a detailed account of Ibn Al Arabi's metaphysics, which pervades South Asian Islam, see William Chittick 1989. For a related South Asian Islamic tradition, see Ernst and Lawrence 2002.

(mis)labeled under the all-encompassing term "Sufism." For those of us whose gendered religious subjectivities have been, and are, formed in and through the historically and culturally specific intertwining of spirit, belief, and body, I placed an importance on bringing together the Sufi-inspired condition of (human) being with the politics of being a Muslim. More important, some of the scholarship that approaches Islam through notions of a discursive tradition displays a marked tendency to rely on texts and traditions that reflect the more puritanical and dogmatic inter-pretations of Islam's discourses that have been adopted by many contem-porary Islamist movements.[7] This involves the risk of centralizing certain discourses, dispositions, and practices that many South Asians associate with the (nineteenth-century South Asian reformist) Deobandi, or even the (official Saudi) Wahabi, schools of Sunni Islamic thought. Both these schools, which have achieved almost sectarian status in contemporary Pakistan, are at variance with other more historically widespread schol-arly and popular Islamic traditions in South Asia.

In this book I situate the Jamaat-e-Islami Women's Wing and the Jamaat women's moral self-cultivation within and against the historical formation of Islam in South Asia, a formation that is historically dynamic and flexible, with important social, cultural, and material effects on the lives of Muslim women (Jalal 2008; Alam 2004; Jalal 2002; Said Khan 1994). While I respect and understand the religious, and at times anti-imperialist, underpinnings of the Jamaat women's project, I do so as a Muslim woman who does not identify with what is referred to as Islamist politics, a position within which the religious politics of Jamaat women can be situated. I use the term "Islamist," as does the extant literature on political Islam, to underline the political and ideological, rather than sim-ply "religious," character of movements such as the Jamaat-e-Islami. It also draws attention to their attempts to redefine Islam (faith and belief) into a system of moral prescriptions and correct practices by yoking the Sha-riah (Islam's guiding principles) with political power (Esposito and Burgat

---

7. For example, as I point out in chapter 6, Asad and Mahmood privilege the ideas of the puritanical Hanbali scholar Ibn Taymiyya to represent Muslim "pious" subjectivity.

2003; Reza Nasr 1996). In the South Asian context the use of the term "Islamist," in contrast with "Islamic," is a useful way to signal a divergence from the region's traditional devotional and intercessionary practices of Islam as well as from the objectives of nineteenth-century movements for Islamic modernism that attempted to reconcile Islam and colonial modernity mostly by progressive reinterpretations of Islamic prescriptions.

Entanglement of Feminism and Fundamentalism in Pakistan

Islamic identity, while not always put forward as an impediment, has usually been assumed by the writers of Muslim women's emancipation narratives to be in need of redefinition to successfully bridge what we might now refer to as traditional notions of tradition and traditional notions of modernity. Indeed, many Muslim women have written of their negotiation of the private/public divide in the early and mid-twentieth century as indicative not of a conflict between Islam and modernity but as evidence of the possibility of enlightened, even modern, interpretations of Islam. The underlying demand of such Islamic modernism was for new readings of Islam that would redeem its essentially progressive nature and thus open limitless possibilities for women's interchange with the modern world. Muslim women writing about their lives in the early and mid-twentieth century presented their narratives as testimonies to the enlightened nature of Islam, which permitted the kinds of engagement with modernity that could allow a Muslim woman to value her religion and culture and yet access such fruits of modernity as secular education and public mobility (Ikramullah 1963; Shahnawaz 1971).[8] In other words, elite modernizing Muslim women argued that Islam provided, within itself, possibilities for intercourse with the modern world and was, in spirit, fully compatible with modern citizenship.

---

8. Pakistan was created in 1947 through the partition of India in response to the demands of a political movement of modernizing nationalist Muslim leaders. Many Muslim women were enabled to participate in public politics through involvement in the "Pakistan Movement."

In the 1950s and 1960s, as the nationalist modernizers in Pakistan fully imbibed the discourses of global modernization theory, there was no longer much need to make the case that Islam must keep pace with the needs of modern society.[9] A modernist reinterpretation of religion was seen as an unquestionable prerequisite for the emancipation first of middle-class women and later for the rest of the female population. An unarticulated but central idea of this philosophy was the construction of a modern Muslim women's identity in ways that made some previous markers, such as purdah, redundant in a newly imagined public nation-space that could claim to be termed "secular."[10] Implicit in this always-contested and never-completed project of womanhood was an idea that the proper place for religion, and thus for purdah and veiling, was the (lower) middle-class family and its private spaces, which had yet to imbibe the development ideology.

At the start of the twenty-first century, the guiding principles of Muslim women's emancipation-as-unveiled mobility in public life are being put to the test as larger numbers of lower- and middle-class university-educated women move into the social-political space of Pakistan's crowded urban centers and even its portals of political representation. As in many Muslim societies, many of these women are not, as once expected, casting off the tropes of culture and religion, but rather defiantly taking them along as symbols of a revitalized Islamic identity. Muslim women's political journey once epitomized as the move "from purdah to parliament" (Ikramullah 1963) may now be described as purdah *in* parliament.

Islamist women who enter into nationalist politics claim, in significant numbers, the modern to be Islamic, and no longer need to justify their entry into public politics with modernist reinterpretations of Islam. In

9. For elitism in the modernizing project, see Rashid and Shaheed 1993. Reforms in divorce and marriage laws undertaken by many Muslims states, including Pakistan, such as the Muslim Family Laws Ordinance of 1961, were part of the effort to bring Islam up to date with modern citizenship.

10. I am drawing here on the recent insights of Talal Asad, Partha Chatterjee, David Scott, and others who have problematized "the secular" as a time-space produced through the class-consolidating, gendered, and colonial practices of modern state power.

the past decade a number of feminist scholars in Pakistan have attempted to theorize this phenomenon, sometimes deploring the undermining of secularism (Zia 2009; Said Khan 1994), sometimes acknowledging the significance of religion in women's lives (Shaheed 1998). An important issue that remains to be underscored is that religiously identified movements seem to have accelerated some of the very objectives for which Pakistani women's groups have long fought and attained with limited success. Movements for Islamic renewal and reform, especially those with an overtly political agenda, facilitated the insertion of large numbers of Muslim women of the middle and lower middle classes in political and economic spaces in a manner that the women's movements never imagined. Thus, while not a realization of the feminist project of gender equality, there is nonetheless a hitherto unseen presence of headscarf-clad women as factory workers, shop clerks, immigration officers, and municipal representatives in Pakistan's urban spaces.[11] Although only a minority of such women engage in formal politics, those who join politico-religious parties such as the Jamaat-e-Islami are strident critics of the claims of the women's movement to represent "Pakistani women" in local and national political bodies. Women members of politico-religious parties are also most vocal in undermining the authoritative claims of the nongovernment organization (NGO) movements to define Muslim women's social and economic priorities. This confrontation frequently translates into the familiar conflict of "feminism versus fundamentalism," which invariably elides into dichotomous politics of secular versus religious, Islamic tradition versus Westernized modernists, and so on.

There is a need to reorient Muslim feminist scholarship in South Asia toward a critical scrutiny of the multiple negotiations and newly reconstituted entanglements of the secular and religious that is subsumed in

---

11. I am not suggesting that all these women are influenced directly by the politico-religious parties, but there is no doubt that the contemporary emergence of veiling in Pakistan is linked to the changed social and cultural terrain due to the influence of these movements.

the feminism versus fundamentalism framework; this is in addition to existing accounts that have engaged separately with Islamism and feminism. Important studies of agency and subject formation among women in Islamist movements by Muslim postcolonial feminist scholars (Baykan 1990; Ahmed 1992; Gole 1997; Badran 1999; Mahmood 2005), although a good starting point, need to be developed beyond their comparison with secular feminism, and situated also within the specific historical and cultural conditions of Islam in South Asia. This necessitates a feminist space clearing for the possibility that contemporary expressions of Islamism and secularism in South Asia do not simply collide; they might collude in reducing the multiply located and heterogeneous historical understandings of piety and freedom among Muslims.

South Asian Islam, as Muzaffar Alam (2004), Ayesha Jalal (2002, 2008), Barbara Metcalf (2005), and Francis Robinson (2000) have emphasized, must be understood in its own right as a particular social, cultural, religious, and political formation in which large numbers of Muslims have lived for extended periods as both rulers and subjects, and of course compatriots, of non-Muslim populations. Alam and Jalal have drawn attention more specifically to the classical traditions of religious dissent that operated in Muslim rule and in colonial conditions as mechanisms for defining and redefining notions of community and authority, self and other, public and private; they also emphasize the intersection of Turko-Persian currents, in addition to Arabic religious tradition and South Asian socialcultural conditions, in constructions of Muslim identities and understanding of Islam. Scholarly interventions like those by Jalal and Robinson critically highlight Islamism's role in foreclosing access to the polyphonic discourses of Islam that served generations of Muslims in South Asia as the basis for building religious, cultural, and political communities (Jalal 2002, 2008; Minault 1982; Robinson 2000). Ultimately this framing, as Jalal's extensive historical political studies have shown, enables dichotomous formulations of Muslim subjects (Bose and Jalal 1997; Jalal 2008, 2002). In so doing it tends to reduce Islam's inherently humanist subjectivity (Smith 1957) to a set of market-style choices available to Muslim subjects: religious/secular, pious/impious, traditional/modern, scriptural/Sufi, elite/folk, and so on.

What is important for South Asian feminists is to consider whether such framings may position "the secular" in many Muslim communities not simply as a guarantor of democratic participation, representative government, and human rights that progressive Muslims associate with it, but also, as Talal Asad has argued, as a standard for evaluating and expelling fellow humans from civilization, modernity, and citizenship (Asad 2003). It is through such unfortunate representations that the secular has often entered feminist discourses in Pakistan, thus being undermined in its ability to challenge the equally formidable and discriminatory discourse of political Islamism. To explicate and understand the assumed connection between feminism and secularism in societies such as Pakistan, it is important to engage with the genealogies of the secular and with what is deemed to be its opposite, the religious.

Feminisms and Islamism

The liberal political and cultural ideas that many Western scholars and ordinary citizens tend to associate with secularism were adopted by upper- and middle-class Muslim women in South Asia amid the conflict between British colonialism and anticolonial movements seeking to inspire ideas of Muslim nationalism. The successors of these women in postcolonial Pakistan became defined as the "women's movement," signaling the activities of mostly professional women to gain state protection in areas of marriage, inheritance, education, employment, and law (Mumtaz and Shaheed 1991; Haq 1996). Since 1981 the group that may be considered to be the public face of this movement is the Women's Action Forum (WAF), a group formed to protest the so-called project of Islamization imposed top down by the dictator General Mohammed Zia ul Haq (1977–88). Zia's understanding of Islam, which in fact was inspired by the conservative ideology of Maulana Maududi, consisted of wide-ranging social, political, and legal changes in Pakistani society. The epitome of this belief system was the institution of repressive laws such as the Hudood Ordinance. The leaders of the present cohort of feminists in Pakistan emerged as a women's movement primarily through their noteworthy opposition to the Hudood laws at a moment in Pakistan's history when formal political parties were almost immobilized by the military regime (Mumtaz and Shaheed 1987; Weiss 1998). The contemporary women's movement may be referred to as "feminist" since it defines its struggles through universal notions of "women's rights as human rights" in contrast to earlier groups that situated women's status and women's rights within the national interest or within modernization and development projects of the state. This makes the present women's movement even more vulnerable to verbal and even violent attacks by politico-religious movements, militant groups, and extremist Islamic forces, who have traditionally positioned themselves as guardians of "Muslim womanhood" in contrast to "Western womanhood." In many Muslim societies, including Pakistan, women's feminist encounters with Islam-claiming groups are disputed sites for multiple understandings of individual/community and private/public that then take the form of political and social struggles.

Why Engage with Jamaat-e-Islami Women?

In this book I engage the experiences of some Jamaat women who, from 2002 to 2008, served as elected representatives of citizens in local, provincial, and national political bodies in Pakistan. I trace the conditions of possibility—economic, social, cultural, and political—that enabled Jamaat women to move from marginalized objects of modernization discourses to self-proclaimed agents of an Islamized modernity and ideal representatives of Muslim women citizens of Pakistan.[12] My observations about Jamaat-e-Islami women are based on interviews and interactions with women politicians, parliamentarians, party activists, workers, and supporters of the movement in Karachi and Lahore from 2003 to 2008. Many of these women were well-known leaders of the Jamaat Women's Wing and some were daughters, wives, and relatives of top party leaders. In this work pseudonyms are used throughout and all identifying characteristics

12. For discussion of the elitist and class-based nature of the state's modernization projects, see Rashid and Shaheed 1993.

have been removed, although most of the women interviewed gave their consent to be identified.[13]

My work corroborates some of the contemporary scholarship on what is referred to as "political Islam" in arguing that Islamist movements, rather than simply being interlocutors in Muslim societies, are catalysts of modernization (Esposito 2003; Utvik 2003). Jamaat women's processes of social and political organizing entail particular interrogations and the reconstituting of identities, which, I propose, changes their thinking about both "the Islamic" and "the modern," the latter being one of the names by which secularism circulates in Pakistan.

Unlike earlier groups of Muslim women entering the public sphere, the women members of the Jamaat-e-Islami justify their political participation not through modernist reinterpretations of Islam, but rather with the avowed objective of harnessing the forces of modernization and bringing them into conformity with Islam. This position presents many epistemological, representational, and political challenges for feminist poststructuralists. And within Pakistan itself, their politics are seen as a threat by other Pakistani Muslim women confronting an opportunistic state, misogynist politicians, and oppressive interpretations of Islam.

Jamaat women, like many other participants in the contemporary Islamic revivalist movements, consider the cultivation of a religious subjectivity and the restoration of Islamic political, economic, and legal systems as not simply a reaction to Western colonialism and imperialism. They see it primarily as *a necessary part* of the project of decolonization and recovery from processes of degeneration of Muslim subjectivity that began after the early centuries of Islam and culminated in the complete subordination of Muslim societies by Western imperial powers in the eighteenth and nineteenth centuries. It would be judicious not to dismiss Jamaat women's discursive reconstructions of the relationship of Islam and modernity as adaptations de rigueur or uphold them as instantiations of piety whose

---

13. I have nonetheless decided to use pseudonyms because of the unavoidable time lag between the interviews and the publication of this book.

significance may be accessed only through particularly sited nonsecular readings. We must refrain from reinscribing a simple framework of secular universalism versus cultural/religious particularity and instead attempt to understand Jamaat women's religious agency as attempts to bring together the culturally marked particular with unmarked universalism, including at times the universality associated with the name of "the West."

To map the spaces carved out by Jamaat-e-Islami women in Pakistani society is to also track the fissures of class, sect, religion, ethnicity, and region that distort the modernizing project of the elite nationalists in Pakistan. There is no denying that many aspects of the lifestyles of the secular elite, who are also the traditional face of the ruling class of Pakistan, are disavowed by the majority of the population.[14] This is evidenced on occasions when public anger as violence directs itself at such symbols of affluence and lifestyle as banks, cars, jewelry stores, or restaurant chains. While it would be untenable and flawed to suggest that the failure of the secularizing project in Pakistan, if ever such a project were intended by the modernizing leadership, is the cause of the emergence of Jamaat women, it is not too farfetched to propose that Jamaat women's successful mobilization of a modern Muslim women's identity marks the limitations of the secular modern as a cultural/political project in Pakistan. Though the contemporary popularity of head and body covering by young Pakistani women cannot be attributed simply to the persuasive powers of Jamaat-e-Islami women, there is no doubt that their activism has contributed to the successful linking of Islamic modesty and freedom of mobility by the scarf-wearing women who are appearing in larger numbers in public places as university students, clerical and retail workers, professionals, and, most important, political representatives at the local and national levels.

---

14. Here I use the term "secular" advisedly, reflecting the popular usage of the term in Pakistani society, since most of those within the elite may be considered secular mostly in matters of lifestyle and cultural taste rather than through any commitment to key principles of secularism such as individual liberty, equality, women's rights, and universal human rights, etc.

Gendering the Assemblies

Women's visibility in the arena of public politics, even without effective power or authority to influence events, is seen by Pakistani feminists and modernizers as a key element of the project of national modernization (UNDP 2005). It is also considered by national and international development bodies to be a way of facilitating a greater acceptance of women's role in public processes and their social status. Indeed women's presence in politics in itself is considered a catalyst for betterment of their social status and therefore of national progress and development. "In a country where women are largely perceived as belonging to the domestic sphere, their visibility at the highest levels can by itself lead to a greater social acceptance of their role in the public sphere and enhancement of their status" (UNDP 2005, 4).

Because of the increased participation of women in politics, women's and human rights groups in Pakistan consider the general elections of 2002 a turning point for women's participation in political and public life. These elections brought a total of 232 women into the legislative assemblies of Pakistan, including 73 in the national assembly, 18 in the Senate, and 141 in the four provincial assemblies. In a recent report prepared for the United Nations Development Programme in Pakistan (UNDP) and endorsed by significant feminist groups, women's involvement in politics and their presence in public bodies were emphasized as a route to the greater involvement of women in lawmaking and budgetary bodies and in influencing decisions on issues with the state (UNDP 2005). Authors of the report included the feminist human rights lawyer Shehla Zia, as well as other feminist and human rights groups, notably the Aurat Foundation. The report "Political and Legislative Participation of Women in Pakistan: Issues and Perspectives" sought to assess the situation of women's participation in the political and legislative processes in Pakistan in pursuance of the aims of the Convention to Eliminate All Forms of Discrimination Against Women (CEDAW), Beijing Platform for Action (PFA), and the national plans of action, such as the National Plan of Action for Women 1998 and the 2002 National Policy for Development and Empowerment of Women. The report considered the 2002 elections to be a step forward for women's rights in Pakistan, since in these polls "the largest ever number of women contested and won general seats and political parties also gave more tickets to women to contest general elections than ever before" (UNDP 2005, 4).

The 2002 elections followed measures that the UNDP considered to be significant improvements in favor of enhancing women's participation in the formal political arena. Among the measures considered most beneficial was the reservation of almost 33 percent of seats for women at all three tiers of local government, district, tehsil (second administrative unit), and union, and 17 percent of seats in the legislative bodies (the Senate, national, and provincial assemblies). All these measures were taken prior to the general elections of 2002. This was a substantial increase in quotas reserved for women in these bodies compared to previous years (UNDP 2005).

While some of these developments were due to the advocacy work and activism of women's and human rights groups, the report also attributed them to affirmative action measures by the government. The UNDP report noted:

> The overwhelming presence of nearly 40,000 women in local councils since 2000 contributed enormously to mainstreaming women into politics. Women's enthusiastic participation in local government elections in 2000–2001, in fact, provided the impetus for women's effective participation in general elections 2002. (UNDP 2005, 9)

At the same time more women than ever participated in the elections, taking advantage of reserved seats for women, and by competing with men for general seats, taking women's overall legislative representation to 20 percent.

The role of women from politico-religious groups in the politics of the nation became dramatically evident to Pakistani feminists following the national assembly elections of 2002. From the viewpoint of the Jamaat-e-Islami, these elections may be considered a historic event since they signaled Jamaat women's official entry into the field of electoral politics. Twelve female members from the Muttahida Majlis-e-Amal (MMA) secured seats out of a total of sixty reserved in the national assembly or parliament for women members of political parties. In addition, women from Jamaat-e-Islami and other politico-religious parties were among hundreds of female councilors in local municipal councils. Overall, these elections are an important instance of the role of women in religious parties and the role of religion in politics.

The unprecedented success of politico-religious parties in electoral politics has been attributed to many local, national, and transnational developments. Partly because of the machinations of President Pervez Musharraf to sideline the major national political parties and partly to a unique show of unity among the diverse politico-religious parties, but also because of resentment of Musharraf's support for the US-led war against terror, the MMA, a coalition of six politico-religious parties led by the Jamaat, was able to secure a quarter of the seats in the national assembly.[15] The MMA was also able to win majorities and form governments in the provinces of Khyber Pakhtunkhwa (formerly North West Frontier) and Baluchistan. This was a significant accomplishment for politico-religious parties since they had never before nor since experienced any significant success in electoral politics despite boasting tremendous support at the street level. Politico-religious parties appear to rival and, sometimes, exceed the ability of nationalist parties to draw masses of people on to the streets; however, their persistently low performance at general elections suggests that their appeal is strongest when centered on specific issues that are publicly perceived to be "Islamic." This is different from the support garnered by the nonreligiously defined political parties that draw people on the basis of their political and economic agendas or ties of ethnicity, religion, kinship, and so on.

Awareness of this inability to persuade the Muslim masses of Pakistan led the Jamaat-e-Islami to undertake an ongoing internal discourse of

15. There are many studies on the complex political relationship between the military and the religious parties, especially Jamaat-e-Islami and the manipulation of politics by the military. Some recent examples from Pakistani authors include: Haqqani 2005; Waseem 2006; Siddiqa 2007.

change, which began to be implemented with the election of Qazi Hussain Ahmad as amir from 1987 to 2009.[16] This was indicated by a more flexible attitude on the part of the party, marked by practices such as the playing of songs at political events and tolerance for foreign journalists.[17] It was this newly envisioned identity that many of my interlocutors appeared keen to promote, although they always made sure to add that this flexibility was in tune with, rather than a departure from, the party's original mandate. Some women had been introduced to the message of the Jamaat-e-Islami through their family environment, others came to know about it during student activism, while a few had sought out the party in response to social and political conditions of the country at a particular moment. Every woman emphasized her personal conviction in the ideology of the party and the training imparted by it as being decisive for her entry into the field of formal electoral politics.

Feminists in Pakistan perceive the high level of women's participation to be a result of a legislative change, but also indicative of an attitudinal and behavioral change. They note that it contradicts conventional ideas that women in Pakistan are not interested in political participation or that political parties are ambivalent about offering support to female candidates. The high level of women's participation in elections "has destroyed the myth that women are unwilling participants in the electoral process on the one hand and on the other the idea that there is low acceptance among political parties for women's role in politics" (UNDP 2005, 9).

Women's Wings of Political Parties

Almost all of the major political parties in Pakistan set up women's wings during the last several decades. Although these groups are usually weak and ineffective in decision making or representative power, the women's

16. Qazi Hussein Ahmed was the Amir of the Jamaat-e-Islami during the period of my research.

17. For a discussion of these changes see Mateen 2010.

wings of political parties are seen by many as an essential way to main-stream Pakistani women in politics (UNDP 2005). Lamenting the prob-lems of women workers in political parties, the UNDP said that most ordinary women party members, despite being dedicated to the leader-ship and party ideals, were taken for granted and seldom rewarded with nominations and electoral tickets. The UNDP regretted that the women who reaped the most benefit from the party and were allotted top party positions were not directly involved in politics. The report stated that women from elite or feudal backgrounds who inherited power from their families tended to be "dismissive of gender issues while dealing with pre-dominantly male-dominated party structures and governance institu-tions, which are deeply entrenched in patriarchal standards and values" (UNDP 2005, 17).

Although it was not explicitly acknowledged by the feminist writers of the 2005 UNDP report, it was evident from the information provided that the only political party in which the members of the women's wing are clearly elected rather than nominated is the Jamaat-e-Islami. The Jamaat-e-Islami Women's Wing is a totally separate entity, since women have no representation in the main party. Like the secular progressive political parties, the general secretary of the Women's Wing is an ex-officio mem-ber of the central consultative committee of the main party.[18]

The Jamaat-e-Islami Women's Wing has central, provincial, and district structures. The office bearers are chosen through elections for a period of two years and are limited to two terms in office. The Women's Wing has a separate charter on women's rights issues and gets a small allocation of funds from the main party. This budget, while small, is an improvement on other parties. For instance, the Pakistan People's Party (PPP) has no separate budget for the women's wing. The Muttahida Qaumi Movement is the only other party in Pakistan that elects its office bearers through internal elections.

18. For the organizational map of the Jamaat Women's Wing, see http://jamaat women.org/site/page/8.

This marks the Jamaat Women's Wing, indeed the Jamaat itself, as distinctive among political parties in Pakistan, since even the parties most vocally dedicated to the democratic process have not yet adopted any mechanisms for democracy within their own ranks. In sharp contrast to the Jamaat-e-Islami, women's wings of most parties, including the prominent national ones such as the Pakistan People's Party and the Pakistan Muslim League (comprising several factions), are rife with dissatisfaction and demoralization of workers mainly because access to power, involvement in decision-making processes, and appointments are not based on ability or proven record of service but rather on family ties, social class relationships, or personal friendships (UNDP 2005). Thus women's wings of political parties in Pakistan "lack any significant decision-making power, tend to toe the party line with barely any autonomy, and play a minimal role in defining or influencing party agendas. Political parties use them to mobilize women voters during elections and provide polling agents in women's booths or to demonstrate on behalf of the party when directed by the leadership" (UNDP 2005, 26).

Women's wings have their own hierarchy; and presidents, vice presidents, general secretaries, and other office bearers in different regions, districts, and cities depend on the outreach and strength of the party. Almost all positions are filled through nomination by party leadership, sometimes in consultation with women party leaders. The UNDP report expressed skepticism about the so-called election process of office bearers and found data on women members to be mostly unreliable. Even a major party such as the PPP, which was led by a woman at the time, was unwilling or unable to provide the authors with figures about the share of women in their membership (UNDP 2005). The Jamaat-e-Islami was the only party in which women were officially accorded a recognized role and were included in the membership figures maintained by the party. According to the UNDP report, there were 800,000 members and 1,500 core members (*rukn*) in the Jamaat Women's Wing in 2005. My interlocutors, however, preferred not to provide exact membership figures.

With regard to organizational structure, the website of the Jamaat-e-Islami Women's Wing prefaces its information on the Women's Wing organizational structure by the following assertion:

"Shura" or "mutual counseling" has great importance in Islam. In both the Quran and Hadith, Muslims have been instructed to counsel. In matters of mutual counseling, the Women's Wing makes use of the collective genius, which diminishes all the possibilities of individual and personal supremacy and paves the way for decisions made in the light of collective thought and interests. (http://jamaatwomen.org/site/page/8)

The Women's Wing is organized around the country's prevailing governance structure including wards, union councils, towns and districts, provinces, and center. Each level has a consultative council, thus there is a central Majlis-e-Shura (consultative council), followed by a provincial Majlis-e-Shura, local Majlis-e-Shura, and district Majlis-e-Shura. The districts, provinces, and center are managed by a Nazima (administrator), Qaiema (organizer), and her advisory board (Shura). The Nazima is selected from the recommendations of the members.

The level of membership is defined according to the degree of commitment to the party. This is reflected in two general assemblies of workers: Ijtama-e-Arkan, the congregation of the Arkan (members), and Ijtama-e-Karkunaan, the congregation of the Karkunan (workers). These congregations, according to the group, are meant to "not only enhance the organizing capability of the Wing but also provide for the accountability of the officials" (http://jamaatwomen.org/site/page/8).

The Jamaat-e-Islami Women's Wing is organized on the same lines as the main party, which is based on different levels of membership. The most responsible members are the rukn, or clerks, who are fewer in number than the other ranks, since they have to be highly educated and well-trained in the party's ideology. The next level consists of those who are on the waiting list to join the party; these are considered to be members who are undergoing education and training by the party. At the third level are all those who are willing to work for the party and who participate in its activities in any way. The fourth and biggest level consists of nonmembers who are supporters of the party. Thus the Women's Wing is organized concentrically around a small group of core members, followed by those on the waiting list and then a wider ring of general workers. All the levels of women attend the major programs, but only the few representatives are involved in the party meetings at which key decisions are undertaken.[19]

Jamaat women are aware of the comparatively superior training facilities and opportunities for women within the party, and many of the party workers that I came across made a point to emphasize this. For example, voting is a compulsory obligation for each member, though women are not obligated to vote for men, only for other women. According to Rabia Alam, who was the Nazima of the Women's Wing in Karachi at the time of this study, this offers Jamaat women an edge over other groups; Jamaat women evince a higher level of political awareness than most Pakistani women, since they are well-trained in voting and political procedures. "What you are doing here [within the party] is practice for political participation in the larger public sphere," she told me at a meeting at the Jamaat-e-Islami headquarters in Karachi in 2004. This was supported by another key woman leader who described the Jamaat-e-Islami Women's Wing as totally sovereign and ahead of women's sections of other political parties: "As far as women and politics are concerned, I consider the Women's Wing to be the only truly women's political party. All others are simply adjuncts of male-dominated political parties."[20]

According to my interlocutors, the Women's Wing is involved in all national issues (economic, political, and legal). In addition there is a separate organization, the Women's Commission, which was set up to focus on parliamentary matters and gender issues. Women also expressed satisfaction with the consultative processes within the party, noting that the leaders of the major decision-making bodies, the Nazm (executive) and Shura (consultative assembly), are all elected by votes of the party's members, and, in the case of the shura, also by votes of workers. All policy decisions are passed through both these bodies. The amir is the head of all bodies in the party. Women elect their own shura through their own votes and

---

19. This information was provided by Jamaat women leaders who were interviewed for this study.

20. Except for communications, speeches, and statements meant obviously for public dissemination, as in the case of Rabia Alam above, I have used pseudonyms to refer to the attitudes, opinions, and positions of interviewees.

their own nazm; while women can vote in men's organizations, men do not vote for women's representatives. According to Hadia, who has served in the past as a nazima for the Women's Wing, almost 70 percent of Jamaat women share in electing representatives to the main party's policymaking bodies, although no woman may be appointed as leader of the party: "We discuss all positive and negative aspects, how to project our point of view, what kinds of handouts and how many to print, how many people to assemble, and so on, all this is discussed and decided."[21]

Most of the Jamaat-e-Islami women who were interviewed for this study ended their term of office in 2008 when the Jamaat-e-Islami boycotted general elections to protest President Musharraf's imposition of a political emergency.

The Research Sites: Gender, Class, and Urbanization in Pakistan

To represent, let alone theorize, the notion of middle class in Pakistan is to take into account the lasting effects of colonial cultural and educational machinations; the relationship of ethnic and linguistic divisions and political, economic, and social structures; and the effects of regional and global political conditions on state and society. In this study I have associated the majority of women members of the Jamaat-e-Islami with the middle and lower levels of the urban middle classes of Pakistani society. This is largely a signifying strategy related to an understanding of women's class and status beyond the relations of economic production to include also relations of consumption, political histories, religious and cultural background, and political commitments.

Postcolonial scholars of gender in Muslim societies and in South Asia have amply explicated how, throughout the nineteenth century in colonial societies, different versions of female emancipation came to be tied to the idea of national liberation and regeneration (Rouse 1988; Sangari and Vaid 1990; Ahmed 1992; Kandiyoti 1994; Said Khan, Saigol, and Zia 1994;

21. Interview with Hadia, Karachi, 2004.

Rouse 2001; Grewal 1996). These accounts also show that religion was used to construct not only anticolonial nationalist identity but also a middle-class identity. Furthermore, many scholars emphasize how middle-class women themselves sought to contribute to this formative process, since they are both simultaneously empowered by their social location and subordinated to the class's patriarchal, gendered organization. Thus, it may be argued that middle-class women's self-formation needs to be understood as part of middle-class formation. Religious nationalism manifested as Islamism and its cultural homogenization processes are constitutive of and constituted by class identity, which is impinged by cultural processes at the local, national, and global levels.

Present-day Pakistani society is a rapidly urbanizing society such that 36 percent of the population, estimated at 185 million in July 2010, lives in cities (CIA 2012; Blood 1994). Urbanization in the form of migration to urban areas is directly related to shrinking opportunities for economic advancement and mobility in rural areas combined with differences in development and quality of life between rural and urban areas (Blood 1994; Qadeer 2006). This has led to "spilling out" and "filling up" of major cities like Karachi and Lahore, which have become megacities (Qadeer 2006, 86). These two cities, along with Faisalabad, house about 13 percent of the total population (CIA 2012).

Pakistani cities are important repositories of the region's complex and troubled political history, and this is well-reflected in the specificity of ethnicity and class that defines each major city. The two cities in this study, Karachi and Lahore, offer different examples of the intertwining of politics, culture, and economics (Blood 1996). Lahore dates from the medieval period and came to glory under the Mughal Empire; Karachi expanded rapidly to become a center of rail and sea transport under British colonial rule and as a consequence of the opening of massive irrigation projects and the increase in agriculture (Blood 1996, 95–96). In 1947, when Pakistan was created through the division of colonial India, Karachi became the desired destination of the majority of the muhajirs (immigrants) who moved, mostly from India's northern states to Pakistan. Karachi is by far Pakistan's largest city and is still rapidly growing. In the early 1990s the population exceeded 10 million (Blood 1996, 95–96).[22] Karachi at first developed in isolation. Relatively few people from outlying areas were engaged in running its factories, and the city had little impact on Pakistan's cultural fabric. But when the economies of southern Sindh and parts of Punjab began to expand, large numbers of migrants flooded the city in search of work (generally low-paying jobs), and Karachi become the hub of the nation's commerce. The city, however, also has serious problems. It has the poorest slums in the country, and it suffers from serious interethnic conflict as a consequence of the influx of many competing groups. It was the site of considerable violence in the late 1980s as muhajirs solidified their local power base vis-à-vis the Pakhtuns and native Sindhis.

From the vantage of the present moment, the most important difference between Karachi and Lahore may be located in the significantly different ethnic makeup of each city, and this is reflected in the political situation of each city. Lahore, being the center of Pakistan's largest Punjab province, is predominantly populated by Punjabi-speaking people, the source of both the bulk and the power of Pakistan's most significant economic, cultural, and political institution, the military. The ethnic and cultural difference colors the nature of the violence in each city. While both Karachi and Lahore are sites of major violence, the bloodshed in Lahore is related to religious extremism/terrorism, unemployment, and political turmoil. In ethnically hybrid Karachi, religious militancy and terrorism are overshadowed by the tense ethnic relations between the two major ethnic/political communities, the Mohajirs, Urdu-speaking descendants of migrants from India, and Pushto-speaking Pathans, whose ranks bulked up after the 1979 US-Soviet proxy war in Afghanistan caused massive economic and political disruptions in

22. The last official census in 1998 put the population of Karachi at 9.8 million and Lahore at 5.06 million. With an estimated urban population annual growth rate of 3.5 percent, the population of Karachi is approximately 16 million and Lahore is around 10 million at the time of publication of this book. For more information, see 1998 Census Report of Pakistan, Pakistan Census Organization, GOP (2002).

Pakistan's northwestern regions. The city of 16 million people frequently sees spates of assassinations and "target killings" of doctors, journalists, politicians, and local political officials as different groups vie for political influence.[23]

Lahore, Pakistan's second largest city, is also the home of the Jamaat-e-Islami, which has a strong presence in the city and enjoys ideological affinity with the Pakistan Muslim League (Nawaz) group, a major national political party led by the brothers Nawaz Sharif and Shahbaz Sharif. In contrast in Karachi, the Jamaat-e-Islam enjoyed popularity and a degree of electoral support until the 1970s, when religious identification gave way to ethnic political mobilization, and now the city is the electoral and political stronghold of the Muttahida Qaumi Movement (formerly the Mohajir Qaumi Movement), led by Mohajirs. The Jamaat, which still enjoys street power and intimidatory influence in Karachi, is largely marginalized in the city's politics, which are battled out at electoral moments and in daily bloodshed between the mohajir-backed Muttahida Qaumi Movement, the Awami National Party supported by the Pathans, and the Pakistan People's Party, which draws its supporters from Karachi and from ethnic Sindhi populations in the city's outlying areas.

During this study I was also obliged to visit Mansurah to meet with a number of my interlocutors. Mansurah is an urban oasis on the outskirts of the city of Lahore, where the Jamaat's head office has been located since 1974. In addition to residential homes and a mosque, the Mansurah complex houses the offices of the Jamaat's central secretariat and other party organizations including a degree college, Jami'atul-Muhsinat, a girls' high school, and a welfare hospital.

Overall Pakistan's economy and population expanded greatly in the 1980s in a number of other cities. The most important of these are Faisalabad, Gujranwala, Wazirabad, and Sialkot in Punjab; Hyderabad in Sindh; and Peshawar and Mardan in Khyber Pakhtunkhwa Province.

---

23. For a brief history and some analysis of the relationship between violence, ethnicity, and politics in Karachi, see Rashid and Shaheed 1993.

Engendering Class

An interesting analysis of class in Pakistan and its gendered manifestations is offered by the sociologist Hamza Alavi through his concept of the "salariat." This class was the "product of the colonial transformation of Indian social structure in the nineteenth century," and it acted as the main functionaries of the colonial state (Alavi 1986, 24). This heterogeneous grouping of urban professionals, lawyers, military officers, bureaucrats, and teachers, while not contributing directly to factory or agricultural production, depends on salaries derived from the productive farmers and industrial workers. Alavi emphasizes the heterogeneity of the salariat; groups at the higher levels enjoy good incomes and lifestyles and those at the bottom levels barely meet their needs (Alavi 1986). According to Alavi the partition of India was the result of competition between the two main groups, Hindus and Muslims, that comprised the large bureaucracy needed to run the modern British colonial state. Furthermore, Alavi has argued that ethnic divisions and conflicts that continually tear apart Pakistani society and economy are due to the ongoing struggle among the salariats of Punjabis, Sindhis, Muhajirs, Baluch, and so on. The concept of the "salariat," while largely schematic, certainly explains some aspects of gender and class in urban Pakistani society. For example, it is within the "salariat" that one may situate the English-speaking, Western-aware, economically better-off women who led the demands for improving women's status in marriage, inheritance, education, and employment in the early decades of state formation in Pakistan. However, the concept of the "salariat" does not explain the job and labor market-related battles in Karachi that ravage the laboring and low-income neighborhoods such as Orangi, Korangi, and Lyari, involving pathan and mohajir laborers, transporters, and drug dealers, and so on. Indeed, as Rouse notes in relation to gender (Rouse 2004), there are qualitative changes in the political struggles due to the mobility of groups as a result of economic and developmental transformations. Drawing on Rouse, it may be argued that since the 1970s the leadership of the secular-oriented women's movement for universal human rights in Pakistan has been shared between elite women and middle-class or petit bourgeois women who have benefited from the education and developmental projects of the state.

The Research Participants: Interviewees or Interlocutors?

The epistemological crisis, Sandra Harding and Kathryn Norberg tell us, is also a political, social, and ethical crisis (Harding and Norberg 2005, 2009). By the time I started my research on Jamaat-e-Islami women in 2004, Pakistan was fully involved in the "war on terror" as a frontline ally of the United States. Although then-President Musharraf insisted that his decision reflected the wishes of the silent majority, the state's support for the US-led "war against terror" in Afghanistan and its ambivalence toward the invasion of Iraq intensified a revival in Pakistan of questions around national identity and the demands placed on it by transnational political and economic conditions. It is in this context that I contemplate the methodological and epistemological implications of the following remark addressed to me by a key woman leader of the Jamaat-e-Islami:

> Please think carefully when you write about Islam and Muslims. After all you are one of us. We might be targeted first [the woman pointed to the scarf covering her head and face to indicate that she was talking about veiled Muslim women] but you will not be spared either.

In reminding me of the perils of representing Islam and Muslim women, this woman parliamentarian of the Jamaat-e-Islami encapsulated some of the key issues and concerns that feminist researchers have debated and discussed in their attempt to make social and ethnographic research reflexive, accountable, and political. Her cautionary advice to think carefully what I write about a group of women identifying as "religious" in a world increasingly dichotomized as Islamic and secular may be read as a reminder of the context of our interactions. Her claiming of me, the researcher, as "one of us" may be interpreted as a call to be reflective of my own identity as a Muslim woman. Her qualifying this relationship by pointing to the differences between us was a reminder to be attentive to the heavily implicated systems of power and knowledge in which our communication was embedded.

The post-9/11 local, national, and global context intensified my concern for what feminist researchers consider *reflexivity* in social research, that is, the normative and ethical dimensions of research. It also presented new challenges to my desire to embrace some guiding feminist principles for research across ideological differences, incongruent locations, and the divergent cultural and spiritual investments.

It is by now well accepted that reflexivity in feminist research is not simply a matter of confessing one's location in structures of class, sexual identity, ethnicity, or religion as a mode of making visible one's privilege in relation to those one is "researching." Indeed, informed by Foucauldian theories of power, many disparately located feminists who are grouped together under the label of "postmodern" or "poststructuralist" relate reflexivity to a variety of strategies of making visible and taking responsibility for the power relations that sustain all projects of social research. Feminist academics and researchers, critical of conventional social science research methods, methodologies, and analytical categories, have emphasized that our understanding of social and cultural realities is always already shaped by the relationship between the researcher and the researched and the location of both within larger sets of economic, political, and cultural relations (Strong-Boag 1998; Khan 2001; Harding and Norberg 2005). Reflexive practices help feminist researchers keep normative questions and ethical issues at the center of their knowledge projects and guide us toward modes of understanding social reality in ways that dismantle rather than uphold fixed identities and locations as the nodal points of power.[24] Elaborating these ideas in the context of globally dispersed processes of capitalist production, political secularism, and cultural modernity, postcolonial feminist scholars call for transnational practices (Grewal and Kaplan 1994), deconstructive strategies, and intuitive cartographies in research projects involving women across geopolitical and national contexts. Scholars such

24. See, for example, Spivak 1988.

as Gayatri Spivak, Inderpal Grewal, Caren Kaplan, Chandra Mohanty, and Jacqui Alexander enable us to move beyond the politics of location and identity by proposing that we eschew traditional notions of domination and resistance in the interest of offering more complex accounts of gendered subject formation. They complicate this project even more by asking feminist researchers to understand, as do Grewal and Kaplan, that "complex subjectivities, positions, and power relations are endemic to all groups, whether in the north, south, First World or Third" (Grewal 1988, 523). Thus a project such as mine, purporting to study a group of "Muslim women," is enjoined not only to look into questions of foundations, agency, and subjectivity in their hegemonic or counterhegemonic modes, but also to theorize cultural localities in Canada and Pakistan as translocal sites for the convergence of hegemonic cultural nationalisms and emergent patriarchies both in their secular and religious manifestations.

Throughout my study I was conscious that my Canadian citizenship, my affiliation with first-world academia, and the source of funding for my project served to both enable and impede my relationship with my co-religionists in the Jamaat-e-Islami. At an early meeting one of my interlocutors, whose consent was important to the party's participation in my project, asked me what I thought about the fact that a Western funding agency was willing to spend so much money on helping me in my search for information about Muslim women in Pakistan. The Jamaat-e-Islami's traditional suspicions about "the West" and its informants were no doubt particularly intensified by the tensions engendered by the "war on terror." Jamaat women leaders openly expressed skepticism about the interest of first-world feminists, even "insiders," in representing them accurately; but, aware of the increased global scrutiny of Islam and Muslims, they also added that they were interested in talking to me with the hope of clearing my misapprehensions about them and their project. Indeed, my interlocutors frequently imparted information to me with the stated intention that they wanted it to be communicated to a wider public to which they felt they had limited access. Our very disparate relationships to the hegemonic global systems of representation were never subtle, hidden, or subsumed within the interpersonal connections or the professional relationship that we established in and through the study.

Taking note of my "modern" appearance (in Pakistan denoted by fashionably cut shalwar kamiz, no head covering or face covering, professionally cut and styled hair, makeup, and so on) and my Canadian credentials and citizenship, Jamaat women correctly identified me as a supporter of the mainstream feminist and human rights movements in Pakistan, which organize their projects around universal human rights and fundamental rights of citizens. They also associated me with the "Westernized elite classes," a term that may be used to describe a heterogeneous and economically disparate group of citizens who, for want of a better categorization, may be said to share a commitment to the discourses and traditions of Western political liberalism and are somewhat familiar with Western cultural expressions such as literature, art, music, film, popular culture, and so on. Conversely, while all Jamaat women leaders that I met rejected Western ideas about women's freedom, they were by no means homogeneous in their relationship to Western modernity or the products of capitalist globalization. During the course of this research I attended many Jamaat meetings, public events, seminars, workshops, training sessions, and bazaars, and personally interacted with women followers, supporters, affiliates, and members of the Jamaat-e-Islami in Karachi and Lahore. These women ranged in age from their twenties to over sixty, they differed in terms of economic wealth and prosperity, some wore makeup, a couple even had their hair uncovered in public, but the majority were fully veiled, including a niqab that revealed only their eyes when they were in any space that might include men. Differences in ethnic background, economic wealth, life style, dress, personal grooming, and social/political status and education levels were evident even within my selected group of respondents, some of whom derived their importance in the movement because of their family connections, while others had risen in the party or won respect as individuals. Regardless of their social status, political influence, or economic level, there was not a single woman among the Jamaat women that I met in this study who was more comfortable conversing in English than in Urdu. More than anything else, it may be argued, this dis-ability is an almost irrefutable means of situating a citizen of Pakistan in specific configurations of cultural and social privilege, since Urdu and English are deeply implicated in ideological claims and power struggles between groups and classes in Pakistani society (Rahman 2010, 2002, 2005). Tariq Rahman's studies confirm that fluency in English is associated with a privileged educational background, modern lifestyles, and Western liberal values, while Urdu is associated with values considered Islamic and resonant with state nationalism. Indeed, Rahman notes an increasing awareness among Islamic revivalists, including the Jamaat-e-Islami and underprivileged Pakistani groups, of the need to appropriate English, as it is understood to be associated with worldly success and power in the modern world (Rahman 2005). Thus while my interviewees varied in their educational background, economic means, and political access, it is pertinent to note that they shared a common cultural social terrain that located them outside of the English-speaking privileged elite world, whether they had attended English medium or Urdu medium schools, private institutions or publicly funded institutions, whether their shalwar kamizes were tailored from fine imported cloth or inexpensive Pakistani material.

In reminding me of what they considered to be my duty to Islam and my Muslim identity and my access to Western resources, my interlocutors also gestured toward my intermediary position between "fundamentalism" and "feminism." Though they did not expect me to support their political-religious ideology and positions, I was frequently reminded that I should not add to the plethora of negative representations of the Islamist project; in turn I promised them that I would try to be as faithful as possible in representing their religious and political positions and in translating and transcribing their statements. These discussions added a sense of accountability to my work beyond the requirement of institutional ethics and review processes, which affected my writing strategies in many ways. For example, since all my interlocutors were speaking as public figures expounding a political public agenda, they readily consented to being identified in my published work. Despite their consent I decided to exercise discretion in attributing statements that I considered to be potentially harmful or embarrassing for an individual speaker. This strategy was meant partly to "safeguard" their reputation and partly out of a hope that it might temper positions and remarks that might appear alarming or militant to Western readers.

Negotiations of Faith

Our shared and disparate backgrounds complicate my study of Jamaat women in important ways. Like them, I was shaped by religious, cultural, educational, and political discourses, which we inherited, embraced, reproduced, or rejected as gendered, middle-class Pakistani citizen-subjects. Unlike my interlocutors I write from a position that I understand as feminist; like them I also lay claim to another cultural political site that is misreferenced by the term "religion" and even by the Jamaat's understanding of "Islamic" as the clearly defined component of a dichotomy whose other side is "unIslamic." I was raised in a religious Muslim family that had an established reputation in South Asian history for being immersed in the knowledges, beliefs, and practices of what is often termed "classical," as opposed to "modernist," Islam. My paternal grandfather was Maulana Abdul Bari of Firangi Mahal, a major figure in the history and politics of twentieth-century Islam in South Asia. Firangi Mahal, for the last four hundred years, has been an influential Islamic institution that for many exemplifies a superior level of theological and philosophical scholarship and practice of Islam. Indeed, it is argued this tradition of scholarship was capable of formulating an Islamic enlightenment but was overcome in the nineteenth century by the twin forces of Islamic reformism and Western education (Robinson 2002).[25] In addition to this paternal inheritance in what has been narrowly named "scriptural" Islam in South Asia, I am deeply connected with what Veena Das terms "folk" Islam, since my maternal grandfather was Shah Hayat Ahmed of Rudauli Sharif, the Sajada Nasheen of the Khanqah of the great mystic saint Abd ul Haq (Robinson 1986).[26] It is through my parents and within these family affiliations that I claim most of my knowledge about what it means

25. Robinson's history offers interesting insights into the different responses to colonialism between the Firangi Mahlis and Islamists.

26. For details, see the well-known debate between Robinson and Das and Minault in Robinson 1986.

to be a Muslim. While my formal education, in Pakistan and Canada, was largely in the Western humanist and social science tradition, I have also received lifelong training, with some degree of formal learning, in Islamic history, scriptural texts, and their doctrinal implications. This training is both similar to and very different from the training and education of the Jamaat-e-Islami women with whom I interacted. Thus, in a sense that is crucial to the understanding of Islam and Muslim history in South Asia, Jamaat women and I represented two different, indeed oppositional, currents that became evident in Muslim politics in India in the twentieth century and continue to influence all religious discourse in Muslim South Asia.[27]

Islamism that emerged in twentieth-century British India, while a response to colonialism and Hindu nationalism, was also a fundamental challenge to centuries-old beliefs and practices of Islam in South Asia as well as its traditional knowledge producers, the ulema (Alam 2004; Jalal 2002; Zaman 2002). For most of the ulema, even more so those scholars/ philosophers allied to the mystic traditions of Islam, as were my ancestors, the Jamaat's founder, Maulana Maududi, and his reformist project were seen as anathema to the pious and spiritual principles developed by classical Islamic scholars and embraced by ordinary Muslims since the thirteenth century (Robinson 2000).

Islamic modernism may be deemed to refer to the movements of Islamic reform and renewal in the eighteenth and nineteenth centuries that tried to bring about compatibility between Islam and modernity. Scholars of Islam and modernity tend to differentiate between "Islamic modernism" and "Islamism"; the latter term is used to refer to Islamist movements that emerged in the mid-twentieth century. However, there is a great deal of disagreement over the relationship of Islamic modernism and Islamism to (Western) modernity. Some scholars such as Masud (2009) and Zaman (2002) have persuasively argued that while Islamic modernism was an attempt to develop a new theology capable of responding to modernity,

27. For an excellent discussion of the relationship between classical and modernist Islam, see Smith 1957.

it was not a rejection of modernity. In contrast, they argue that Islamism, such as represented by Maududi and the Jamaat-e-Islami, signaled a rejection of modernity even though it produced new interpretations of tradition in the interaction with modernity. Others such as Reza Nasr (1996), Robinson (2000), and Hatem (1998) suggest that the Jamaat does not reject modernity but rather seeks to appropriate and Islamize modernity. They note that while Islamic modernists wanted to reinterpret Islamic theology to reconcile it with modernity, Islamists such as Maududi sought to reinterpret modernity and subsume it within an Islamic framework. In this process they form a new Islamic modernity and, one may argue, new modes of being Islamic and Muslim subjects. I propose that the postcolonial and transnational feminist reworking of Western modernity in the late twentieth century has amplified the cultural and political significance of women for Islamist movements, such as the Jamaat-e-Islami in Pakistan. This process has also intensified women's activism within Islamism.

I frequently identified myself to my interlocutors by referring to my family background and in the process emphasized the strong influence of South Asian mystical and devotional Islam on my Muslim subjectivity. This signaled to my interlocutors the wide distance that separated me from the Islamic position of Maududi and the Jamaat, and therefore their own. It situated the cultural and political differences between us not only in the comfortable contrast of modernity and tradition, secular and religious, Western and Islamic, but also in the more discomfited realm of faith or *din* in which Muslim identification invokes contested histories and conflicted meanings for contemporary South Asians, and for many Muslims elsewhere.

Whenever we discussed an issue of concern to Muslims in relation to the configurations of global Western political power, my interlocutors and I seemed to converge in a commonly shared project, namely, Islam. However, this commonality was usually temporary and tentative, as our different attachments to and understanding of Islam quickly intervened to draw us apart. My interlocutors' exposition of din through correct practice and bodily enactments seemed removed from my intuitive and subjective conditioning; their model of morality (*taqwa*), overwhelmingly cast in terms of embodied acts as "sinner" and "abstainer," was a disjuncture to my proclivity for the more intersubjective notion of *khush aqeeda* (beautiful in knowledge/creed); their eschatological iterations of *iman* (belief) and *kufr* (heresy) as matters of obedience and punishment were jarring to my sensibility accustomed to the infinite play of these notions in Islamic mysticism and poetry, as, for example, in the following verse of Allama Iqbal: *Moti samajh ke shaan-e-karimi ne chun liyay / qatray jo thay mere araq-e-infiyal ke* ([The] Majestic Mercy gathered up like pearls / the [sweaty] drops of my shame.)[28] I insisted on a certain legitimacy as a gendered Muslim subject of politics, culture, religion, and history, derived from my inherited and present positioning in the Urdu-speaking cultural-scape of North India. It was a negotiated process as to whether and to what extent they were able to grant me that legitimacy. In contrast to the intimacy reported by feminist anthropologists in their encounters with nonfeminist women (e.g., Deeb 2006; Mahmood 2005), I cannot construct my interactions with Jamaat-e-Islami women as anything more than a respectful, often friendly, debate across a deep emotional, ideological, and political divide.[29]

The reserve between my interlocutors and me was perhaps due to a mutually shared sense of accountability and relationality that may not be present when researchers spend two years in a city or village, usually in the "non-West," and eventually return to their "normal" place of work and life, usually in the geographical and cultural West. I did not move into the far-flung middle-class suburbs of Karachi in an attempt to "understand" what it means to be a part of "their" world, in part because their world was heterogeneously constructed by class and economic differences and in part because in some ways our worlds were entangled spatially and culturally. For example, sometimes a place or home to which I was invited by Jamaat women for our meeting was in a neighborhood I knew to be the

---

28. This couplet emphasizing Islamic mysticism's prioritizing of divine mercy over divine wrathfulness is well cited in Urdu and attributed to Allama Iqbal. However, as is the case with other instances of the oral tradition of Urdu poetry, I could not locate its exact occurrence in recently published works of Iqbal's poetry.

29. For an introduction to the Islamic notions referenced in this paragraph, see Chittick 2000. Also see Schimmel 2006.

home of a cousin or relative of mine, with its accompanying associations. At others a woman would claim an individual or institution, for example, the poet-philosopher Allama Iqbal or the "father" of the nation, Moham- med Ali Jinnah, as part of her formative ideology, which I also understood very differently to belong to my own cultural geography. I continued to live in my parents' or friends' homes in upper middle-class neighborhoods in Karachi and Lahore and from there traversed the distance between me and my interlocutors. This distance was sometimes cultural and ideologi- cal, sometimes spatial, and sometimes both. However, there was a divide between us that both sides appeared to be conscious of traversing every time we met, whether it was a five-minute drive for me to the Clifton office of the Jamaat's Working Women's Organization or two-hour journeys to the northern suburb of Gulistan-e-Jauhar.

Most of my meetings with Jamaat women, including some prear- ranged interviews, were never privatized affairs in which I asked ques- tions and my respondents replied. Although my appointment was to meet a particular individual, there were usually others present, including party members, clients, workers, and other visitors who happened to come by to meet with my interlocutor at that particular moment. Women often dropped by to discuss some matter and were invited to join the discus- sion or to contribute their opinion on a particular topic that we happened to be focused on. While these contributions added to the richness of my understanding, and deepened my insights into the party, and increased the number of women I was able to meet, it also introduced a level of unevenness to the information I could elicit. Whether it was party policy to discourage private interviews, as some of my acquaintances in Pakistan suggested but which I did not find convincing, or simply the culture of the party, I did not feel it polite to request my interviewees to dismiss their visitors and acquaintances, whom they invited with great enthusiasm into our discussions. When an interview, or parts of it, turned into a group discussion, often involving different sets of people, it sometimes became difficult to "control" the direction it took. On occasion, I came away feel- ing that I had not been able to abide by the interview guide that I had pre- pared. On the other hand I often got information that I may not have had if I followed a strict guideline.

In this book I refer to my interviewees as "interlocutors," as other postcolonial feminists (e.g., Deeb 2006) have referred to the subjects of their ethnographic projects. In its etymological traces, the term "interlocutor" conveys the sense of a dialogue between two speakers; in this case, subjects not placed in identical spaces as might be the individuals in a Habermasian rational, communicative public sphere. Unlike the ideal citizen-subjects of a modern public sphere, Jamaat women and I were not equally situated in the public space of this study but rather asymmetrically located in the histories of colonialism, nationalism, feminism, and modernization. "Interlocutor" is a term that hints at the inevitably political character of the public time-space of this study; I consider this term appropriate for my relationship with Jamaat women in Karachi and Lahore. This time-space was inclusive of limitless possibilities for communication between feminist and fundamentalist women in Pakistan, but it also delineated the very limited probability of consensus between widely divergent visions of self and society.

During the course of this research I encountered and engaged in discussion with over fifty women followers, supporters, affiliates, and members of the Jamaat-e-Islami in Karachi and Lahore. However, the observations and insights in this book are based primarily on in-depth interviews with fourteen women. These interviewees are significant because they are part of the key political and moral female leadership of the party/movement. Some of them derived their importance in part because of their family connections, in addition to their own capabilities; others had risen in the party or won respect as individuals. These women cannot be termed "elite," since they represent different levels and complexities of power and privilege. They differ widely in cultural and class experiences ranging from "lower middle class" to "upper class," as these terms are understood in the Pakistani context. To identify someone as lower middle class in Pakistan would be to situate them in a very different category from working-class, manual laborers, peasants, and farmers in terms of educational expectations, income levels, lifestyles, and notions of status and respectability. "Upper middle class," as I deploy the term here mostly to refer to feminists and NGO leaders, indicates an economic and social power that does not match that of the elite or super elite, as they are sometimes referred to in the media and Pakistani scholarship, but that also differentiates between sections of the middle class.

As well as the heterogeneous group of fourteen women, varyingly located in terms of privilege, cultural experience, and income levels, whom I engaged in this study through in-depth and multiple interviews, my observations and analyses are also importantly shaped by interactions and encounters with many others who are not directly represented here. However, it is pertinent to note that this project reflects the deep-seated views, analysis, and aspirations of a small group of women who belong to the critical core of the gendered leadership of the party and count among the main women exponents of the movement's ideology. Therefore, this study does not offer an insight into the extent and expanse of the influence of the Jamaat-e-Islami among women in Pakistan. This is due to a number of reasons. In addition to the obvious difficulty of enlisting interviewees from a group that is so hierarchically regimented and centralized as the Jamaat, the availability of a large pool of participants was not integral to the implementation of my research objectives. My intent in this research was to understand the publicly stated political and cultural position on "women's issues and interests" that dominated the discourse of women leaders and supporters of the Jamaat-e-Islami, as these ideas were understood by them, both as individuals and collectively. In-depth interviewing with key informants rather than broader, less specific discussions with multiple women was more likely to provide me with the insights I needed.

The Gendered Vanguard of a New Modernity

The principal aspect of the conceptual/theoretical issues shaping this project was the notion of a "gendered vanguard" that I developed from Seyyed Vali Reza Nasr's groundbreaking study of the Jamaat-e-Islami in its founding years.

In his seminal text on the Jamaat-e-Islami, Reza Nasr (1994) described the party as the "vanguard of the Islamic Revolution," signaling both the ideological and the political dimension of the movement. One of the main arguments made by Reza Nasr is that in the early twentieth century Maududi envisioned an anticolonial movement that was different from both the secular-oriented nationalist Muslim League and the traditional groups that were preoccupied with religious concerns. A motivating factor in Maududi's vision was to reverse the political inertia of colonized Muslims in South Asia and to differentiate a Muslim polity from the Hindu nationalist subjectivity that was emerging with the decline of colonial power in the 1930s and 1940s. In his study Reza Nasr traces the complex processes involving appropriations of multiple ideological trends, including Western intellectual and Leninist ideologies, through which Maududi was able to reconceptualize the traditional relationship between religion and politics in South Asia.

According to Reza Nasr, Maududi's was a dialectic view of history, which would be decided by a revolutionary struggle between Islam and the West, in which the Jamaat would be the vanguard. It was this ideology, Reza Nasr elaborates, that developed into the political project of demanding an Islamic state in Pakistan in the 1950s. Thus Reza Nasr emphasizes that in spite of its basis in the Islamic tradition, "the Jamaat-e-Islami is a modern party" whose organizational strength owes much to the European models on display in the 1930s: "fascism and, even more, communism" (Reza Nasr 1994, 41). Therefore, he proposes that we view the Jamaat not as a political party in the conventional sense but rather as an organizational weapon in the Leninist tradition, with which Maududi had become familiar owing to his reading of communist literature and his exposure to communist movements in southern India in the 1930s and 1940s. Drawing upon the monumental work of W. C. Smith, Reza Nasr observes:

> For Lenin the vanguard was won over by the doctrine and then charged with the task of maneuvering the masses into position for the struggle against the economic and political order. The Jamaat fulfilled the same function with the difference that it focused its attention not so much on organizing the masses as on maneuvering the leaders of society. This was a significant departure from the Leninist model and one that muddled the meaning of revolution in the Jamaat's ideology. (Reza Nasr 1994, 46–47)

According to Reza Nasr, Maududi considered politics to be an integral and inseparable component of the Islamic faith and believed that Muslim political action should establish an "Islamic state" that would solve all the problems facing Muslims. While the integration of Islam and politics was not entirely new, it was always anomalous to the main current of Islamic history in which Muslims have tended to separate religious institutions from political ones to avoid contamination of the former by the latter. The ulema have tended to act as an institution that works with and mitigates the power of the ruler to contain the excesses of judicial processes in the Muslim state (Reza Nasr 1994; Alam 2004; Zaman 2002). However, Reza Nasr observes that Maududi had no patience for the classical Islamic tradition, which had developed a "sober understanding of the relative weight of normative ideals and the imperatives of exigent realities in the life of man" (Reza Nasr 1994, 52). Ultimately, in Maududi's interpretive and political reading of Islam, religious piety became transformed into a structure of authority under which "faith became ideology and religious works social action" (Nasr 1994, 18).

Building on Reza Nasr's insight that middle-class, modern-trained *Muslim men* were considered by Maududi to be the vanguard of the Islamic revolution in the South Asian subcontinent in the early and mid-twentieth century, I propose that a set of local, national, and transnational conditions have enabled the construction of middle-class, modern, educated *Muslim women* as the gendered vanguard of the movement in the present moment. Thus I draw attention to a new cohort of women members of the Jamaat-e-Islami whose identities and practices cannot be theorized through the conventional categories of "modern" versus "traditional." The contemporary generation of women protagonists of the Jamaat are challenging the very terms through which the debates around freedom and progress were framed by modernizing nationalist elites for most of the twentieth century in Muslim South Asia. I suggest that it is one of the antinomies of Islamic/Muslim social life in the contemporary era that the gendering of what has been termed "political Islam," in this case the Jamaat-e-Islami, has become a necessary condition for securing the Islamization project, and this in turn has secured the continued engendering of the movement's vision of an Islamic public space, certainly in Pakistan and possibly in other states.

The idea of the vanguard reflects Maududi's vision of the party as a top-down structure rather than a grassroots movement. As Reza Nasr points out, the Jamaat's structures and organization reflect those of the European models that were predominant during the 1930s, particularly fascism and communism. Reza Nasr therefore emphasizes that the Jamaat may be understood as an "organizational weapon in the Leninist tradition devised to project the power of an ideological perspective into the political arena" (Reza Nasr 1994, 13). This implies a limited number of individuals, who shape the ideological priorities of the project, considering themselves best able to lead a larger population. Furthermore, from the viewpoint of the party, the ideological commitment and training of key individuals and groups are the most important projects rather than the dissemination of the ideology among larger numbers of people or the masses. This is reflected in the gendered vanguard embodied by the Jamaat-e-Islami Women's Wing.

A Transnational Feminist and Sociological Inquiry

The fundamental concern of this book is the interrelationship of religion, politics, and gender in Muslim South Asia. A key site for the rehearsal of the secular versus religious conflict is the relationship between the individual Muslim believer and the community of Muslims constructed as the modern nation-state. It is through the modern nation-state and its development projects that Muslim women in postcolonial societies have traditionally sought to enhance their status as autonomous citizens and it is toward the nation-state that today's Islamist women turn in their project of Islamizing society through widespread legal and political measures. Despite the divergent opinions about the exact nature of the relationship between Islam and national identity, there is no doubt that Islam has always been part and parcel of the public discourses and discussions of nation and identity in Pakistan. Thus it is misleading to discuss Islamist politics in Pakistan through ideas about the deprivatization of religion, as is deployed in studies of Western societies, or as a crisis of secularism, as has been used in contemporary debates about Indian politics. It is not the public emergence of religion that is at issue in the politics of gender, Islam, and citizenship; the issue, I propose, is a new disciplining of Muslim identity and the narrowing of the meanings of public Islam that has become a marker of the experiences of the religiously governed in Pakistan. I approach Jamaat women through feminist insights into the fashioning of modern citizen-subjects and theories that seek to understand the cultural, economic, and political effects of new forms of global dominance and sovereignty. I propose that an intertwined set of historical, political, and economic conditions, including the neoliberal rhetoric of gender and development and the power regimes of transnational Muslim identity, have enabled Jamaat women to imagine themselves as privileged political-cultural subjects who can claim to be agents of both modernization and of Islamization in Pakistan.

While I emphasize some of the challenges being posed by Jamaat women to the secular feminist project in Pakistan, I draw attention also to the implications of gendered Islamism for classical and devotional forms of Islam in South Asia. This way I acknowledge that Jamaat women's innovative invocations of both Islam and citizenship are reversing secular assumptions and opening new spaces for middle class and lower middle class women in Pakistani society. At the same time I also emphasize the crucial ways in which women's appropriation of Islamism and its disciplinary practices are narrowing the possibilities of self and community construction that were available to South Asian Muslims through what one may call "customary" Islam with its intercessionary practices, mystical dimensions, and humanist impulses. As Jalal has justifiably asserted, feminist complacency toward theorizing Muslim religious and secular subjectivities has discouraged a new generation of South Asian Muslims from engaging with the roots of the Islamist modernist project in South Asia and therefore from confronting its role in shaping definitions of Muslim identity.[30]

This work intends to be read as a transnational feminist and sociological inquiry into the "making" of Jamaat women as modern, Muslim,

---

30. Ayesha Jalal, "Partisans of Allah: Jihad in South Asia," talk given by Jalal on May 15, 2009, at the Ontario Institute for Studies in Education, University of Toronto, and organized by the Canadian Muslim Union, the Committee of Progressive Pakistani-Canadians, the Left Institute, and the South Asian People's Forum.

gendered individuals and community members who occupy a particular space in Pakistani politics as the self-appointed religious interlocutors of self-defined secular feminism. The notion of "transnational" I invoke here refers not to comparative analysis of different societies or differently placed women, although I do discuss the specificity of Jamaat women's activism and the situation of Islam in Pakistan compared to other sites. Transnational is used here to emphasize the functions of globalizing discourses, including feminism, modernity and development, and Islamic revivalism, that are relevant to discussion of contemporary Jamaat women's agency as well as their cultural political positioning. This project is sociological since it engages issues that have become, though they were not always, the concerns of social theorists and sociology as a discipline. Exploration of gendered agency, the relationship of religion and other "nonmodern" forces to modernist sites of identity such as the nation-state, the university, and civil society, and the explication of culturally constructed difference may be considered to be the legitimate concerns of contemporary sociology as much as issues of order and action or structure and agency. Investigating religion and spirituality as a ground for political action, not simply cultural identity, disturbs the conventional idea of "the social" as a secular space of transformative development and action.

The Chapters

In chapter 1, I review some of the feminist approaches taken up by Muslim women in Western institutional sites in their attempts to theorize women in Islamic movements. In chapter 2, I trace the newly opened space of the public-religious that has resulted in Pakistan because of the entanglement of the Jamaat's project of an Islamic state with the global discourses of women's empowerment. In chapter 3, I describe an urban development project implemented by the Jamaat women in Karachi and compare it with the early history of women's involvement in the Jamaat-e-Islami. This is further developed in chapter 4, in which I examine the present era as a complex of local, national, and global restructuring that has enabled contemporary Jamaat women to profess a new engagement with modernity. Chapter 5 theorizes the transnational public sphere constructed by local-global discourses of gender and development. Chapter 6 focuses on the social-religious space constructed by discourses of the gendered Islamic self and national community. I review the possibilities and limitations of Jamaat women's gendered project of Islamic modernism when situated in the historical discourses of Islam and Muslimhood in South Asia. In the conclusion, chapter 7, I draw attention to some alternative modes of political organizing and community construction that are available in the historical tradition of religion, ethics, and politics in South Asia, and compare Jamaat women's project in the light of these other possibilities. I conclude that Jamaat women's project of bringing together Islam and modernity is ambiguously positioned between opening new spaces for the enactment of middle-class women's economic and social aspirations and stifling the possibilities of practiced modes of spiritual and cultural expression that resonate with the vast majority of Muslim women and men in Pakistan.

As noted earlier, all the interviews in this study were conducted in Urdu and audiotaped. While I tried to be as faithful as possible in transcribing and translating the narratives into English, the possibilities for multiple and discrepant meanings cannot be ruled out.

While this is by no means a complete picture of the organization or activities of the women of the Jamaat-e-Islami, it is an account of the coming together of the modern-political and the modern-religious in the shaping of a group of gendered Muslim citizen-subjects.

1

Newly Emerging Subjects

Feminism, Islamic Feminism, and Post-Islamic Feminism

Many Muslim women, such as me, acquired feminist consciousness through the discourses of global liberal feminism in its local manifestations, and were reoriented toward the convoluted relationship of "modern" and "Islamic" through transnationally dispersed theories of postcolonialism and poststructuralism. In turn, the re-presenting of Islamic and Muslim to feminists concerned with questions of gender, Islam, and modernity has become an important project of contemporary poststructuralist feminist practices, involving complex interconnections at multiple levels (Spivak 2004; Brown 2005; Razack 2007). The juxtaposing of postcolonial and poststructuralist theories with the transcendental assertions of religious and pious subjects offers a credible foothold inside/outside Western thought, inside/outside the secular polity nurtured by such precepts, and inside/outside the notions of citizenship that have become globalized in the contemporary world. For some scholars, the staging of poststructuralist readings of Islamism involves the desire to comprehend alternative processes of subject formation as much as it does the desire to signal the limitations of liberal notions of agency, autonomy, and freedom. Generally, the linking of poststructuralism and Islam with gender is a cultural-political space from which to disrupt some deeply entrenched teleological conceptions of history and subjectivity that continue to dominate social science research in many first-world academic institutions.

From such a position, representations such as Islamic feminism, Muslim feminism, and secular Muslim feminism become legitimate modes of challenging hegemonic forms of feminism, and also for integrating the political agency of Muslim women into contemporary first-world feminist discourses. Chandra Mohanty's well-known and oft-cited argument demonstrates that the analytical practices of feminist cross-cultural scholarship can lead to the "discursive colonization" of third-world women's experiences in a manner similar to the linguistic and cultural practices of male orientalists illuminated by Edward Said. It affirms the constructed superiority of the West, and defines the West's normality by relegating to the Orient all that is abnormal, forbidden, and dangerous (Mohanty 1988). Mohanty alerted feminists to the scholarly uses of the material and historical experiences of third-world women that served to produce a "composite singular representation: Third World Woman" (81). She demonstrated that in feminist theory, Asian, and particularly Muslim, women were depicted as powerless individuals who needed to be guided by Western feminism in order to become politically mature. Following Mohanty, similar interventions from a variety of positions have, over the past few decades, pushed feminist theory to present a more complex view of how gendering processes occur, or "how women become women," and other kinds of gendered subjects around the world (Grewal and Kaplan 2000, 9).

Continuing this trend, feminist scholarship on women in religious and rightwing social and political movements has moved from a reductive focus on causal or motivational factors to more sophisticated analyses explicating processes of agency and subject formation. Informed by poststructuralist accounts of subjectivity and agency, scholars of the interrelationship of Islam, gender, and modernity have advanced our understanding of the religiously identified (Muslim) woman as an active agent and subject instead of the traditional conception of visibly observant Muslim women as passive and oppressed victims of religion or culture (Najmabadi 1998; Mahmood 2005; Badran 1999).

Much contemporary feminist scholarship in this area tends to be critical of approaches that posit religious women as a problem awaiting feminist resolution. Due to these important scholarly interventions we now have access to elaborate accounts of veiling, bodily practices, and religious practices of women in Muslim societies that cannot be unproblematically understood to be oppressive simply because they do not fit Western liberal notions of freedom or autonomy (Najmabadi 1998; Mahmood 2005; Badran 1999).

These gendered accounts also bring to light an assumed dichotomy between religion and modernity in women's lives that is invoked most frequently in relation to women in so-called developing societies and communities. According to this narrative of development, religion is seen as a residue of traditionalism that will disappear or at least retreat into the sphere of the private as societies become modern. On the contrary, ethnographic, sociological, and historical accounts of Islamic feminism (used here in its broadest meaning as the invoking of Islam by women for their own interest) testify that woman's struggles, and therefore their agency, may proceed through recourse to Islam as much as to liberal notions of rights and freedoms.

Evident throughout feminist scholarship on Islamic feminism is the endeavor to dismantle the dichotomy of religion and secularism in women's lives in Muslim societies, and to look for correspondence rather than conflict in secular and religious feminist projects. This impulse was evinced in the early writing of Iranian feminist scholars such as Haleh Afshar (1998) and Afsaneh Najmabadi (1998). These scholars began promoting the notion of Islamic feminism after the Iranian Revolution of 1979 to refer to the specific methodologies, analytical practices, and political strategies of a particular group of Iranian women. Afshar referred to alliances between secular and Islamist women in Iran over constitutional changes related to women, family, and the household (Afshar 1998). Najmabadi provided the important insight that the assumed opposition between secular and religious feminism is a recent one (twentieth century), since nineteenth-century women struggling for their rights did not define themselves in these terms; instead they rhetorically used any position that enabled them to invent a female-friendly discourse. Najmabadi proposed that "Islamic" and "secular" are "comforting categories" projected not only by Islamist feminists but also secular feminists. She put the onus on Iranian secular feminists outside the country to work with Islamic women and reconfigure a new cultural political space rather than try to safeguard their diminishing secular space (Najmabadi 1998).

Scholars of Islamic feminism in Iran have paid special attention to the activities of women editors and contributors to the journal *Zanan* as an example of Islamic feminist practices. Afshar provides an important corrective to the conventional binary of Islam as oppression and secularism as liberation by arguing that Islamic feminism should be celebrated as not simply a challenge to patriarchal Islamic authorities but also as "the culmination of over a century-long critical engagement by Islamist women with Western liberal and Marxist perspectives" (Afshar 1998, 16). According to Afshar, the Islamist women in her study displayed a range of opinions and strategies, but they shared a common critical contestation of Western dominant definitions of women's rights. Afshar concluded that Iranian Islamist women were "reconstructing a multifaceted Islam [that is] increasingly delivering what elsewhere could have been called feminist demands" (Afshar 1998, 215).

Like Afshar, Najmabadi approached Islamic feminism as a discourse in its own right rather than a reaction to Western feminism or state repression. In her analysis of *Zanan*, Najmabadi explained the journal's explicit appropriation of feminist discourses as a shift from the traditional strategy of Iran's religious feminists who rejected the feminist label. By doing so, according to Najmabadi, the Islamist contributors of *Zanan* broke down the secular/religious dichotomy among Iranian women (Najmabadi 1998).

Meanwhile, Margot Badran's study of "Islamic feminism" indicated that this term was being used in a variety of sites and by different feminist scholars in the Middle East to refer to new feminist practices that were emerging in the 1990s in their contexts and that seemed to define themselves against the secular (Badran 2002). In an article published in *Al-Ahram Weekly* in January 2002, Badran referred to the expansion of the concept of Islamic feminism to regions outside the Middle East, as, for instance, in the case of the South African activist Shamima Shaikh, who employed the term "Islamic feminism" in her speeches and articles in the 1990s. According to Badran, by the mid-1990s, the term "Islamic feminism" was being used by Muslims in "far-flung corners of the global umma [Islamic community]" (Badran 2002). For Badran, Islamic feminism could be defined as the discourses and practices of feminism that may be articulated within an Islamic paradigm:

> The basic argument of Islamic feminism is that the Qur'an affirms the principle of equality of all human beings but that the practice of equality of women and men (and other categories of people) has been impeded or subverted by patriarchal ideas (ideology) and practices. Islamic jurisprudence, *fiqh*, consolidated in its classical form in the 9th century, was itself heavily saturated with the patriarchal thinking and behaviors of the day. Thus a priority of Islamic feminism is to go straight to Islam's fundamental and central holy text, the Qur'an, in an effort to recuperate its egalitarian message. (Badran 2002)

Scholars have delineated a variety of methodologies, analytical practices, and political strategies that characterize the work of women who are referenced by the term "Islamic feminist" (Badran 2002; Kandiyoti 1996). Badran observes that some women focus exclusively on the Quran, others apply their rereadings of the Quran to their examination of the various formulations of the Shariah, while others focus on reexamining the Hadith (recorded traditions of the Prophet Muhammad). The basic methodologies of this Islamic feminism are the classic Islamic methodologies of *ijtihad* (independent investigation of religious sources), and *tafsir* (interpretation of the Quran) (Badran 2002). Used along with these methodologies are the methods and tools of, for example, linguistics, history, literary criticism, sociology, and anthropology (Badran 2002). Badran concludes that Islamic feminism may be seen as a project, an analytical term, and as a term of identification.

In addition to Islamic feminism, scholars sometimes attempt to differentiate between groups of Muslim women on the basis of their differing relationships to Islamic injunctions and secular precepts. Some of the terms suggested are: "Muslim feminist," "secular Muslim feminist," and even "atheist Muslim feminist." Some of those who are identified as Muslim feminists argue that the dominant versions of Islam, constructed by a patriarchal vision, are not reflective of an authentic Islam. This is evident in the following statement by the Pakistani scholar Riffat Hassan, who describes her mission to inform Muslim women of their rights in Islam that have been denied by patriarchal forces in their own communities:

> The more I saw the justice and compassion of God reflected in the Qur'anic teachings regarding women, the more anguished and angry I became, seeing the injustice and inhumanity to which Muslim women, in general, are subjected in actual life. I began to feel strongly that it was my duty—as a part of the microscopic minority of educated Muslim women—to do as much consciousness-raising regarding the situation of Muslim women as I could. (Hasan 2002)

Muslim scholars who may or may not identify themselves as feminists adopt an explicitly feminist stance, that is, a concern with gender equality in all areas of life, to argue that we should focus primarily on the teachings of the revealed text, the Quran, because much of Hadith and Shariah are imbued with patriarchal assumptions. Indeed, Margot Badran concludes from her extensive work on feminism in Middle Eastern societies that Islamic feminism may offer more radical insights than most Muslim women's secular projects (Badran, 1999). In an almost celebratory mode, she argues:

> Islamic feminism stands to benefit us all, Muslims of both sexes, as well as non-Muslims living side by side with Muslims everywhere. It seems important to focus on the content of Islamic feminism, on its goals, and not to get bogged down with distracting issues about who has the right to think/analyze and to speak. Let us not be too defensive or proprietary about Islamic gender equality, about Islamic feminism. The way I see it, Islamic feminism is for all. (Badran 2002)

This inclusionary gesture on the part of secular feminists does not seem to have persuaded many of those women who identify themselves as Islamist or Islamic. While some women, such as the producers of the journal *Zanan*, accept the feminist label, the majority of women who have been categorized as such do not use it for themselves and some reject it outright. The Muslim scholar Asma Barlas questions the efficacy of Western discourses, including feminism, for a morally relevant conceptualizing of Islam (Barlas 2002); the Egyptian Islamist scholar Heba Raouf Ezzat rejects the use of the term "feminist" because it obscures the strong differentiation of secular and religious that is the basis of her arguments (Ezzat 2002). In an article posted on the website On Islam.net at about the same time as Badran's, Ezzat insisted there was a fundamental difference in the frame of reference between those who espouse a secular worldview and those who see Islam as an all-encompassing system. Arguing that secularizing processes signify fundamental changes in human identities and subjectivities, Ezzat contends that it is a mistake to propose, as feminist groups tend to do in Muslim societies, that secularization can be defined as merely the separation between religion and politics or church and state. The difference for Ezzat is that the secularist outlook tends to marginalize God and place the human being at the center of the universe. Most important, Ezzat asserts that feminism is but a stage of secularism and hence presumably irreconcilable with a religious subjectivity (Ezzat 2002).

In many cases women in Islamist movements see secular feminists in their countries as collaborators with the modernizing state, which has traditionally been an agent of repression in these societies. At the same time, feminist projects are also frequently attacked for bolstering the dominance of international organizations and aid agencies over national interests (Ezzat 2002). Skepticism about the motives and the interests of secular/liberal feminists in Pakistan were expressed to me by many women who reject feminist identification. For example, a woman leader of the Jamaat-e-Islami said: "The issue of the oppression of Pakistani women was initiated outside [in the West] and then it was conveyed to us through NGOs."[1] The capabilities of secular and NGO feminists are often considered suspect because of their disconnectedness from the "authentic" culture. At times even their sincerity to the movement is doubted as they are seen to be motivated by greed and professionalism rather than egalitarian or patriotic impulses. This suspicion is evident in the following remarks of the same key leader of the Jamaat-e-Islami Women's Commission in Karachi:

1. Interview with Jamaat Women's Commission leader, Karachi, June 2003.

[secular feminists groups] . . . have workers who are "professional" people. We say to them we are willing to cooperate with you since we have people who can do jobs that you cannot do. But you have aid from the UNO [United Nations], which we do not receive. Such aid [from the UN] also carries with it a certain agenda to which we do not subscribe. . . . We want to tell them (the secular NGOs) that we have a lot of workers at the grassroots level. If you come into the limits prescribed by Quran and Sunnah then we are willing to work with you and we are ready to prove that what we are doing is strictly in line with Quran and Sunnah and this is in women's interest.

These remarks, which may not be an accurate reflection of the state of the women's movement and the commitments of feminists in Pakistan, are nevertheless representative of the suspicions of many women in the Jamaat and to some extent the wider community. In these representations, feminism is constructed as intrinsically oppositional to religion and religious identity, and thence to the national culture and identity, which derive from Islam.

Comments such as these, different versions of which were reiterated by my interlocutors during this study, also point to the ongoing construction and reconfiguring of what may be the Jamaat-e-Islami's position on women and gender. As I show later in this book, this developing position can be understood only in its interaction with class, ethnicity, local and national politics and its entanglement with economic and political processes of globalization, and not simply as the "gender consciousness" of Jamaat women or evidence of emerging Islamic feminism among them.

Islamic Feminism: Beyond Tolerance

Building on and problematizing the groundbreaking work of scholars such as Afshar and Najmabadi, more recent contributions to the study of women, religion, and secularism prod us to think beyond, and in some ways against, preliminary analyses of Islamic feminism by questioning the very presuppositions that construct the notion of women's agency in a postcolonial world. These interventions propose that, inclusionary intentions notwithstanding, existing approaches that seek to reinstate the agency of religiously defined women may obfuscate rather than clarify our understanding of these gendered subject-agents (Konchar Farr 1994; Mack 2003; Mahmood 2005). While poststructuralist accounts may disrupt the ungendered autonomous subject of liberal social and political thought, these scholars argue, they reinscribe liberal assumptions about agency by understanding it in terms of resistance to constraining structures. Thus they conclude that poststructuralism, like liberalism, tends to reauthorize the subject of secular feminist thought in ways that erase the religious subjectivity and agency of Islamic women (Mahmood 2005; Mack 2003). Indeed, scholars such as Saba Mahmood, in her study of women in Egypt's mosque movement, or Phyllis Mack, in her reading of eighteenth-century Quaker women, seek not simply to restore the agency of religious women, but also ask us to recognize that it may be of a different nature than secular agency (Mahmood 2005; Mack 2003). Mahmood and Mack, writing from different positions and referring to very different contexts, maintain the possibility of conceptualizing women's subjectivity and agency through alternative formulations that question not only the liberal subject of freedom and autonomy, but also the feminist subject of resistant agency.

Mahmood and Mack argue that agency may be thought of not necessarily in secular terms but also in religious terms. Religious agency may be apprehended not through secular feminist notions of responsibility, self-fulfillment, resistance, negotiation, or subversion, but rather in terms of passion, ecstasy, virtue, fear, and hope. They ask us to recognize a different conception of agency when women ascribe their historical acts to the fulfillment of a divine will than of that related to the (Foucaultian) subject of modern disciplinary processes. For Mack and Mahmood, practices involving painful emotions, acts of self-disempowerment, charismatic performance, and prayer can indicate the existence of an agency of a different kind than secular conceptions associated with modern citizenship. While an agent understood in the secular sense struggles for individual fulfillment, they argue that for the believer individual faith and community action are seen as integral to each other.

Women in the Jamaat-e-Islami must be understood within their own sociohistorical, geopolitical, and discursive context, which is different from both that of Islamic feminists in Iran and pietist women in Egypt. Jamaat women's agency is not identical to the Islamic or Muslim feminists in Iran who are actively engaged with the nation-state in pushing forward women's rights, sometimes in direct collaboration with secular feminists, sometimes separately from them. In contrast with the Islamic feminists in the Iranian journal *Zanan*, Jamaat women are not interested in undertaking novel, women-friendly, and progressive interpretations of scriptural texts. They uphold only one interpretation of the Quran as expounded in the *Tafhim ul Quran*, a commentary produced by the Jamaat's founding father, Maulana Abul Ala Maududi, whose ideology Pakistani feminists consider misogynist and oppressive to women.[2] Jamaat women do not acknowledge patriarchal domination as an issue for women and therefore state no commitment to reinterpretation or alternative understandings of Islamic texts, even though in their actual practices they may display some flexibility regarding what is Islamic or patriarchal. Unlike the Islamic feminists in Iran, Jamaat women cannot be valorized as Islamic feminists and they actively reject such a classification.

Neither do Jamaat women prioritize the construction of a pious or religious self in the manner that Mahmood has described for women in Egypt's piety movement, in which gendered agency emphasizes self-transcendence instead of self-fulfillment. Mahmood challenges conventional feminist understanding of women's agency as resistance by arguing that "pious" women's agency may be apprehended as a mode of inhabiting norms, not only of subverting norms. In Mahmood's study, women in an Egyptian mosque movement are shown to be unconcerned with women's rights vis-à-vis the state or self-determination in competition with liberal feminism; rather, they are predominantly focused on membership in an Islamic community that may be formed through cultivating virtuous conduct in oneself as well as imminent others (Mahmood 2005; Asad 2003). Women's political project in this context is thus deemed to bring into focus

---

2. The *Tafhim-ul-Quran*, written over the course of thirty years, is an exegesis of the Quran in which Maududi also includes discussions of history, social and cultural issues, economics and politics. It is available at http://tafheemulquran.org.

a different kind of agency than is associated with the interrelationship of the gendered individual and modern nation-state. Mahmood, therefore, emphasizes agency for Muslim women in Egypt's mosque movement as related to the cultivation of correct bodily practices rather than as a struggle for identity, rights, or justice. She deems the mosque women's self-focused practices and their efforts to reform others to be a type of politics, since it displaces male authority in the religious sites they inhabit.

While Jamaat women similarly relate individual morality and agency to constructing a moral community, they do not consider this to be possible outside of the formal sphere of national politics. Jamaat women explicitly and unmistakably declare the political, not simply the personal/communal, as the focus of their struggle, which is to bring about Islamization of law and society in Pakistan through the power of the state. They invoke and assert not only religious agency but also political rights and entitlements that are associated with modern citizenship and the public sphere of the modern nation-state. While Jamaat women defy categorization within the secular framework of resistant and self-fulfilling subjects, they also exceed the conceptions of a purely Islamic and pious self. They profess not only submission to Allah and the requirements of religion, but also claim the rights and entitlements of citizen-subjects that are being globalized through projects of national progress and development. Furthermore, they seem to understand themselves as modern rights-bearing subjects and act accordingly in the community and nation-state.

The need is, therefore, to theorize Jamaat women's subjectivity and agency through the relationship between microlevel studies of women's agency and motivations within the Islamic social context and the implications for the larger social-political project of political Islam that seeks a particular kind of transformation of the individual and society. It is here that contemporary Jamaat women bear some resemblance to their Islamic feminist or pious sisters in Iran or Egypt, since their moral selfhood is entangled with the construction of a righteous community. Like Ezzat, Jamaat women reject the notion of an autonomous individual in matters of religious beliefs and practices, and consider as inextricable the disciplining of their selves from the nature of the larger community of Muslims that the moral self needs in order to fulfill its divinely ordained duties.

"Islamic" and "Secular" Feminisms in Pakistan

The present cohort of Jamaat-e-Islami women is one of several religiously defined women's groups, having widely differing constituencies, that are noticeably active at different levels in contemporary urban societies in Pakistan. Subsumed for a long time within the conventional Muslim women-versus-male fundamentalists mode of understanding that dominated women's politics in Muslim societies, the differing agendas and the vision of different religiously identified Muslim women's groups in Pakistan neither interested nor challenged Pakistani feminists. Although Jamaat-e-Islami women have been the most vociferous opponents of liberal feminist politics, they were largely ignored by liberal or leftist feminists who perceived the main opponents of secular and progressive politics to be rightwing religious men. Liberal progressives in Pakistan, although they resort frequently to Islamic texts for support of particular positions, tend to identify themselves as secular, meaning that they advocate the separation of religion from politics. In defending their secular position, Pakistani feminist scholars challenged the monopolistic claims of Islamic cultural authenticity made by the politico-religious parties (Mumtaz and Shaheed 1987; Said Khan 1994; Rouse 1996). They tended to explain the mobilization of women in political religious parties such as the Jamaat-e-Islami by recourse to the effects of uneven development and failed political, economic, and cultural policies of the state.

Writing in the 1990s, the Pakistani feminist scholar-activists Farida Shaheed and Khawar Mumtaz attempted to theorize the appeal of the veil among women and linked it to changes in the country's socioeconomic conditions. They contended that the appeal of Islam was mostly among women who belonged to cultural social backgrounds in which gender segregation was practiced and who found themselves forced to share spaces and interact with men once they were compelled to work as a result of economic changes (Shaheed and Mumtaz 1992; Mumtaz 1994). These women were brought up to believe that men would provide for them, and yet were being compelled by socioeconomic conditions to supplement the family income (Shaheed and Mumtaz 1992; Mumtaz 1994). Thus these feminists pondered the implications of the visible popularity of hijab and other symbols of Islamic identification among women in Pakistani cities by attributing Islamist women's practices to the cultural hegemonic power of fundamentalist men. While acknowledging the role of the religious as a form of identification and affection in women's lives, Shaheed and Mumtaz theorized women's political mobilization for Islamization as a failure of their adaptation to modern life (Shaheed and Mumtaz 1992; Mumtaz 1994). Mumtaz and Shaheed considered this to be particularly valid for women of middle-class and lower middle-class background in Pakistani society, who tend to segregate socially from men and who seem to be caught in the economic dilemmas presented by the processes of globalization that compel them to leave the domestic sphere for economic reasons. This economic, cultural, and social space is the space most identified with the politico-religious parties, among whom Jamaat-e-Islami is a major player. Yet the political mobilization of these women did not concern Pakistani feminists, as these women were largely understood as objects of a patriarchal project.

The possibility of women's activism within, rather than against, Islamic politics became a concern for feminism in Pakistan when noticeable numbers of elite and upper middle-class women began to engage in Islamic courses and workshops offered by Al Huda, an Islamic school for women set up by Dr. Farhat Hashmi in Islamabad in 1994. It was then that Pakistani feminists and secular-liberal forces noticed Hashmi's conservative interpretations of Islam that valorized women's veiling and unequal gender roles within the family and community (Mushtaq 2008; Ahmad 2009). Al Huda, which is a competitor for both the feminist women's groups and for the Jamaat women, is now the International Institute of Islamic Education for Women, with branches in cities and towns across Pakistan as well as in other countries including Canada. Described as a "social movement," Al Huda represents a unique approach to Islamic education for women that has propelled the study of Islam from an occupation once deemed suitable only for poor urban and rural girls who could not afford a "proper" (institutionalized) education, to a runaway trend among urban upper middle-class and elite women of all ages in major cities (Ahmad 2009). Sadaf Ahmad suggests that Al Huda's successful mobilizing of these women is due to the institute's novel approach to religious education and knowledge and its perceived flexibility toward dress code and lifestyle (Ahmad 2009, 70–71). Acknowledging the popularity and significance of Al Huda in Pakistan's urban centers, Ahmad describes Al Huda as a "school-turned movement" (1). Based on her ethnographic study of Al Huda in Islamabad and Lahore, Ahmad has especially under-lined Al Huda's teaching philosophy, which has enabled it to delink the practice of religious instruction from its earlier association with "unedu-cated, unkempt, misogynist and extremist" mullas to "something very modern" (71). This repackaged image is further supported by tools such as the use of PowerPoint, other audiovisual aids, and the fact that the group's founder, Dr. Farhat Hashmi, has a doctorate in Islamic Studies from overseas rather than from a local madressa or dars group. Another distinguishing factor noted by Ahmad is that while imparting a similar message about women's status and rights as the other Islamist women's groups, Dr. Hashmi is able to present it in a framework of "rationality," science, and scientific facts that heightens the "empirical credibility" of her teaching and adds to her charismatic appeal for many students (77).

Besides Al Huda and the Jamaat-e-Islami, other women's groups engaged in offering religious instruction in Pakistan's cities and towns include the women's branches of Tehreek-e-Islam and Jamaat-ud-Dawah. Each of these groups considers itself unique and distinguishable from oth-ers in its ability to understand and impart "true" Islam and to prescribe the correct practices of the faith. None of the three other groups have been able to match Al Huda's significant impact in the lives of women from elite and upper middle-class groups, who tend to acquire their education in English-language private schools and are comfortable with Western life-styles and consumer trends (Ahmad 2009). Thus it is only Al Huda among the Islamic women's movements in Pakistan that has found a substantial following among those women who were traditionally understood to be the main constituency and followers of the liberal progressive women's movements in Pakistan.

In my own interactions with Jamaat-e-Islami women, it was clear that Jamaat women were aware of the success achieved by Al Huda in urban con-texts and that Jamaat women were borrowing, consciously or otherwise, many of Al Huda's pedagogical methods and its promotional strategies to modernize their own image. Indeed it was evident that the Jamaat-e-Islami Women's Wing, especially through its newly set up Women's Commission, seeks to exude a similar attitude of flexibility toward dress and lifestyle and adopt similarly "modern" modes of research and pedagogy. Despite these measures the Jamaat-e-Islami cannot claim similar success among women of the elite English-speaking classes in Pakistan. Unlike Al Huda, Jamaat-e-Islami women's ability to destabilize liberal feminism and progressive politics does not derive from claims to a social cultural constituency, but rather from a fundamentally different social, cultural, and economic position. Jamaat women's political advantage and their weakness lie in their cultural difference from the conventional women's movement, since they easily engage in street activism and mass politics of the male party. However, like Al Huda, they have also resorted to borrowing heavily from the mainstream women's movement and NGOs in the use of technology, social media, and feminist practices of activism and advocacy.

The Jamaat-e-Islami Women's Wing may be better compared to Jamaat-ud-Dawah women, whose burqa-clad figures received substantial coverage in Pakistani and foreign media because of their remarkably organized and comprehensive relief efforts following devastating floods in Pakistan in July 2010. While largely ambivalent about expanding their message to elite upper- and middle-class women, Jamaat women are similarly engaged in vigorous efforts to mobilize and undertake welfare and relief work among poor and rural women. Jamaat women in their self-definition as enlightened often contrasted their more urbane sartorial style and greater mobility with the women of Tablighi groups and religious "extremist" groups who they considered to be excessively constrained. Jamaat women tend to wear a long straight full-sleeved coat reaching their ankles, which is topped by a head covering and a burqa or veil that covers the face except for the eyes. They consider this adequate for moving about in public and engaging in public discourse. In contrast, women of Tablighi Jamaat and Jamaat-ud-Dawah tend to wear loose chaddar-like coverings and sometimes cover their hands and feet with gloves and socks (Iqtidar 2011, 124–28). My interlocutors often compared themselves to the women in these groups, whom they considered to observe an extreme form of veiling that, in addition to covering oneself, involves avoiding interactions even with close male relatives such as younger brothers-in-law and fathers-in-law. Jamaat women's somewhat lesser rigidity in women's purdah may be reflective of the orientation of the Jamaat-e-Islami, which though obviously influenced by Wahabism, does not define itself in this way as does the Jamaat-ud-Dawah. In her comparative study, Iqtidar found male members of the Jamaat-e-Islami to sport a more urbane appearance than Jamaat-ud-Dawah men, who refrain from trimming their beards, which gives them an "unruly" look (Iqtidar 2011, 125–28). As did Iqtidar, I found among Jamaat women a tendency to distance themselves politically and ideologically from extremist groups such as the Jamaat-ud-Dawah and thereby situate themselves within mainstream politics and civil society. It may be recalled that the Jamaat-ud-Dawah, which also works as the charitable organization Falahi Insaf (Social Justice), is considered by the United Nations to be related to the banned terrorist group Lashkar-e-Tayyeba.[3]

Rather than a coherently linked community, Islamist groups and politico-religious parties in Pakistan need to be understood as markedly different in their ideologies, their political objectives, and their social agendas and interests. Indeed, the differences of faith and principles of its application among the leaders of various religious parties was emphasized as far back as 1954 by the Munir Commission Report, which bemoaned the inability of Pakistan's religious elite to agree on a common understanding of what defines a Muslim (Munir 1954). Iqtidar noted the existence of competition between Jamaat-ud-Dawah and Jamaat-e-Islami in Lahore, which, she argued, has engendered many changes, transformations, and characteristics within these groups. It is likely that this competitiveness has worked to the advantage of women in Jamaat-e-Islami, as these women have started engaging in the kinds of activities that take them outside their family and community zone and beyond the parameters that defined the scope of *dawah* and activism of the previous generations of Jamaat women. For example, in addition to organizing and participating in massive relief operations during floods and earthquakes in rural and mountainous

3. For an interesting account of women's role within the Lashkar-e-Tayyeba, see Haq 2009.

regions outside their home provinces, Jamaat women frequently informed me that they were traveling for workshops, for conferences, and for mobilizing engagement in outreach activities. This is in contrast with the policy of earlier generations of women in the party who attempted to abide more strictly with Maududi's dictum that women should avoid staying away from their homes overnight even for religious work.

Before moving toward a discussion of Jamaat-e-Islami women in relation to the feminist/progressive women's movement, it is important to dwell further on differences in the kinds of politics that define the major Islamist women's groups. Here a comparison of Al Huda and Jamaat-e-Islami is particularly pertinent, since both groups consider their aim to be the transformation of gender and society so as to enable Muslim women to be righteous within modern life and eschew what they consider to be the extreme religiosity of Jamaat-ud-Dawah and Tablighi Jamaat. The major distinguishing characteristic that separates Al Huda from both the Jamaat-e-Islami and the mainstream feminist women's movement is Al Huda's overtly and insistently nonpolitical image and character. Thus the women practice what Mahmood (2005) has described as a "politics of piety," which focuses on embodied practices as a mode of self-transformation. In this process Al Huda, similar to other such groups in other Muslim societies, has created a new space for women in Pakistan that disrupts the male-dominated domain of religious instruction. Indeed, Hashmi has received widespread criticism from both Pakistan's secular feminist groups who denounce her message as misogynist and patriarchal and male religious leaders who discredit her qualifications to interpret religious texts, condemn her novel pedagogical style, and challenge her right to occupy a traditionally male role of religious teacher and preacher (Mushtaq 2008).

Yet Al Huda continues to attract women, especially from the upper and middle classes, and is now spreading to women of the lower middle classes. Ahmad's characterizing of the group as a social movement is validated by anecdotal accounts I hear every time I visit Pakistan, where stories abound of formerly Westernized and fashionable elite or upper middle-class women who joined Al Huda and brought about a minor revolution in their own home or household by adopting the veil, avoiding gender-mixed parties, eschewing alcohol, television, sleeveless dresses, and so on. Despite effecting these disruptions in the traditional power imbalance that characterizes the relationship between the modern/secular and backward/religious in Pakistani society, Al Huda functions firmly as a nonpolitical organization. In contrast, other women's groups, such as the Jamaat-e-Islami, who may offer similar types of pedagogy in women's religious education, are linked with politico-religious parties and thus with electoral and state-oriented politics. This may be a key factor in their failure to attract middle-class and upper middle-class women who hesitate to engage in formal public politics, even avoiding the women's movement, where they may be enjoined to take part in street marches, protests, and other traditional modes of political participation. By locating classes, seminars, and workshops in fashionable neighborhoods and in hotels, clubs, and malls, a strategy for which, according to Mushtaq (2008), Al Huda receives considerable criticism from various quarters, the group makes it possible for these women to remain within their geographic and cultural comfort zone. Furthermore, the "politics of piety" associated with Al Huda, while it may cause annoyance among husbands and relatives, does not in most cases cause major shifts in power within elite and upper middle-class families where fathers and husbands are most likely to be associated not with the politico-religious parties but rather the progressive/secular or nationalist ones. This enables middle-class women to avoid either engaging in formal politics altogether or maintaining a clear divide between the political and the religious-personal. Islam thus fits into the private and domestic domain that is a main site of social and cultural experience of middle-class and upper middle-class women in Pakistan and elsewhere (Ahmad 2009, 155–80). Involvement in the "politics of piety" allows middle-class and elite women to obtain indulgent tolerance from their families, while active involvement in politics such as feminism or religious politics would trouble the stability of the middle-class domestic, cultural, and social life.

Since Farhat Hashmi's father was a former amir of the Jamaat-e-Islami and she was also associated with the Jamaat before she went to study abroad, I asked one of my interlocutors to comment on the project of Al Huda. My respondent conceded that Hashmi was "doing good work," especially noting her successful engagement of elite women, but appeared to be skeptical of Hashmi's refusal to engage in conventional politics, which is a cornerstone of the Jamaat-e-Islami today. My interlocutor noted that Hashmi, possibly to maintain her legitimacy for elite and bourgeois women, avoids engaging in any national or state issues and on occasion refuses to lend her support to the Jamaat women even when it would boost the latter's position against "secular" women. This Jamaat official noted that this gave Al Huda an edge over the Jamaat women preachers, since "their adherents do not feel too burdened by their teachings. . . . I want to go further and ask people to change their lives." However, she acknowledged that Al Huda had brought about significant changes in society, as it "has taught the upper class to wear a scarf on their heads and enabled them to become acquainted with Islam, with which they were previously unfamiliar."

I would add that the differential appeal of these various Islamist groups for women of different classes needs to be tempered by the recognition of flexibility in women's own motivations and movement toward different messages. There is evidence that Al Huda is now drawing followers from women of the urban lower middle classes (Ahmad 2009), as is the Jamaat clearly attracting the attention of women from the middle and upper middle classes.

Feminism and Islamization

While diverse groups of women are engaged in struggle at a variety of levels and spheres in Pakistan (related to specific ethnic, labor, cultural, or civic issues), references to "the women's movement" in literature, politics, and media specifically denote the activities of upper- and middle-class, usually professional, women to gain state protection in areas of marriage, inheritance, education, employment, and law. Since 1981, the feminist women's movement in Pakistan has been represented by the Women's Action Forum (WAF), a group formed to protest the sentencing of a man and a woman under the *zina* laws of the Hudood Ordinance.[4] Although

---

4. The word *Hudood* stems from the root word *hadd* or limit: crimes under Hudood are punishable because they have crossed societal limits. The Hudood Ordinance consists

the ordinance was issued by General Zia in 1979, it was not until the death sentence of this lower middle-class couple that elite women realized the full implications of Hudood laws for social control and their effect on the status of all women in Pakistan. A Karachi-based group, *Shirkat Gah*, organized meetings of women's organizations and individuals to discuss the sentencing, and it was there that the *Khawateen Mahaz-e-Amal* (WAF) was formed (Mumtaz and Shaheed, 1987, 123–42). Farhat Haq describes the formation of WAF as the "most important challenge" to the Islamization policies of Zia ul Haq. She notes:

> Though it was small in number and limited to the major cities of Pakistan, WAF was very successful in starting a national debate on the inequities of the proposed legal changes, becoming the only force, at the height of martial law, to challenge the policies of the military government. (Haq 1996, 169)

The founding of WAF is considered significant for feminism in Pakistan since it was the first time in history that elite women mobilized to protect their rights as women and not in the interest of anticolonial or postcolonial nationalism (Rouse 2004; Haq 1996; Mumtaz and Shaheed 1987). Furthermore, it also marked a fundamental change in the relationship of the urban educated upper and middle class to the state; these women had to confront an Islamizing state that sought to curtail women's rights rather than protect them from the conservatism and patriarchal pressures of the ulema, cultural elite, and illiterate masses (Haq 1996). WAF defined its aims as follows:

> Women's Action Forum (WAF) or *Khawateen Mahaz-e-Amal* is a consciousness raising group aimed at enabling women to fight for their rights. It is also a lobby cum pressure group committed to protecting and promoting the rights of women by countering all forms of oppression.

---

of five criminal laws covering rape, adultery, theft, robbery, and use of narcotics. The ordinance on zina (unlawful sexual relations before or outside marriage) has had the worst impact on women. See Khan 2007.

It is non-hierarchical, non-governmental, and non-political. It seeks to bring together individuals and organizations on a common platform for women's rights. (WAF Charter, in Mumtaz and Shaheed 1987, appendix 4, 183–84)

The impelling force behind WAF's arguments against Islamization was the curtailment of rights so far acquired to some degree by mainly middle-class and elite women in Pakistan. These rights included education, professional training and employment, relative freedom of movement and speech, and so on (Mumtaz and Shaheed 1987; Weiss 1998). As Mumtaz and Shaheed point out, while low-income and rural women suffered most directly from the legal and physical impact of the laws, elite women were most outraged by the loss of legal, political, and social status that ensued from Islamization of law and society. It is true that WAF's discourses focused on the issue of women's equality and autonomy, and that women who had some public or legal status in society had much to lose from relinquishing such status. It is also correct that the leadership of WAF was, and to some extent continues to be, in the hands of upper middle-class Western-educated women who uphold universalist notions of human rights and the fundamental rights of citizens. However, what may be referred to as the women's movement in Pakistan no longer coalesces as it once did around the WAF or any one group. Indeed, the composition and character of WAF itself has undergone significant changes since its founding and it may now involve more lower middle-class women and be less dominated by elite or upper-class women, many of whom have started their own NGOs or issue focused groups for research, consultation, and project implementation (Bari and Gul Khattak 2001; Said Khan 2002; Rouse 2004). It is difficult to speak of the women's movement in Pakistan today, as "women's issues" are currently taken up by heterogeneous actors at many different levels and diverse sites, including journalists, television personalities, and politicians who may mobilize as a force at particular events. However, it would be disingenuous to argue that the feminist or secular women's movement in Pakistan, whether embodied by middle- and upper-class women or not, is inconsequential for the rights and experiences of the mass of Pakistani women. The women's movement has also now integrated women's rights with other social justice issues such as the rights of ethnic and religious minorities and major human rights issues. The most important contribution of women's rights and human rights groups has been to continually disturb and on occasion dislodge the fixed and unitary construction of Muslim identity and Pakistani citizenship that lies at the heart of the project of politico-religious groups in Pakistan. It is no coincidence, therefore, that secular feminists regularly feature in organized projects to uphold the rights of women and of ethnic, sectarian, and religious minority groups that are victimized by the so-called Islamic laws such as the Hudood laws or the Blasphemy law, and so on.

As I have argued elsewhere (Jamal 2005), the activities of groups, such as WAF, that received attention in the 1990s through their challenging of state-imposed "Islamization" have indisputably linked the concept of "woman" to notions of "human" and "citizen" in a way that was never evident in Pakistani society. For the first time in Pakistan, through the dialogic relationship of "feminism and fundamentalism," a space was opened and continues to remain open wherein it is possible for media, individuals, and groups to debate entrenched understandings of women and family, tradition and honor, community and nation. This political/cultural/social space is also replete with all sorts of possibilities that are discounted when women are understood through simplistic frames of Western versus native, traditional versus modern, or religious versus secular. It is this space that must necessarily be underscored in an attempt to engage with the present cohort of Jamaat-e-Islami women in Pakistan, since they are configured by it, and which they seek to reconfigure through their politico-religious project.

Indeed, it is this nexus of feminism and fundamentalism that grants legitimacy to the discourses and projects of contemporary Jamaat-e-Islami women. These women construct their position as one that rejects both the untenable extreme positions of those male religious voices who would deny women access to the benefits of modernity and of the feminist champions of women's rights who would lead Pakistani women toward an uncontrollable modernization, exemplified by women's social and economic mobility, political rights of the individual, universal human rights, cultural diversity, and so on, whose empirical reference is available in Western societies. They present themselves as ideally situated—as educated middle-class professional women and believers—to offer a balanced solution to the contentious issue of gender and development in Pakistan. As my study indicates, important aspects of the Jamaat women's project become most credible when understood through their interactions with women's rights and human rights activists.

Islamizing Transnationality

We need to understand both Islamization and its counter struggles as modern discourses of those who have been defined as two opposing "sections of the elite" in Pakistan in order to dispel attempts to romanticize either the secular or religious parties as the authentic voice of the masses (Said Khan, Saigol, and Zia 1994). This may also be taken as a caution against conceptualizing women's agency, whether pious or secular, without reference to class, religion, ethnicity or region, as well as the historical local, national, and international contexts.

In examining Jamaat women's Islamism as a mode of modern Muslim women's self-construction and site of agentive action, it is also important to situate them within other global discourses—citizenship, nationalism, development, modernization. This is necessary to understand the operations of what Grewal has termed "transnational connectivities," which she uses to draw attention to the variety of ways in which geopolitics and biopolitics collude and combine to produce gendered and racialized bodies and subjects in diverse spaces (Grewal 2005, 3). It also enables us to understand the question of gendered agency and resistance, as does Grewal, and apprehend Jamaat women as agents enabled to move "in all kinds of directions and mechanisms that did not remain pure of their conditions of possibility, but created contradictions, tensions, and struggles" (Grewal 2005, 19). Therefore, I highlight the ways in which women appropriate a variety of discourses, including both secularism and religion, to assert their autonomy as citizens and as religious subjects.

I propose that an engagement with Jamaat women's discursive attempts to conceptualize, delineate, and operate in and through a space of the public-religious enables a mapping of the religious *and* expands our insights into how to fathom "the secular" in a Muslim society such as Pakistan. It is to this issue that I turn next.

2

The Spaces of the Public-Religious

Juda ho din siyasat se / to reh jati hai changezi [politics without faith is tyranny]. Invoking the authority of the poet-philosopher Allama Moham-med Iqbal, a key woman leader of the Jamaat-e-Islami, who I will refer to by the pseudonym Samina, responded to my request to explain her under-standing of the term "politics." At the time of this discussion Samina was one of the women from the Jamaat-e-Islami who was elected to the National Assembly of Pakistan (2002–8). She said:

> I consider politics to be a component of religion. This is how I have been trained . . . as the poet-philosopher Allama Iqbal said: Separate reli-gion from politics and all that is left is tyranny; tyranny may take many forms—whether it is the fury of empire or the authority of democracy.[1]

This Jamaat leader's understanding of the imbricated nature of poli-tics and religion appeared to speak to the ongoing struggle over the role of Islam in the nation-state in Pakistan. Her response challenged the given position of those Pakistani scholars, historians, and activists who are fre-quently referred to as the secular or liberal or progressive forces in this Muslim-majority society. For the latter groups, the state can offer social justice and equality to all citizens only if there is a consensually agreed on, if not actual, separation of the political public sphere from another sphere that is deemed to be more private and appropriate for the expression of

1. Interview with "Samina," a leader of the Jamaat-e-Islami Women's Wing, Man-surah, Lahore, March 2006.

religion. The Islamist construction of "the religious" (see chapter 6), and its mirror opposite, the liberal progressive construction of "the secular," both hinge on a bracketing of the unique historical political-religious experiences of the Muslims of the Indian subcontinent. This bracketing has enabled the upholding, in present-day Pakistani society, of a particular relationship between religion and politics that is a key source of friction between groups of citizens who may describe their politics as secular and others who describe themselves as religious parties (*mazhabi Jamaatain*).

Therefore, before we can map the contours of the "public-religious," we need to understand the "public-secular" in this officially designated Islamic Republic of Pakistan. Such a mapping of the discursively constructed, and therefore motivated, nature of both secular and religious in Pakistani politics is needed in order to bring the present discussion into dialogue with some important observations about the complex functions of secularism in the destruction and construction of subjectivities and communities in many widely different societies (Chatterjee 1993; Foucault 1982; Spivak 2004; Asad 2003; Scott 1999; Razack 2007).

A variety of postcolonial, poststructuralist questions directed at the secular-modern alert us to the assumptions about liberalism, secularization, and modernity that have been transplanted around the world, including Muslim societies, through colonial, nationalist, and postcolonial projects of modernization. Reflecting a Foucaultian understanding of modern state power as the practice of governmentality or the process of managing populations through the discursive construction of different groups as subjects and objects of political-cultural discourses, some scholars have suggested that we understand secularism as a project that refers to much more than a separation of religion and politics in the business of the nation-state (Chatterjee 1993; Foucault 1982; Spivak 2004; Asad 2003; Scott 1999; Razack 2007). Given the privileged status of the secular in Western philosophical, political, and social discourse, these scholars argue that secularism is not simply the opposite of religion but rather a more powerful force since it carries the power to define and regulate religion and its possibilities of expression in modern public social and political life. Thus they point out that the secular is global and encompassing and capable of valorizing subjects and spaces as modern or denigrating them as pre-modern (Asad 2003; Spivak 2004; Razack 2007). One may infer that religion, in particular Islam, given its beleaguered status in contemporary global power relations, cannot be said to enjoy the same kind of power in public life.

From this view the cherished project of Pakistan's secular, liberal, and progressive forces, including the nation's founding father Mohammed Ali Jinnah, to construct communal and sectarian harmony via a separation of religion and politics is another manifestation of the powers of the secular in contemporary lives. And this is certainly one mode in which ideas about secularism, mostly in the euphemism of the "modern," seem to have shaped the lives of women in Pakistan based on their class, caste, family background, ethnicity, religion, and political connections. The scrutinizing of secularism and the secular as modes of subjugating religious "others" is intellectually and politically appealing to those of us committed to postcolonial and poststructuralist critiques of colonial and nationalist modernity and its hegemonic discourses. However, despite their theoretical rigor and political morality, such conceptions of secularism tend to flatten the multiplicity of associations and functions that the secular is called on to perform in Pakistani political-social life in both quotidian and unusual conditions. For many transnational feminists, it is important to note that some contemporary scholars, notably Scott (1999) and Chatterjee (1993; 2004), have explored possibilities for disruption of the powers of the secular-modern by subjects acting from within the secular spaces of the postcolonial modern without necessarily reinscribing normative versions of religiosity or piety as the counter of secular hegemonies. For example, Chatterjee points to the strategies of economically and culturally marginalized Muslims in Bengal as resisting contemporary forms of governmentality through the exercise of democratic rights in a manner that may confound the political projects of civil society (Chatterjee 2004). Indeed, the Jamaat women's explication of their public role resonates with the activities of groups that operate in what Chatterjee has theorized as "political society," that is, a space excavated and occupied by those who are excluded by traditional civil society and that serves as a platform for the assertion of rights that are conventionally reserved for full citizens (2004, 39–40).

Building on Foucault's conception of governmentality, Chatterjee differentiates between citizens who are subjects of governance and those populations that are the objects of the practices and projects of governance. While civil society is the domain of citizens, "political society" is occupied by populations or communities. Chatterjee suggests that in this space politics may occur in different forms than the official, homogeneous, and universalized one as marginalized groups assert their rights from within the space of community rather than the state. This space also marks the emergence of a range of new political claims as well as new rhetoric for articulating these claims that Chatterjee calls the "politics of the governed" (2004, 50–60).

For example, according to the dominant thinking of modern history exemplified by Benedict Anderson's imagined communities, the national community is seen to comprise large anonymous social groups that experience a simultaneous existence through a conception of time as undifferentiated and empty and that are connected by print capitalism (Anderson 1991). Chatterjee argues that the notion of "empty time," which is integral to capitalism, constructs all impediments to its flow as extrinsic and as remnants of pre-modernity that will eventually be overcome by the tide of modernity and development. Related to the sense of homogeneous national history is the idea of politics as a unitary process that is enacted similarly and simultaneously in multiple sites. Chatterjee states that such a conception folds time into space, enabling the idea of the "time-space of modernity." "Thus, politics in this sense inhabits the empty homogeneous time-space of modernity" (2004, 6). Against the unvarying conception of politics associated with the time-space of the nation, Chatterjee proposes other forms of activities that communities may undertake in spaces that cannot be encapsulated within the imagined national utopian time-space, but rather in a space that may be more aptly described by Foucault's concept of heterotopia (2004, 6). In this "real space of modern life," Chatterjee argues politics may mean very different things to different people. He suggests that the heterogeneity of politics and the ambivalence of the concept of "the nation" are an inevitable part of modern politics itself, not simply its marginalizations or exclusions that may be contained and embraced within the idea of the people (2004, 6–7).

Drawing on these insights, it may be argued that Jamaat women's politics constitute not an exceptional or extraordinary form of citizenship, but rather an inevitable aspect of postcolonial citizenship, and that the space of the public-religious is a context-specific and historical instance of the politics of the governed. We may argue that the dominant discourse of the postcolonial neoliberal nation-state and global modernization projects cannot impose participatory and representative rights on unwilling subjects. They are constructed as part of the populations targeted by the discourses of reform through education and development used by both the secular modernizing elite feminist and global projects of development. To a limited extent, Jamaat women, acting through and somewhat against the patriarchal, elitist, and male-dominated politics of the party and the nation-state, may be seen as excavating a public space that has potential for the kind of politics that Chatterjee theorizes. In these politics "the demands of electoral mobilization, on the one hand, and the logic of welfare distribution, on the other, overlapped and came together" (Chatterjee 2004, 135).

The entanglement of civic ideals and political activism, on the one hand, and of electoral mobilization and social justice, on the other, became most poignantly evident in the meshing of Islam and global politics after September 11, 2001. In Pakistan, the Jamaat was often seen to be supporting extremist groups. I asked Samina about reports that the Jamaat-e-Islami's Women's Wing was involved in sheltering and hiding people who were fighting against the United States. In response, she related a meeting with a visiting US political secretary after 9/11 who had asked her a similar question. She told the American official:

Look sister, your people provide shelter to homeless dogs and cats . . . and if a woman comes to me at this moment in front of you—an American political secretary—and no matter which party she belongs to, whether it is JI or Al Qaeda, and whether she is a Muslim or Christian, no matter if she comes alone or with children, and if she comes to me as a woman and asks for help I will accept her. I may not do the same for a man; I have no dealings with men, they may go elsewhere. But if a woman comes to me for help, no matter who she is I will extend help to her.

Here this woman leader seems to be gesturing toward a sisterhood that, as I discuss below, is to be distinguished from the global women's movement; it is based not on ideas about shared oppression or experiences or social justice, but rather on humanitarian pragmatism. According to Samina, the US official was appreciative of her frankness and honesty, and one may add, by her seeming feminism. Contradicting news reports about the Jamaat's aid to Al Qaeda militants, Samina argued that the two or three people (Al Qaeda suspects) that had been found in Jamaat women's homes were women and children, and if they were to ask for shelter again Jamaat would offer them protection again. Regardless of the accuracy of this attempt to vindicate the party, it would be hard to disagree with her argument that many of the people who were being hunted down in Pakistan had been invited to the region by the United States to fight against the Soviet occupation of Afghanistan in the 1980s.

For very different reasons from the marginalized economic groups described by Chatterjee, Jamaat women are often seen as outsiders by what is understood as the civil society in Pakistan; in fact they are, albeit tenuously, its members. Unlike the communities of Chatterjee's political society, Jamaat women's priorities are not issues of habitation and livelihood and their claims challenge the very heart of the modern state itself. This is because, unlike the marginalized populations of the untouchables and shelterless, Jamaat women are fully inserted into capitalist globalization processes, global Islamic revivalism, and global development discourses. As well, they desire to live a religiously defined life not outside of but within traditional civil society and the national and international politics of democracy. Furthermore, Jamaat women express a strong commitment to constitutional forms of democratic politics that they use in civil ways to make claims that feminists, liberals, and progressives consider fundamentally uncivil. In terms of objectives, therefore, their project is more contentious than the socially, though not legally, acceptable aims of those who must subsist on society's economic and social margins (Chatterjee 2004).

Yet I propose that Jamaat women's politics deserve feminist attention for a deeper appreciation of some of the "entanglements and the contradictions" that Chatterjee has noted in his account of the relationship between modernity and democracy in India, and which I extend to Pakistan (2004,

44). By using the notion of "political society," Chatterjee was able to delineate important changes in the relationship between elite and subaltern politics that, according to historiographers of the Subaltern Studies project, characterized the anticolonial nationalist phase in South Asia.[2] Thus Chatterjee could expand the space for examining the nature of groups and politics in the contemporary era when many more spaces of social life and more social groups must depend on the postcolonial national state for their survival or subsistence. Drawing on Chatterjee's methodological insights for reading the political spaces of the postcolonial nation as much more entangled and disorderly enables us to discern the kinds of compromises that he has noted between normative modernity and popular desire.

In Pakistan, nothing offers more insights into the nature of these entanglements—of elite and non-elite demands for rights and pleas for interests, legitimate demands, and moral claims—than the pervasive but diverse presence of Islam as religion, as politics, as spirituality, as culture and poetry, as identity and history. For it is the experience and consciousness of Islam that binds civil society and political society, elite and subaltern, formal and informal politics together in the national culture. Despite the widely divergent opinions about the exact nature of the relationship between Islam and national identity, there is no doubt that Islam has always been part and parcel of the public discourses and discussions of nation and identity in Pakistan. This consideration adds another gloss to our understanding of citizens as subjects and populations as objects of the discourses of governmentality (Chatterjee 2004) as these relate to some contemporary questions about the place of culture, religion, and identity in the modern nation-state.

When we decide to make visible and theorize through the forms of political violence constitutive of the categories of gender, race, religion, and sexuality in addition to class, we may achieve a more complicated reading of the politics of the religiously governed. While it is not my intention to represent Jamaat-e-Islami women as subaltern, their gendered cultural-political

2. Chatterjee is associated with the school of Indian historiography known as the Subaltern Studies project. For an introduction, see Guha 1982.

positioning, as I have argued in this text, is clearly distinct from both the male Islamist leaders and mainstream feminists.[3] Indeed, in the interest of a strong feminist analysis of South Asian cultural-political contexts, it is worth remembering the analytical interventions of scholars like Gayatri C. Spivak, who suggests that women's relationship to constitutionality, that is, the secular-modern, may itself, under certain conditions, be theorized as an important site for a kind of politics that challenges regimes of gender, class, caste, religion, and so on (Spivak 1996). Thus we may wonder whether some of the regulatory practices of secularism, especially its ability to elevate and denigrate individuals as moral, rational, modern, or not, pinpointed by these scholars, are also implicit in aspects of what is presently promoted as Islamic in South Asia. This contextualizing is needed to bring into focus the variegated texture of secular dominance as well as the multi-hued tones of religion-based misgivings about the secular, the modern, and the Western. Both secular and religious may be best approached in Pakistan as different—but linked—political spaces whose functions and effects may vary depending on historical context and the agents who deploy them. This scrutiny is needed in the interest of developing a complex understanding of both the extent and the limits of the powers of the secular as a modernist project and for understanding important connections between Islamist politics and modern nationalism. Without placing blind trust in the secular as a sine qua non for better human existence and national progress, it is necessary in the context of Pakistan to scrutinize the assumed dominance of the secular in political life as well as the relationship of religious agents to local secularity. We need to understand how the histories of Islamism and secularism in their South Asian Muslim formations converge and close off each others' emancipatory possibilities for Muslim women.

While remaining attentive to the complex cultural-political nature of "the secular" and "the religious," I examine in this chapter the manner in which Jamaat women understand the gendered nature of the

3. Indeed, I understand the term "subaltern" in Gayatri C. Spivak's more circumscribed usage, which makes it unsuitable for both feminism and Islamism in Pakistan (Spivak 1996).

"public-political." Jamaat women's construction of the space of the public-religious is apprehended by their discussion of their understanding of politics, their reasons for entering electoral politics, the activities undertaken by them as political representatives of women, and their accounts of their role "as women" as enacted through their interactions with other female political representatives. I revisit some of my discussions with members of the Jamaat-e-Islami Women's Wing who were serving in political representative positions at the local, provincial, and national levels at the time of our discussion. Before I proceed to my interactions with Jamaat women, I offer a quick reprise of the muddled relationship of politics, Muslim identity, and varied understandings of Islam in the history of Pakistan.

Islam and Politics in Pakistan

Official historical narratives trace the politics of the term "secular" in its nationalist mode to a statement made by Mohammed Ali Jinnah, Pakistan's founding father, in which he declared that while people may cherish their religious identities in their private lives, the ideal of the new state was that

> in the course of time Hindus would cease to be Hindus and Muslims would cease to be Muslims, not in the religious sense because that is the personal faith of each individual but in the political sense as citizens of the state. (Asghar Khan 1985, 136)

The nation-state in Pakistan shares many of the assumptions about modernization, democracy, and progress that are deemed to be intrinsic to secularism projects elsewhere, and this is evident in some constitutional provisions such as fundamental rights of citizens and equality of individuals regardless of class, gender, religion, or race. However, it is, along with perhaps Israel, unique among twentieth-century nation-states in being based not only on secular principles of modern statehood but also on religious principles of particular nationhood.

According to the official narratives of Pakistani history, which have been subjected to multiple contestation by postcolonial theorists, an anticolonial nationalist movement of Indian Muslims, relying mostly on universalist and modernist principles of rights, freedom, and autonomy, argued for the partition of India into separate states for the Hindus and Muslims of the subcontinent amid the impending departure of British colonizers in the early twentieth century. The establishment of Pakistan on August 14, 1947, is widely represented as a testimony to the legitimacy of these demands. However, the political subjectivity, on whose basis these claims of Muslim national identity were made, was not simply a modern/secular one but also had a religious and communal identity (Muslim) into which were collapsed heterogeneous class, regional, linguistic, sectarian, and other differences.

Despite recent scholarly interventions to deconstruct this representation, the notion of Muslim as national identity retains salience. In this society and its associated political culture, it may be argued that secularism has never existed as the unmitigated antithesis of the religious. If it functioned at all in this guise, it was in the imagination of two small groups of people occupying culturally opposite corners—the leaders of politico-religious parties such as the Jamaat-e-Islami and a smaller fraction of people who may be correctly identified as the "secular modernizing elite."[4] Indeed, even when self-proclaimed secular progressives reiterate the words of Mohammed Ali Jinnah to argue for a notion of citizenship unmarked by religious identity, many do so either to defend the basic citizenship rights of religious minorities or the fundamental human rights of other citizens, such as women, sexual minorities, and the poor. Unlike similar attempts in self-styled secular Muslim countries such as Turkey

---

4. The interconnection of "secular," "modernizing," and "elite" is mostly used derogatively in Pakistan to homogenize for the purpose of condemnation a heterogeneous group of liberal and left-thinking people, but also some religious thinkers who challenge the cultural ideological prescriptions of "Islamists." I use this term, because of its potential to signal a historical and discursive class-specific position, with caution and a great degree of ambivalence. I also use the term "secular-progressive" to refer to feminists, human rights activists, and other groups opposed to Islamism, since "secular" and/or "progressive" appear to be the preferred terms of self-definition in many of their verbal and written statements (Mumtaz 1994; Said Khan 1993; Shaheed and Mumtaz 1992).

or Egypt, or European states such as France, the secular is rarely invoked to stamp out representations of religious identity in the public space of Pakistan or to impede the entry of all that is religious into an imagined nation-space of homogeneity (Anderson 1991). What may be identified as a secular impulse, one that is undoubtedly permeated with exclusionary ideas about class, gender, and ethnicity, is usually enacted not so much to expel the religious from public life but rather to restrain the excesses of politico-religious discourse in the domain of public politics. In the case of Pakistan, furthermore, I propose that many appropriations of the secular may be read not simply as a testimony to the global dominance of the secular, but also as a palimpsestic reminder of the dissenting tradition of Islam in South Asia.

The Islamic tradition in South Asia, encapsulated in the prayer of the revolutionary poet Faiz Ahmed as "the courage to dissent, the audacity to criticize," enjoins us to situate Muslim and Islamic subjectivity beyond the various discursive constructions of the religious-versus-secular and to subject both the religious and the secular to moral scrutiny and an overwhelmingly sanguine conception of human and divine.[5] Faiz's mystical ideas are emblematic of the poetics of South Asian Muslim culture, in which the political authority stands as the prime signifier of deviation from spiritual purity and piety, deserving of disapproval and ridicule, though not always to be altogether shunned (Mukhia 1999). From this perspective, dissent expressed through mysticism and devotional affect and

5. Faiz Ahmed Faiz, "Dua" (prayer), written on the occasion of Pakistan's Independence Day, August 14, 1967, in Faiz 1986, 429. In this book, Faiz uses the term "kufr" for dissent/interrogation. Kufr or disbelief is a significant concept in Islamic thought. According to the *Oxford Dictionary of Islam*, the word "kufr" or one of its derivatives appears in the Quran 482 times. It also means "ingratitude," the willful refusal to appreciate the benefits that God has bestowed. Modern reform and revival movements invest the concept with new significance: current Muslim beliefs and practices have been so corrupted from true Islam that they constitute *shirk* (idolatry) or *jahiliyyah* (ignorance). Pre-modern reformers tended to see kufr in popular Islam, including Sufi practices; some modern reformers see the pervasive influence of the West as a cause of kufr. "Kufr," in Esposito 2003, http://www.oxfordreference.com/views/ENTRY.html?subview=Main&entry=t125.e1323.

circulated widely through poetry and music is oppositional to both dog-matic and institutionalized religious authority and the political authority encapsulated in the modern state. Expanding on this role of mysticism in social and political life and epitomized in poetry, Mukhia emphasizes that the counterpoising of mind and body, head and heart, in Sufi poetry should not be seen as "one of rationality and irrationality, but of argumen-tation and feeling, of hegemonic ambition and [humanist] universalism" (1999, 873).

It is not surprising that a recurring theme of mystical art, as in the poetry of Faiz that I have cited, is the expression of disdain for the cal-culated religiosity embodied by the middle-ranking Islamic subject or the *vaez* (preacher), whose misguided disciplinary overtures may reflect above all his ignorance of the nature of ecstatic piety that transcends ritu-als or practice.[6] I suggest that in the space of contemporary state-centered politics in Pakistan, poetic dissent, inflected not simply in poetry, music, and art per se but in the poetics of our lives as well, is also an attempt to dislodge the enduring authority of the modern Islamist-religious, and thereby its spokespersons, to affect the terms of Muslim identity, and defi-nitions of belonging based on that identity. As I discuss in chapter 4, the Islamist project in Pakistan, and feminist responses to its power, are better understood not as the insertion of the religious into a normatively secu-lar public space, but rather as the imposition of a particular, contentious vision of community on a host of sometimes separated but at times over-lapping or interlinked ambivalent political-cultural spaces. A small but intensely visible space among these is the cultural-political configuration that is often misnamed liberal/secular where religion and the secular have interacted with various unresolved outcomes. The space of Muslim anti-colonial nationalism in South Asia was thus much more complex than its historical representations. And it is because of this multihued complexity that the project of the Jamaat-e-Islami was unacceptable to many Mus-lim nationalists who were widely represented as secular modernizers but

6. For a good introduction to the mystical dimensions of Islam, see Chittick 2000. For a gendered South Asian account, see Dehlvi 2009.

included a wide stratum of traditional ulema (scholars), maulanas (theologians), and Sufis (mystics). It is through these understandings of "Islam" and "Muslim" that the political project of the Jamaat-e-Islam needs to be approached.

Jamaat Women, the Public-Political, and Purdah

A key to Jamaat women's understanding of public space, and therefore of their own role in its politics, is the manner in which the modernist Islamic reformer Maulana Maududi theorized it in his seminal work *Purdah and the Status of Women in Islam* (1939). Jamaat women frequently urged me to read this book or at least its chapters relating to social and public life. They emphasized that it was here that Maududi encapsulated the identity and role of the Muslim individual and delineated its gendered boundaries and differences.

In this book, which was written in India under British colonial rule in the early twentieth century, Maududi seeks to address clearly and unambiguously the modern Muslim public subject that, for the Jamaat, is normatively male. Against the cultural and social changes wrought in Indian Muslim society due to the colonial encounter, Maududi exhorts Muslim believers in the twentieth century to rectify themselves and attain a specified standard of righteousness or else "be prepared to face those disgraceful results towards which the Western way of life will inevitably lead them" (Maududi 1939, 25).

The institutional practice that Maududi identified as critical to righteousness for Muslim men and women was the system of purdah, or the seclusion of women and the restriction of interactions between women and men. Purdah as a social system dividing the pure and the tainted, private and public, and home and the social/political world is placed at the crux of the Islamic social system and as the cornerstone of being a Muslim. In contrast to prevailing South Asian understanding of women's seclusion as cultural routine, Maududi theorized purdah as Islamic practice. Even as he conceded that no specific mode of veiling was inscribed in the Quran, he insisted that purdah "is Quranic in spirit" and incumbent on Muslim society (Maududi 1939, 194).

Maududi's theory of purdah was produced through his class, his gender, and the experience of being Muslim in South Asia while coping with colonial rule and the expanding project of Hindu nationalist modernity. Rejecting the predominantly affective and intuitive bases of individual and communal piety that characterized the dominant traditions of Islamic theology and Muslim philosophy in the Indian subcontinent, Maududi argued that Islamic identity derived from its social system. And this social system relied on three foundations: moral purification, punitive laws and preventive measures, and the rules and regulations of purdah (Maududi 1939, 217–18). Owing to the expansion of print and other media, he said immorality had increased in Indian Muslim society and moral purity had dissipated. At the same time, the experience of colonial rule had undermined the force of the "punitive laws of Islam"; therefore, two of the three foundations of the Islamic social system were destroyed. In these conditions, Maududi emphasized the importance of purdah as the only remaining structure of Islamic society in India in the early twentieth century.

In this text Maududi defined purdah as the veiling of women, but also as the sequestering of Muslim women in the home and exclusion from the public sphere of male activities: "Islam allows a woman at the most to uncover her hands and face and leave her home for genuine needs only in the utmost need" (Maududi 1939, 21). Indeed, in this text more than anywhere, Maududi stretched the meaning of purdah to denote a whole set of injunctions that for him constituted the most important part of the Islamic system of community life. Purdah was thus conceptualized as much more than a social, cultural, or even religious practice; it signified an ideal of a social system based on a strict gendered separation of the spheres of public and private lives.

Maududi blamed the decline of the purdah system, above all, on the cultural influence of colonialism and the "slavish mentality" of Muslims who had succumbed to the force of Western standards of civilized behavior and modern subjectivity (18). He was critical of the efforts of reformist Islamic scholars to offer reinterpretations of the Quran and Hadith regarding gender relations and women's rights to encourage the community to adapt to the social, educational, and political systems imposed by the colonizers in India. Although Indian religious reformers of the period tended to support their reformist strategies with reference to Islamic traditions such as scholarly consensus and deductive or analogical reasoning, Maududi distrusted their intentions. He begins his theorizing of purdah by denigrating previous Muslim reform attempts, saying they were not related to perceived practical or religious needs, but rather "arose as a result of being overwhelmed by the attractive culture of a dominant power and its vehement propaganda against Islamic culture" (Maududi 1939, 21). This clearly indicates an anticolonial impulse in the Islamist vision of Maulana Maududi, and it is evident also in the politics and discourses of present-day Jamaat-e-Islami women. It needs emphasizing that this anticolonial Islamist impulse, like its secular nationalist counterpart in India and elsewhere, was a fundamentally gendered one, since Maududi identified Muslim women's purdah/segregation from the public as the pillar on which rests the "whole superstructure" of the social system of Islam (218).

In the effort to establish purdah as defining Muslim identity, Maududi's text delineates what he terms "three positions" that characterized the attitudes of Indian Muslims in relation to modernity and the issue of veiling. At one extreme were those Muslims who had begun to oppose purdah, and Maududi described them as "Oriental Occidentals," since he believed they had intellectually accepted Western social and philosophical ideologies. At the other extreme, he situated the "foolish and thoughtless people who cannot think and form independent opinion" (1939, 83). According to Maududi these were the masses of Muslims who did not deserve the attention of scholars and reformers and may, therefore, be ignored.

The main concern of the reformers of the Jamaat-e-Islami, according to Maududi, were those whom he termed "Lip Service Muslims," or a section of people who claimed Muslim identity but were ambivalent in their observances of Islamic social practices: "Women of these people neither observe full Purdah nor are wholly unveiled. . . . Their blend of the Western and Islamic ways and observance of the so-called Purdah is no solution at all." Maududi urges this group of Muslims to consider whether they are fully prepared to face the challenges of Western life. If not, then they should "not even look towards the Western way" (1939, 80–81).

It is thus the emergent Muslim middle classes in the 1940s and those of the present era that are the main object-subject of the Jamaat's vision of

Muslim public subjectivity. The political vision of Maududi and that of the Jamaat may be understood through examination of Maududi's specific use of the term "revolution," which was different from Western social and political thought. Although Maududi drew freely on Western ideas and concepts, he modified them to the conditions of Islam and Muslims in South Asia (Reza Nasr 1996). For the Jamaat, revolution does not symbolize a violent overthrow of the existing order, but rather a gradual cultural and political transformation aimed at society's leading classes. Rather than begin at the grassroots, this was a type of social change that was seen to begin at the top and permeate downward. Therefore, as Reza Nasr (1996) emphasizes, if Maududi's message was aimed at any particular social group, it was to society's leaders or those who were aspiring to become leaders. Referring to an address given by Maududi to a party gathering, Reza Nasr states: "It is not the people's thoughts which change society, argued Maududi, but the minds of the society's movers and leaders" (Reza Nasr 1996, 77). These groups comprising not the elite but rather middle-class professionals are also the main objects of the modernizing and developmental discourses of the nation-state of Pakistan. Both the political project of nationalism and the religious project of Islamism are gendered, classed, and culturally specific discourses whose main concern is men and women of the emergent middle classes in Pakistan. Today the Jamaat-e-Islami's reach into the professional classes in Pakistan is by no means encompassing, but contemporary events suggest that significant populations of the nation's lawyers, doctors, journalists, and soldiers are imbued with a variety of ideologies that may resonate with the social-political visions of the politico-religious parties. We may situate the present cohort of Jamaat women among these middle-class professional groups and understand them as citizen-subjects who lay claim to both the Islamist discourses of Maududi and the developmental discourses of the nation-state.

Jamaat Women and Electoral Politics

According to Maududi, the only legitimate sphere of activism for Muslim women is the domestic and social space where women interact with other women in charitable activities, social welfare, and religious reformism.

While the members of the Jamaat Women's Wing have always supported the main party and its political activities and on occasion demonstrated this support through public protest, the Women's Wing categorically declares the space of public politics, government functions, and public office to be the domain of men. Metcalf (1994) has argued that women's bodies have become particularly potent symbols of Islamic norms in movements such as the Jamaat-e-Islami, which became involved in nationalist politics and imbibed modern nationalism's discourses of women's roles and feminine nature as well as its differentiation of public and private roles. Metcalf states that unlike some other twentieth-century movements for Islamic reform such as the Tablighi Jamaat, the Jamaat-e-Islami is to be understood in the context of the institutions of the nation-state, "which examines and reconfigures Islam to adapt to the principles of a social order mandated by modern national politics" (Metcalf 1996). Questions related to women have figured prominently in public discussions on law and politics in Pakistan, and the Jamaat-e-Islami has been a significant player in shaping these discussions. Consequently, for the Jamaat-e-Islami, women are a key public symbol for its project of institutionalizing an *Islami Nizam*, or Islamic order in the nation-state (Metcalf 1996). Despite this symbolic significance, the Jamaat had always been able to curtail women's political participation to protests, electoral support, and canvassing of female voters instead of direct participation in elections as political representatives of the party.

This changed in 2002 as Jamaat women were forced to confront a new reality when the government of President Pervez Musharraf increased the space for public participation of women by allocating special seats for women representatives in local, provincial, and national bodies. At first the increase in women's seats was vehemently opposed by the Jamaat-e-Islami and its coalition partners in the Muttahida Majlis Amal, the MMA, who argued that the involvement of women in the political sphere would disrupt the Islamic family system with its specified gendered roles.[7] Ulti-

7. According to information provided by a Jamaat Women's Wing leader, Lahore, March 2006.

mately the Jamaat and its co-members of the Majlis voluntarily decided to drop their longstanding opposition to women's political participation and put forward candidates at all levels. The leaders of parties emphasized that the decision on women's political participation was antithetical to the aims of the movement and needed to be understood as a strategic reaction to a particular political condition rather than a change in gender policy. Even those women who got elected to significant political positions in the local and national bodies, such as Samina, described their political responsibilities as an unwelcome imposition on their traditional roles in the party and home. According to Samina,

> In the name of empowerment, women are being pushed into political decision making and economic participation, in the belief that women will become powerful through economic and political independence. However we believe, and this is evident in Allama Iqbal's *Israr-e-Khudi* and *Javidnama* [monumental philosophical works], that if women venture out of the homes they will neglect their creative [reproductive] role.

In a similar vein, another key leader of the Jamaat Women's Wing emphasized that it was not the objective of the Women's Wing to promote women's access to power at the party or national level, nor was it to facilitate women's entry into public spheres of the economy, law, or politics. Their main focus was to create awareness among women of their rights and duties in Islam, promote women's education, including health education, create institutions and organizations that would serve women, and, above all, to save them from vice and educate them about virtue.

Even while they spurn the space of public politics, Jamaat women appear to be fully conversant with the discourses of democracy, citizenship, and modern nationalism that frame their struggles for a particular vision of an Islamic nation-state in Pakistan. While Jamaat women observe the veil and emphasize the public segregation of men and women, they are fully capable, even more so than so-called secular middle-class Pakistani women, of operating in the public sphere of electoral politics. They are advantaged by access to the Jamaat's superior intellectual and ideological training opportunities and the benefit of being completely proficient in the languages of mass politics (that is, Urdu), which, for many English-educated secular-progressive women, has become a major stumbling block in contemporary Pakistani politics. Indeed, Jamaat women's involvement in street politics (protests, demonstrations, strikes, and so on, which are a key aspect of the public face of politics in Pakistan) occurs only with the endorsement and support of the party's male leaders. This is in contrast to women in feminist and gender-focused politics who tend to be marginalized if not opposed by the leadership of liberal and leftist parties. A distinctive ambivalence reflecting modernist political strategy and rejection of cultural modernity pervades the discourses and actions of present-day Jamaat women as they seek to redefine and reshape the political/public nation-space as the gendered space of the public-religious.

Politics as a Religious Vocation

Samina and Hadia were two Jamaat women leaders who became members of Pakistan's National Assembly from 2002 to 2008. In the next sections I will discuss some of their views about politics, feminism, and their understanding of Muslim women's role in the public-political spaces of the nation. I will also revisit my discussions with some other women who were elected to other bodies.

I met Samina in the summer of 2006 at her home in a small community located on the outskirts of Lahore. In her well-appointed but simply furnished drawing room, she entertained me with cups of tea accompanied by trays of fruit, quiche, sweets, cakes, and sandwiches. Widowed at a young age, Samina lives with her teenage daughter and son a few minutes from the home of her brother. An academic by profession, Samina graduated from Punjab University and at the time of our interview in 2006 was undertaking postgraduate work in Islamic studies. In addition to institutional studies, she was also learning languages so that she could speak and write Arabic, Urdu, and English. When I met her she was studying Persian and engaged in the study of *Iqbaliat* (the writings of the poet-philosopher Mohammed Iqbal) under the guidance of her father.

Like many Jamaat women, Samina started her political career as a student leader, in Lahore College, which later became a university. Before

General Zia ul Haq (1977–88) banned student councils in universities, Samina was one of the leaders of the Islamic Jamiat Talibat in Lahore, but also an informal mentor of the female students, for whom she organized religious and welfare activities. For Samina, it was the influence of her close relatives, first her father and later her husband, that directed her toward the politics of the Jamaat-e-Islami. She started her career through what she described as "nonpolitical" activities in the nongovernmental sector and set up her own nongovernmental organization, which now has branches all over Pakistan.

Referring to her motivation for being involved in the Jamaat-e-Islami Women's Wing, Samina expressed deep admiration for the amir, Qazi Hussain Ahmed, who she believed had changed the political orientation of the Jamaat from negativity and censure to love and service. She told me:

> So for me and for Jamaat-e-Islami, politics means that power should be used for the benefit of people. Not to be used indiscriminately in the sense of might is right. But to use power for the welfare of people. This is what Maulana [Maududi] preached and what we have learned from him, that the aim of politics is to serve people.

Like other Jamaat women, Samina blamed the nature of politics in Pakistan for the repeated electoral failures of the religious parties rather than their ideologies or their political agenda. Jamaat women also believe that while their movement enjoys greater support among the masses of Pakistani women than is commonly perceived and reported, they are not seen by the media as the legitimate representatives of women in Pakistan. Speaking in the background of the "war on terror," women believed that their project was being undermined, and their accomplishments ignored, because of the heightened public and media discourse on the then-president Pervez Musharraf's project to present a "liberal" face of Islam and Muslims to the West.

According to Jamaat women, the political processes in Pakistan and the actors who operate within these processes have distorted the nature of politics from a form of service to the art of governance or managing people through the exercise of power. They argue that this has undermined the correct meaning of politics in Islam. Against such conceptions of the political, Samina said Maududi's attempt to link the moral and the political was a "unique contribution."

For Samina one of the important insights of Maududi was to establish the Prophet Muhammad himself as "the greatest of all politicians." Maududi's ability to understand this aspect of the Prophet's life, she said, was his major contribution to Muslims "in this modern age and in this subcontinent," and one of his reasons for establishing the Jamaat-e-Islami. Samina noted that although there had been many Islamic reformist movements in the past, "it was only the Jamaat that was able to offer a vision of a complete Islam with all its various components." She explained:

> Maulana Maududi has done a great favor to our generation in that he has shown us the true face of Islam and the real message (*dawat*) of the Prophet Muhammad, that religion and politics are not necessarily contradictory aspects of life. In fact, politics are a component of religion and such an important component that were it to be removed from the Quran, two-thirds of the Quran, *Astaqfir ullah* [God protect us], would be inapplicable.

Elaborating on the pious intention behind Maududi's linking of politics with religion, Samina argued such an impulse could be gleaned from a serious study of the life of the Prophet Muhammad. She said that Maududi's vision for Jamaat as a religious-political movement was based on the example of the Prophet, who first meditated in isolation in the cave of Hira, then came back to bring the word to his family, and eventually turned to the entirety of humanity so that all of humankind could join him. Therefore the Jamaat considers politics both a key element of religion and the means by which religious order may be established in the world. Samina argued that although the Prophet Muhammad emphasized mostly *dawat* (invitation) and *tabligh* (proselytizing) in the early years of Islam, this changed when he migrated with his followers [from Mecca] to Medina, where according to Maududi, he set up the first Islamic state. Drawing on Maududi's monumental text *Tafhim-ul-Qur'an*, Samina said Maududi had demonstrated an inextricable relationship between political power and social life, which thus established the true mission of the Prophet: to establish the dominance of Islam.[8] She argued, "The ascendance of Islam happened only after the Islamic state was set up. The [system of the] Quran cannot be established until it has the support of power."

Samina dismissed the idea that by prioritizing politics the Jamaat had moved from its original orientation as a religious movement. Indeed, many followers of Maududi, most prominent among them Dr. Israr Ahmed, left the movement when Maududi directed the Jamaat-e-Islami to take part in national elections in the 1960s. Samina defended the party's increasing involvement in electoral politics, saying that the Jamaat had "not shifted an inch" from the vision of Maududi, whose objective was "to establish Islam as a complete system, in the same form as that preached by the Prophet Muhammad and to accomplish this neither through violence nor through surreptitious means." Therefore, Samina said, "I consider politics to be a component of religion. This is how I have been trained."

I met Hadia at her modest home in a middle-class suburb of Karachi.[9] I was struck by the simplicity of her home, a sharp contrast to some of the mansions of the top leaders of democratic progressive parties that stand out in upscale neighborhoods in Karachi. Our discussion took place in an upstairs room of the two-story house. The floor of the large room, covered with carpeting, was otherwise almost totally bare, devoid of chairs or couches or any seating arrangements. In the middle of the room was a long low table laden with party pamphlets and other materials. There were about five or six women there and we all sat around the table. Two women went downstairs and brought us bowls of pistachio ice cream and bottles of 7-Up. Hadia urged me to take both refreshments, pointing to the extremely hot and dusty weather that afternoon.

Hadia is the wife of a key leader of the Jamaat-e-Islami, but she traced her interest in religious politics to the influence of her father. At the time of the struggle for Pakistan in the 1940s, she said her father had been a

---

8. Samina was referring to Maududi's commentary on Quran Surah 17:15 in *Tafhim-ul-Quran*, http://tafheemulquran.org/Tafhim_u/017/surah_all.htm.

9. Interview with Hadia, Karachi, May 2004.

supporter of the anticolonial nationalist movement led by the Muslim League. This was also the period of the emergence of the Jamaat-e-Islami, which emphasized religion in contrast to the "secular" nationalist politics of the Muslim League. Hadia's father was an admirer of publications of Maulana Maududi, in particular the party's monthly journal *Tarjuman-ul-Quran*, and this had a lasting influence on her family. After 1947 when Pakistan was formed, Hadia's father became a part of the Jamaat-e-Islami. As is a common pattern among many other middle-class women in the subcontinent, Hadia's introduction to the Jamaat was through its vast range of publications.

The defining moment in national politics, and in Hadia's own life, came in 1971, when Pakistan was split into two countries (Pakistan and Bangladesh) after a bloody civil war and the massacre of thousands of Bengali citizens by the national army. The Jamaat-e-Islami was one of the devout supporters of the unity of the two Muslim majority regions that constituted pre-1971 Pakistan and of the theory that Muslims and Hindus were two distinct nations. The Jamaat had also provided volunteer and vigilante groups to the Pakistan army in its attempts to repress the Bengali nationalist movement that eventually led to the creation of Bangladesh in December 1971. At that time Hadia was a student in a local college in Karachi, where she studied economics, political science, and Islamiyat. She recalls:

> At the fall of Dhaka I began to wonder why this has happened? At that time I was also undertaking some reading of texts, in particular the *Tafhim ul Quran* of Maulana Maududi—and related books—in order to understand whether it was our own fault or was there a political situation that had led to this huge disaster in our country. I began to realize that our claim to be Muslims was an empty one—Islam has also placed some responsibilities on us, which require us not simply to sit in our homes but to become actively engaged. That is why the sadness that I experienced after this tragedy led me to read more and I started this work.

Hadia appears to understand the economic, political, and cultural marginalization of Pakistan's Bengali citizens as a result of the weakness of the nations' leaders to develop a religious subjectivity among the people. This was clarified by her contention that although the Pakistan People's Party came into power after the army defeat in 1971, its response to the division of the country was "defensive" in that it did not adequately focus on the ideological damage to the nation but rather on the survival of the nation-state. According to Hadia: "They said, 'Thank God Pakistan has been saved'—as if they had saved something—whereas I felt that we had lost something." Hadia explained that while the British colonizers had done a deep injustice to the Muslims of subcontinental India by giving them a country that was divided by one thousand miles of Indian territory, once Pakistan was created as a Muslim state, it was incumbent on us all to defend its integrity. This, she said, required all political parties to support the Pakistan army in East Pakistan (Bangladesh) against the Bengali struggles, as the Jamaat-e-Islami's Bengali counterpart had done with its "No to Bangladesh" campaign. Amid this political and cultural background Hadia said she was drawn to the political stand of the Jamaat-e-Islami, which had organized and trained groups of youth, mostly Urdu-speaking non-Bengalis, into civilian militias to assist the Pakistan army. She said:

> If anyone was willing to die with the Pakistan army it was JI [and] their paramilitary organizations—Al Badr and Al Shams. Our youth felt that we were one nation and India had no right to intervene in our affairs. . . . I still have regrets that our troops surrendered.

This reflects a defensive view of the brutal military actions against Pakistan's ethnic Bengali population that led to a civil war and the eventual establishment of Bangladesh in 1971.[10] It also resonates with the Jamaat-e-Islami's

---

10. The Jamaat-e-Islami was banned in Bangladesh soon after the country's independence from Pakistan in 1971 because of its vehement opposition to the liberation struggle. Later on it was included in several coalition governments. In July 2010 the government banned all publications by Maududi, saying they encouraged Islamic militancy and terrorism.

staunchly nationalist ethos, which both contradicts and also upholds the idealization of a transnational Muslim *ummah*.

After the events of 1971, Hadia said that she began to realize that Islam placed responsibilities on individuals, including women, and that therefore it was a responsibility to "use our spare time for religious purposes." Her induction into formal politics was part of this process of understanding her own role as a Muslim woman, which, she emphasized, was not "simply to sit in our homes but to become actively engaged." Hadia said that the present political condition of Muslims worldwide was considered, among Muslim men and women, to be due to a failure to engage in politics and develop a strong Islamic political system; otherwise, "we would not have been under US domination the way we are now and we would not be shedding tears over Iraq."

Hadia emphasized that for social transformation to occur there was a need to adhere to three Islamic principles: obedience to God and abiding by His rules, eliminating wrong and promoting virtues, and situating power in the hands of rightly guided (*sualeh*) individuals who would be able to guide the masses, as did the rightly guided caliphs. Hadia defined dawat as a political issue of great importance to the party, because it is only the virtuous who should be in power, whether male or female: "We believe that tabligh without politics is not enough. . . . We are all involved in this struggle and we give tremendous importance to this political issue of our dawat so that our authority in power should be good. Our objective is to bring into power those who are virtuous, whether male or female."

In addition to Samina and Hadia, two of Jamaat's female politicians whom I met several times were Farida and Maria, both members of the Karachi City Council from June 2001 to 2005. The circumstances of their joining the Jamaat were different from those of Samina and Hadia, who were exposed to the Jamaat's ideology and politics through their family and home environment. Farida and Maria said that their decision to become actively involved in the politics of the Jamaat marked a departure from their family traditions and environment. They meant that their families were Muslims in the classical South Asian sense, that is, they observed the basic obligations, such as prayers, fasting, pilgrimage, and so on, but did not engage with religion in the rationalized and self-conscious manner as did Jamaat women. In becoming critical of the traditional mode of being a Muslim woman, women like Farida and Maria and some of their relatives represented a new subjective process in which individual reiteration of faith became the primary ground for religious practice and observances. This was also evident in their more activist and programmatic approach to politics, in which they were involved at the municipal city level. Farida was interested in bringing about changes in the urban environment in Karachi through legislation for media, advertising, and promotional activities, as well as in the moral guidance of its citizens through educational curricula.

The two women were very good friends and I usually met them together in the Karachi Civic Center, where the city government offices are located. Farida's office was typically full of women who had come to see her about issues related to their neighborhood. Because she observed purdah, outside her door was a notice announcing that only women were permitted to enter; a woman in a burqa opened the door when I knocked or rang the bell. This was a departure from the normal experience of government offices in Pakistan, where even the offices of female officials are served by male secretaries and other administrative staff. Often I reached the office a little early for my meeting and, if neither Farida nor Maria were present, the woman always brought me a cup of hot tea, sometimes accompanied by biscuits. There were usually other women in the room seated on large sofas grouped around a coffee table, and there was invariably a discussion among us about children, women's issues, religion, or politics.

With Farida and Maria my meetings were mostly in the form of a three-way discussion rather than conventionally structured research interviews, even though I carried a list of questions to keep me on track. Very often it was Maria who was able to give me more attention, since we met in Farida's office and Farida was often interrupted by visitors, petitioners, and other citizens, mostly women seeking her help. While Maria and I were engaged in discussion, Farida would frequently interject to support or elaborate on a point Maria made by sharing an incident from personal experience or relating a Hadith. I shared a special affinity with these women since they had studied in my old alma mater, a degree college in Karachi run by Catholic nuns. Like me they had also studied in the Department of Journalism of Karachi University, and we had many experiences to share about our department and faculty.

Their understanding of politics and women's role in it were developed during the high era of Islamization in Pakistan when the Jamaat became a major force in Karachi's colleges and universities. Their ideas about the legitimacy of gender in bringing about social change reflect some of the ideas that became normalized in Pakistan through the NGO movement. Some of this may be evinced in their accounts of their reasons for joining the Jamaat-e-Islami.

Farida described her home environment as traditional but not really religious. She became interested in the mission of the Jamaat through exposure to the students' organizations affiliated with the party in Karachi University. This led her to engage in a special study of the Quran and Hadith by going to Mansurah (Jamaat headquarters) and completing a course at the college for women. She realized then that most Muslim women are devoid of what she regarded as basic knowledge about the Quran and Hadith, even those from educated and religious-minded families like herself: "I came back to Karachi and told my parents, why didn't you tell me that such and such a thing was so important and that these are the limits [set by Islam] in this matter?"[11]

Maria described herself as someone who had never been interested in the Jamaat-e-Islami or its politics. Before joining the Jamaat, she said, "My hair was cut short and I used to often wear T-shirts and jeans when I went abroad with my husband." She became interested in the Jamaat when she started dropping in on a Quran discussion group that met at the house of a relative. "I used to think: 'Burqa and me?'" she said, emphasizing that she had been an unlikely candidate for the Jamaat's politics until she went through a complete transformation. Both women usually followed up such comments by describing how their own families and friends were skeptical of their decision to join the Jamaat since it was commonly (mis)understood as a restrictive and oppressive environment for women. The women described with amusement the surprise and amazement of their

---

11. Interview with Farida, Karachi, June 2003.

relatives and friends when they learned how emancipating Maria and Farida found their actual experiences of the Jamaat. They also emphasized that their own experiences of being in the Jamaat were in contrast to what they deemed to be commonly held misperceptions about the party, even among their families and friends. For example, Farida laughed that people often found it surprising that she had managed a boutique and could bake Western-style cakes and desserts—implying that purdah was often perceived to be incompatible with modern skills, even those related to domestic life.

Explaining the rationale for their involvement in the Jamaat's political activities, Farida said: "Activism is a kind of jihad." Both women said while they had been involved in the Women's Wing they entered electoral politics at the behest of the leadership of the Women's Wing rather than through their own inclination. They rejected my suggestion that since they themselves seemed to be active both at home and in public politics, it was contradictory of them to oppose women's public participation for fear that it would destroy their family obligations. They argued that Muslim women had historically played a role in nation building, recalling that the Khalifa Omar had appointed a woman, Hazrat Bibi Sauda, to monitor the market in order to ensure that prices were stable. Therefore, they argued, it was wrong to suggest that Muslim women should "waste" their time at home.

Interestingly, it was not an aversion to the public or political that seemed most evident in the responses of Farida and Maria. For these women, who were comfortable in both the religious environment of the Jamaat and the more worldly society outside, it was the political that must change in order to accommodate the personal or domestic and religious. Thus their notion of a public space and formal politics focused on transformations that would open more spaces for both women and religion.

They described some of their efforts, often with success, to change structures and practices in government bodies in order to Islamize and feminize "secular" political spaces to make them appropriate for women like themselves. Indeed, Farida emphasized that she found the Jamaat an ideal political public environment for women since here, unlike other political parties, women's domestic responsibilities were integral to the party's political agenda. She noted that since their election as councilors,

Jamaat women had demanded and managed to bring about many changes to reduce conflict between women's political activities and family responsibilities. Among the successes she described were the establishment of a daycare center in the Karachi city government complex, and demands for reorganizing the hours of offices, clinics, and other public service facilities according to women's domestic schedules. Citing her own example, Farida said she had difficulty participating in the city government assembly sessions since its schedule conflicted with the routine of her school-going children. She said women councilors had been successful in changing the schedule of the assembly sessions from morning to afternoon so that women could meet their children when they came home from school, feed them, and put them down for an afternoon nap before leaving the house.

According to Farida, although there were only 58 women out of the total 265 members in the City Council, the body had agreed to this schedule, which was proposed by the women. Farida emphasized that this was part of the vision of the Jamaat that prioritized women's family responsibilities:

> We believe that our children are a very important resource and we cannot afford to neglect them. You see, even if a woman is a doctor and she neglects her daughter, the daughter will never want to be a doctor when she grows up. If my children get hurt by the kind of work I do then they will never want to have anything to do with this kind of work.

At the same time women party members are also offered training workshops to enhance their public and domestic roles; there are regularly organized time-management workshops to train women who are working outside the home about how to adjust their home and other responsibilities, how to raise children, and how to organize their children's lives and activities. Referring to the benefits of this training for herself, Farida said: "For instance, now I am working, I have enrolled my two older children in the summer camp—I told them you should go there and you will learn all kinds of important things about politics and economics."

Both Maria and Farida were elected from and lived in Nazimabad, a middle-class suburb of Karachi mostly populated by Urdu-speaking muhajirs, a term used in Pakistan to refer to all those who had migrated from India to Pakistan in the partition of 1947. Since the 1980s, this sub-urb has been the stronghold of the Muttahida Qaumi Movement (MQM), a Karachi-based party originally organized on the basis of muhajir as an ethnic identity. Indeed, the Jamaat women were mostly successful in the city elections of 2001 because these polls were boycotted by the MQM. In 2006, when the MQM decided to run for local and national elections, the Jamaat lost most of these seats. Since both Maria and Farida appeared to be ethnically muhajir, I asked them why they had not joined the MQM, which has strong support not only among the Urdu-speaking working class and the urban poor but also among middle-class and lower middle-class groups in Karachi. In response, they drew attention to the MQM's well-known record of violence in Karachi and its deliberately secular ideology.

Maria, reflecting the Jamaat's universalist and nationalist stance, was critical of the MQM's ethnic populist approach, since it encouraged the division of Muslims who should be a single ummah. She argued that ethnic identities are divisive and weaken religious identity, and therefore harm national identity. She reiterated that she had joined the Jamaat for religious reasons but also political ones:

> Ethnic tensions are a reflection that people are straying away from din. Our din taught us to be fair and to be just, but when the din itself has disappeared from within us, then it doesn't matter whether one identi-fies as a Punjabi or Muhajir. One ceases to be a Muslim—the same kind of thing happened in Bangladesh.

The ruminations of Hadia, Maria, and Farida on the reasons for their gravitation toward the Jamaat's religious ideology, as opposed to ethnic nationalist ideologies of other parties, refer to a particular historical-ideo-logical period and its lasting aftermath. Their repeated disavowal of their ethnic and cultural particularities, and their privileging of a transcen-dental nationalism based on Islamic identity, binds them closer to, rather than releases them from, the history of Muslim nationalism, the Islamiza-tion of the Pakistani state and society, and the ethnic, linguistic, and sec-tarian divisions fueled by politico-religious and militaristic politics that weave into the texture of the ethnographies discussed in this text. Their comments are saturated by their experiences of life in Karachi, which has become the center of easily ignitable ethnic and sectarian tensions related to Pakistan's involvement in several decades of war, including the military crackdown on Bengalis and war with India, the Soviet–United States proxy war in Afghanistan, and the ongoing US-initiated "war on terror." I problematize some of these events and the religio-social and political implications for Pakistani society and gendered Muslim identity throughout this book.

The effect of context, locality, and personal experiences on women's understanding of politics and their own role in it was evident in other instances, such as my interview with Razia in Lahore in March 2005. She was another member of the Jamaat Women's Wing who had been elected to a representative body in 2002. The interview took place in the Jamiat ul Mohsinat (women's college) at Mansurah toward the end of a long day for both of us. During our interview, other women dropped in to discuss some work-related matter or other business and stayed on to add their input to our discussion.

Razia, who had an MA in English from Punjab University, said she was introduced to the Jamaat by her mother, as the latter had been an active participant in the dars given by female members of the party. The eldest of three daughters, Razia said that while all her sisters were involved in the Jamaat none was as committed as her. Reiterating the views that I had heard from other Jamaat women, Razia emphasized her mission to redirect other Muslim women toward the Jamaat's version of Islam. She said: "As you know most people are not really in touch with religion despite being born in a Muslim family or Muslim household. They just assume that whatever they are doing is right."

Interestingly, Razia's understanding of politics and gendered participation seemed to have been layered by the many years she had spent in Saudi Arabia, where her husband worked as a medical doctor for the government. In that society, in addition to her job as a college instructor, she had served the party as an administrator. Since I considered the Jamaat's ideal of Islamic social life—especially its emphasis on gendered segregation and the provision of separate spaces for women's education, leisure, medical needs, and employment—similar to the prevailing system in Saudi Arabia, I asked Razia about the activities of the Jamaat Women's Wing in that kingdom. She informed me that though the party was well-established in Saudi Arabia its mission of religious reform and education was confined to Pakistani immigrants and workers, as the party was not allowed to propagate its ideology among Saudi nationals. This was particularly ironic since the majority of Pakistan scholars, analysts, journalists, and ordinary people link the Jamaat's organizational stability to massive support from Saudi Arabia for the propagation of its puritanical version of Islam among the Muslims of South Asia.

I asked Razia if she found the situation of Saudi women to be different from that of women in Pakistan, since both were Muslims, and what she considered to be the reason for these differences. At this point, other women present in the room, many of whom also seemed to have lived in or visited Saudi Arabia, joined in with their comments. The general feeling was that Saudi women were better taken care of materially by the state, since they enjoyed better living conditions, including free local phone service, no taxes, and government control of food prices. It is worth emphasizing that despite appreciating the materially easier lives of Saudi women and men, my interlocutors were not completely envious of them or uncritical of the issues of gender, citizenship, and politics in that country. The other women joining in with concurring remarks, Razia lamented the lack of political awareness among Saudi women, whom she considered to be better educated than Pakistani Muslim women about their religious rights and obligations given by Islam, but ill-informed about their secular rights as citizens: "Their schools are very good at teaching religious studies. However, they offer their King almost Godlike obedience. They do not have any interest in democracy or fundamental rights or freedom of speech, etc. They may ask about it but are not much interested."

It is clear from the accounts of Razia and her companions in Lahore that, although Jamaat women may covet the cultural and social aspects of Arab women's lives, they do not idealize their authoritarian political systems as representative of the Islamic ideal. Their remarks provide an important nuance to popular and scholarly perceptions about the cultural, social, and economic impact of the massive labor migrations to oil-rich Arab countries that have been a feature of social and economic life in the sub-continent since the 1980s.[12] Jamaat women insisted that democratic politics are an important aspect of their ideology and inseparable from their religious being. Their insights about the difference between their political status and that of Arab Gulf women is a combined product of both their access to modern systems of citizenship and education and the elaboration of the Islamic system of government by the party's ideologues and leaders. They seemed to uphold notions of the party's ideal political system, which, according to a Jamaat leader, is neither identical to that of Saudi Arabia, because it is a monarchy and thus not Islamic according to the Jamaat, nor similar to the Iranian system, where authority lies in the hands of clerics, nor to the Taliban government in Afghanistan, since that was the rule of young madressa-trained men and rural maulvis (Ahmed 2002).

As defined in the Objectives Resolution, which was a preamble to Pakistan's early constitutions, and in the 1990s was integrated into the present constitution, the Jamaat argues that sovereignty belongs to Allah and has been given to the people as a sacred trust (Ahmed 2002). Indeed, it was the pressure of Jamaat representatives in the early constituent assembly debates that led to the adoption of the Objectives Resolution in the constitution of 1956, compelling the secular-oriented nationalists to institutionalize the Islamic character of the state and its laws (Choudhury 1995; Ahmed 2002). According to this resolution, the government is enjoined to create the necessary conditions that allow people to live their lives in accordance with Islam. Jamaat leaders lament what they consider to be

---

12. To deal with a balance of payments crisis in the 1970s, the government of Zulfiqar Ali Bhutto set up a program to promote the export of skilled and unskilled workers and military troops to many of the Persian Gulf states. Many of these workers were forced to return by 1990 because of decreasing employment opportunities and the Persian Gulf War. The migration slowly renewed after the Gulf War. According to a US Library of Congress Country Study (1986), the number of Pakistani workers in the Middle East was estimated at about 4 million in the early 1980s, sending home remittances of between US $1.5 billion and $2 billion a year, or over 30 percent of Pakistan's foreign-currency earnings and almost 5 percent of the GNP. US Library of Congress Country Studies: Pakistan, countrystudies.us/pakistan/86.htm.

a disregard for these injunctions by ruling elites, due to which "Islam and Democracy, which are the foundational principles of Pakistan, are in opposition to each other" (Ahmed 2002, 137). Reiterating the Jamaat's understanding of democratic, electoral politics as a path to achieving Islamization of society, Razia said: "When complete Islamization occurs, democracy too will be Islamized and we will be able to practice it in accordance with Quran and Hadith. People's opinion is also countable. In reality, what Islam offers is a kind of democracy."

Contradictions and Disjunctures: Women's Sense of Solidarity

In describing their entry into the public arena as a major event, many of my interlocutors acknowledged the support and protection of other party women in enabling them to fulfill their tasks. Samina said that the party system was structured to be a protective one that offered support for women in this world and also prepared them for the next. These expressions of solidarity were part of a deeper sense of collectivity that many women described as essential to their personal and political activism. It is this sense of the relationship between individual righteousness and social political activism that endows Jamaat women with a historical consciousness of what Cantwell Smith has described as the idea of a "community in motion," meaning a community both based on and also integral to individual faith (Smith 1957). This relationship between politics, history, and individual agency is reflected in the experiences of Fatima, a media officer of the Jamaat Women's Wing in Karachi. Describing her induction into the Women's Wing, Fatima explained that her initial attempts to adopt an Islamic lifestyle were marred by the criticism and derisive attitude of friends and relatives who were skeptical about her adoption of the burqa and her rejection of social activities that she once enjoyed. She said it was only her awareness of the existence of a strong collective consensus about these matters and the emotional support of other women in the party that enabled her to rise above these criticisms and to survive these difficult social moments: "It was then that I realized that this is a collective endeavor. If I am to continue on my mission then I must become part of a collectivity. Otherwise, on my own, I will not be able to achieve anything. That is why I joined the collective." She went on to add that in addition to the emotional and intellectual support of the collective, she had also gained personal strength, self-confidence, and patience from the frequent training opportunities offered by the party.

Fatima's experience was repeated in many different versions by women from very different classes and various social situations. It was important to my interlocutors that their successful attainment of political or professional power should not be misunderstood as an example of individual fulfillment or success. They relished the idea that they could not have managed without mentoring and support from other women and a continuing tradition of religious education and discipleship/mentorship. Similarly, Samina, in describing her experiences as a young widow in the public sphere, said that she was grateful for the protection and support from women who were older and more established in the party, to whom she referred, like my other interlocutors, as *baji* or *apa*, terms commonly used (by Pakistanis of all stripes) to show respect/affection for an older sister. Samina said:

> I began to deal with all the international issues of women, under supervision of X baji. Then we established a Women's Commission, which is headed by Dr. Kauser Firdaus. Women such as X baji, Y baji, and Z baji, have helped and guided me and, because of the team work of Jamaat-e-Islami, have enabled me to achieve all that I have done.

This solidarity expanded to include women from other politico-religious parties once Jamaat women entered the larger arena of formal politics. Jamaat women recounted for me some development projects that they had undertaken along with women from other politico-religious parties in the MMA that were intended to benefit their constituencies in mostly lower middle-class urban areas of Pakistan's towns and cities. Among their most impressive efforts was a project in which Jamaat women members of the Karachi City Council, along with a couple of women from other parties, pooled their state-allocated development budgets for the construction of a US $1.2 million women's library complex in Gulshan-e-Iqbal, a middle-class suburb of Karachi.[13] In another instance, Jamaat women members of the Assembly decided to donate a one-time salary increment totaling 10 million rupees (US $128,000) to the party's budget. The money was to go to the plan of the Women's Wing to build a multipurpose building for women's development, health, and education, and two or three small projects. Samina informed me: "It will be managed by the Jamaat-e-Islami but we will return it to the nation."

This sense of women's collaboration, however, did not extend to Jamaat women's interactions with women from "secular" or nonreligious parties, with whom Jamaat women acknowledged a communication, cultural, and ideological gap.

The Limits of Sisterhood

The interaction of women across class and political lines, resulting from the structural changes introduced by the Musharraf government in 2002, was experienced and analyzed in an ambivalent manner by my interlocutors. A few saw possibilities for collaboration by the opening up of a shared ground of action—women's issues. Farida conceded that a long-time communication gap between Jamaat women and women from groups like the All Pakistan Women's Association (APWA) and Women's Action Forum (WAF) has narrowed to some degree. "There is now a start of some communication between us and them on some issues." Feminist and fundamentalist women came together for the first time, in large numbers, mostly as political opponents on the floor of the parliament or assemblies but also in many other sites. They met in United Nations–sponsored training and empowerment projects for women parliamentarians that were enthusiastically implemented by women's groups and NGOs such as the Aurat Foundation and Shirkat Gah.

Women parliamentarians from the Jamaat, who participated in state and NGO training projects, said they often outperformed women from

13. I learned later that the project could not be completed because the Jamaat lost most of its seats in the municipal elections of 2005.

other political parties in meeting the goals and objectives of these empowerment and training projects. For example, Maria was recognized among the outstanding participants out of forty thousand women councilors who underwent training in the Women Councilors' Training Project organized by the United Nations Development Program in Pakistan and the Women's Ministry's Women's Participation Project (W3P). Jamaat women pointed to such achievements as testimony both to their superior capabilities over women from secular political groups and their claim to represent Pakistani Muslim women as a political constituency.

Jamaat women generally agreed that their access to legislative bodies and the experience of debating the problems of women helped them develop a greater understanding of what might be considered women's issues, and the causes of problems attendant to those issues, and then engage in lawmaking attempts. However, they were critical of feminist arguments, which to them appeared to be aimed at creating a society that was contradictory to the cultural traditions of Islam as understood by the Jamaat-e-Islami. Indeed, Samina pointed out that a major obstacle between women of politico-religious parties and other secular political parties was the latter's lack of knowledge about Islam and the rights given to women in Islam. She said:

> We believe that the more women become aware of the Quran the more they will know how to gain respect for themselves and attain their rights, and there will be peace in society. They will understand the divine law and we believe that they will understand the system of the world.

Elaborating on this divide, Hadia argued that unlike other women's groups, the Jamaat did not consider the relationship between men and women to be either based on oppression or arising from necessity, but rather "a responsibility" that must be accomplished in accordance with a particular framework:

> As far as Islam's teachings are concerned, for all human beings who inhabit this earth, and especially for Muslims, the concept of life is that in addition to the rights of God, there is a tremendous importance to the

rights of human beings and of individuals. Those who follow this religion are obliged to first fulfill their responsibilities, and then as much as possible, every Muslim man and woman has the social and religious responsibility to undertake this task [of the struggle for rights].

Jamaat women reject the notion of a "gender divide" as a feminist fiction and deny that "women" may represent a different set of political and social interests. Although some of the representatives referred to the work they had done to improve women's legal and social conditions as members of political bodies, they emphasized that meaningful change and progress would only come if women were able to achieve the rights given to them by Islam, not governmental or global ideas about women's rights.

Women's enhanced presence in the assemblies during 2002–8 was marked by bitter contestations between politico-religious women and women politicians from other parties over proposed modifications to legislations specifically geared toward women's status: the Hudood Ordinance of 1979 and the Muslim Family Laws Ordinance of 1961. The two ordinances are the most significant legislations that have affected the lives of women in Pakistan since the inception of the nation-state and are the most serious sites of conflict between Islam and secularism in Pakistan.

The Muslim Family Laws Ordinance was instituted in 1961 by the military government of General Ayub Khan in response to bourgeois women's demands for changes in marriage, divorce, and inheritance laws. It is considered by many Pakistani feminists to be the most significant legal provision for women by the national state (Mumtaz and Shaheed 1987). On the other hand, Pakistani feminist groups are engaged in a struggle for the repeal of the Hudood Ordinance instituted in 1979 by another military regime.

The Hudood Ordinance, covering rape, adultery, theft, robbery, and the prohibition on narcotics, was part of a state-imposed "Islamization" program. The ordinance applies to both Muslims and (differently) to non-Muslims (Saeed and Khan 2000). One of the most detrimental effects of the Hudood Ordinance has been the treatment of zina, or adultery and rape, and the failure to draw a clear distinction between the two acts. Thousands of women in Pakistan, mostly poor and rural women, have been jailed because of the ambiguity; they have been victimized by ex-husbands and family members on procedural grounds for failure to obtain an official divorce before remarrying (Khan 2007). After the zina laws came into effect, cases of reported "adultery" went up from a handful to thousands in a short period of time. According to the Human Rights Commission of Pakistan (HRCP), the number of women prisoners in Pakistan went up from seventy in 1980 to over six thousand in 1988; they were mostly accused of crimes under Hudood (Saeed and Khan 2000). Many Pakistani feminist groups, therefore, argue that the Hudood Ordinance, rather than enshrining Islamic principles, has furthered the exploitation of poor women for a variety of structural reasons that may have little to do with religion (Khan 2007). While not denying the suffering of women that is associated with the zina laws, Jamaat women defend the Hudood Ordinance as "Islamic" and vow to fight the feminist women's movement and human rights groups that are demanding the repeal of the ordinance. They insist that problems related to the Hudood Ordinance are in fact due not to the ordinance but rather to their undermining by the only other woman-friendly move taken by the state (until the time of this study)—the Muslim Family Laws Ordinance of 1961. This latter ordinance, which was bitterly opposed by the Jamaat-e-Islami, was introduced in the 1960s by a modernizing government in response to demands of secular women's groups. My interlocutors argued that by introducing the formal registration of marriage and requiring the written consent of the existing wife in an attempt to limit polygamous marriages, the Family Laws Ordinance had created discrepant marital situations for poor and illiterate people, which became criminalized with the advent of the zina ordinance. Jamaat women counter feminist demands for repeal of the Hudood Ordinance by demands for modification to the Muslim Family Laws Ordinance. These have been major issues of public confrontation between the two groups of women in political and legislative forums and in the media.

On the matter of women's collaboration, some of my interlocutors went beyond commenting on legal and ideological differences to express skepticism about the national and global efforts to encourage women to unite on women's issues. Hadia said she did not believe it was possible for different women parliamentarians to come together on a common platform on women's rights, as was being promoted by the NGOs with the support of the United Nations and global women's organizations. While agreeing that women's representatives should try to bring about change in women's situations, she argued that women politicians should also resist being ghettoized into women's issues. She emphasized: "Political parties have their own ideologies and agendas, which are related not only to women's issues but also to other matters, so women's unity is not happening and will not happen." Hadia said that although the idea of a women's world in which one could discuss women's issues freely was appealing, "We cannot abandon all else and just focus on women's issues—we cannot overlook the bigger agenda in the interest of the smaller one."

The Spaces of the Public-Religious

In a purported project to conserve energy in public spaces such as schools, markets, and shopping centers, the newly formed democratic government in Pakistan introduced "summer time" in June 2008. All clocks were to be put forward by one hour. I was visiting my parents just then and found that my father was having difficulty adjusting to the new time. An attendant looking after him told me that my father found the change so disruptive that he did not eat his lunch for two days because it was too late in the afternoon by the time he finished his Zohr (afternoon) prayers. Upon investigation I discovered what was going on. My father, like thousands of other "religious" and "secular" Muslims in Pakistan, followed a personal routine according to which he first completed his afternoon (Zohr) prayer and then ate his lunch. In the evening, too, most Muslims who pray prefer to offer their Isha (evening) prayers before dinner, since many people feel more relaxed for a meal once they have finished their religious duty. It is also harder to bend and bow on a full stomach. Since religious considerations are not part of official deliberations, the government's energy-saving plan did not bother to take into account the reality of a large number of citizens for whom the new timing presented problems. Eventually my father's attendant, Javed, declared: "Baji, we are not going to follow the new time—we will stick to our old time." So my father and his attendant, like many other people that I met in Karachi, had chosen to live in a different time zone than the official time zone of the nation-space. During my trips to Pakistan I found that this was the experience of many people in homes, bazaars, tailor shops, grocery stores, cleaners, and so on.

As I have indicated in this chapter, gender, class, colonial memory, and cultural experience interact with notions of Islam and Muslim identity to construct spaces that we may call public-religious; these spaces are experienced differently than, but also entwined with and affectively overlapping, the space that is conventionally deemed to be the (secular) public sphere. Jamaat women's claim on such a space in Pakistan highlights that in the present postcolonial moment, representative democracy is not exclusively the monopoly of the secular.

Their oft-iterated transcendent religiosity, their demonstrated capability as worldly actors, their understanding of the party's moral vision and their commitment to its political objectives, their shared sense of sisterhood with other Jamaat women and their rejection of a wider women's community point to the complex experiences of women's religious politics. As I have attempted to establish in this chapter, Jamaat women recounted their experiences as gendered political subjects within Pakistan's representative bodies by pointing to their successful articulation of an Islamist women's vision in opposition to the projects of women's and human rights groups. Their responses also evince an enhanced awareness of the idea of "women" as subjects and objects of political discourses and the relationship of these politics with their own understanding of Islam.

What is noteworthy is that while women almost always emphasized the operation of their own religious-political independence rather than family or male pressure in becoming members of the Jamaat, they also always attributed their entry into electoral and representative politics as a duty imposed by the party leadership in view of or as an act of accommodation to the imperatives of national interest. Politics was almost never described as an avenue for a woman's self-empowerment or the exercise of the entitlements of citizenship, even though Jamaat women clearly considered themselves more capable and worthy of representing and leading the nation's people than the women of other political parties. This contradiction was highlighted by my interlocutors' repeated assertions that their entry into the public political was a religious duty imposed on them by the party, necessitated by local and global political conditions. In the observance of this duty, Jamaat women considered the public to be a religious space and, in some cases, referred to particular instances of their success in introducing organizational change that would facilitate the functioning of religious subjects in these public spaces.

Based on my discussions with women political representatives of the Jamaat at various levels of government, I propose that Jamaat women's entry into the domain of electoral politics entailed a reconceptualization of the public political space, marking a different kind of interaction between the religious and secular, moral subject and citizen, and Muslim woman and political actor. As I have discussed, unlike some other reformist movements such as the Tablighi Jamaat, the Jamaat-e-Islami does not consider the public political nation-space compromised because of its relationship with worldly power. Rather, if the modern public sphere is to be shunned, this is because it threatens to destabilize the movement's idealized conception of feminine uniqueness and the private and public as exclusionary zones of male and female activities. Women's participation in politics and employment is to be abhorred because it offers women the opportunity of social interaction with men, and hence possibilities for sexual immorality, as theorized by Maulana Maududi (Maududi 1939). The civic and communicative possibilities of political participation are seen to be imbued with limitless potential to disrupt the division of domestic moral responsibility and public moral responsibility, as well as the gendered division of purdah. Thus the public space of politics is seen to pose a threat to the family system idealized by the movement.

If the public was restricted for Jamaat women it was not because of its civic possibilities or its secular character, but rather because it was potentially ungendered in character. Jamaat women were able to circumvent their preferred division of (male) public and (female) private only by invoking an Islamic doctrine of necessity whereby a moral imperative may change the immoral character of an act. My interlocutors therefore rejected the possibility that any transformation had occurred in women's own sense of gendered responsibility. They emphasized that women politicians would ensure that their political activities did not interfere with their family and domestic responsibilities, which they considered to be their primary interest. Samina was able to declare: "even if a woman were offered the rulership of the whole world, but at the cost of her family, then she should not accept it." However, the Jamaat's position on keeping women out of political power is marked by ambivalence, as Jamaat women continue to lay claims to modern politics, albeit with the hope of Islamizing the public sphere. Samina said: "We have come into this space with the understanding that politics is religion. Therefore, I do not see the participation of women diminishing but more likely increasing."

3

Politics of Morality

Feminist genealogies of Muslim women's movements in South Asia generally ignore the possibility of women's engagement with Islamism. This is odd, since twentieth-century Islamism, like modern Muslim nationalism, is a product of the same period of mass mobilizations and large-scale anticolonial protest during which ideas about women, nation, and secular nationalism are seen to have developed in Muslim South Asia.[1] Indeed, the history of women in the Jamaat-e-Islami tends to be obscured even by sympathetic accounts of the movement, which tend to focus solely on the male leaders of the Jamaat, despite the recognition of the significance accorded to gender by these leaders. On the whole, histories of the Jamaat-e-Islami as a male-led movement rarely engage in depth with the issues that are acknowledged to be key to the construction of Islamic society in Maulana Maududi's formulations: the definition of private and public, the maintaining of sexual boundaries, and the precisely defined roles of women and men in the middle-class family. As such, even scholars who have done insightful and groundbreaking work on the Jamaat and on Maududi's theorizations have not considered it worthwhile to investigate the implications of the ambiguities, even as they are noted, of his formulations about women and purdah (Reza Nasr 1996). The formulation of feminism versus male fundamentalists has become so universalized in feminist scholarship on Muslim societies, including Pakistan, that

1. Women's involvement in Islamism is almost ignored in mainstream accounts of the anticolonial nationalist movement and in feminist accounts of the Muslim women's movement in colonial India (see, for example, Mumtaz and Shaheed 1987).

it can be argued that an important aspect of the history of Jamaat-e-Islami women is the manner in which their history has been subsumed within these other accounts.

My interest in turning to these histories, however, is not to recover or reinstate the place of Jamaat women in the history of women's politics in Pakistani society. It is rather intended to construct an account against which we might compare and therefore understand the transformative role of gender (as constituted by cultural knowledge, economic class, education, and urban-rural position, among other elements) in the contemporary conditions of the Jamaat-e-Islami. We might then be able to map the movements, the transformations, and the repositioning of women in the party and better understand Jamaat women's social-political trajectory, a trajectory as deeply but differently implicated in notions of progress and modernity as Muslim women who are seen to be associated with secular Muslim nationalism. The positioning of some groups of women as immobilized in their religious identity and unable to engage with modernity contributed to the inability of early women's movements in Pakistan to interrogate the gender, class, sectarian, and regional underpinnings of dominant projects of national progress, and continue to plague representations of gender in contemporary South Asia. I will represent some of this unexamined history, and thereby draw feminist attention to some vernacular modes of women's politics that seem to be reworked successfully by contemporary women's groups identified as "religious" in Pakistan. I sketch this account by way of two women who may be considered the founding mothers of the contemporary members and followers of the Jamaat Women's Wing.

Changes and Continuities in Jamaat Women's Project

Any attempt to recuperate the accounts of Jamaat's early female members suggests that in the 1930s and 1940s, at a time of fervent anticolonial nationalism in South Asia when groups of elite educated women in India were joining the nationalist anticolonial struggle, a small group of similarly educated women, mostly from the (traditional) middle classes, mostly based in smaller towns, were drawn to the call of the Islamic/Islamist movement. These women were from families that did not allow young women the freedom to engage in public activities, even in public gatherings dedicated to discussion of Quran and dars. Young women were expected to acquire religious and other knowledge and capabilities through private interactions and reading rather than public discussion or dialogue with unrelated others (Bano 1999). Thus early Islamist women's political activities were restricted to schools, colleges, neighbor's homes, family gatherings, and weddings (Zubair 1999).

The gendering of Jamaat-e-Islami was traced, by my interlocutors, primarily to the reformist activities of Hameeda Begum, a middle-class schoolteacher from a small town in British India, affectionately remembered by present generations as "Apa Hamida Begum." In addition, a key role in disseminating Maulana Maududi's message through her prolific translation of his works into English was played by Maryam Jameelah, a Jewish American university student formerly named Margaret Peggy Marcus. Aspects of the contributions of these two women provide important insights to our understanding of present-day Jamaat women.

Hameeda Begum: A Benefactress of the Jamaat

It is not anomalous, given the profile of the contemporary Jamaat woman member (young, educated in contemporary knowledge, and also motivated by religious zeal), that the first woman to join the Jamaat and start a women's section in the party was a young woman who was the principal of a girls' school in a small town. Hameeda Begum (1915–84) is seen as the most important of the founders of the Jamaat women's movement. She occupies an almost legendary position in the party's gendered history and is said to have drawn hundreds of young women and men to the movement.

In a tribute to Hameeda Begum, Mian Tufail Mohammed, the former amir of the Jamaat, described her as "a female image of Maulana Maududi in terms of commitment and attitude, intellect and intuition/perception, balance" (Ahmed 1999, 5). To commemorate Hameeda Begum's contribution, the party published *Daur-e-Hazir ki Mohsina* (A benefactress of the present era), which includes tributes from party leaders, family members, friends, and colleagues. The book emphasizes that Hameeda Begum was among the small section of middle-class women who had developed religious and literary awareness in the 1930s and 1940s through exposure to Maulana Maududi's monthly digest, *Tarjuman-ul-Quran*. These women were keen to become members of the Islamic movement for renewal and reform.

Nayyar Bano, a contemporary of Hameeda Begum, recalls that one of the main impediments to women's inclusion was the absence of resources within the party to start a separate women's wing of the movement. Since any correspondence and discussion was possible only through male staff, the Maulana did not think it appropriate that the Islamic movement should facilitate the emergence of any kind of correspondence or any other form of contact between men and women (Bano 1999). In Hameeda Begum, Maulana Maududi found the correct intermediary through which he could initiate women's induction into the movement. The Jamaat-e-Islami Women's Wing was convened in February 1947, and in March 1948 Hameeda Begum was unanimously elected its leader, a position that she retained until her death. Hameeda Begum conceptualized the role of women in the dawat and movement so that they could devote some time to God's work and also fulfill their domestic and childrearing responsibilities (Bano 1999). Bano notes that Hameeda Begum had very little to offer in material wealth or riches, but she offered the movement the love of Allah and invitation to the faith, and this drew many women to the cause. Reflecting the social conditions of young women in many middle-class Muslim families in the 1930s and 1940s, Bano states that in the early days of the movement:

> Young women did not have free permission to engage in public speeches or discussion of Quran and *dars*. They were instructed to increase their knowledge and capabilities in a private manner and to seek answers mostly through reading rather than discussions or conversations with others. (9)

Because of the limited opportunities for mobility, women focused on writing as the main organ for their dawat activities under the supervision of Hameeda Begum (Bano 1999). However, there were other reasons for

Hameeda Begum's emphasis on writing as a revolutionary tool. In another essay in the same publication (Ahmed 1999) "Hameeda Begum and the Establishment of the Writing Front," Bano notes that books were seen as an important medium in the Jamaat's objective of reaching a wide (middle-class) audience and a means to further stimulate the interest of those women who were becoming interested in the movement's publications. Furthermore, there was a perceived need within the party, as it expanded, for literature in accessible language and to supplement Maududi's scholarly writing with popular publications. Most important, women's writing was seen as necessary to confront the challenge posed by the Progressive Writers Movement, which was gaining great popularity in India during that period.[2] Jamaat women led by Hameeda Begum wrote critiques and letters to the editor and protested the publication and popularity of literature they considered secular and irreligious, such as the radical Urdu short stories and plays of Sadat Hasan Manto (1912–1955), one of the best-known writers of the progressive literature movement.

Jamaat women's historical commitment to letters, literature, and publishing explains the abundance of literature and publications associated with the present-day Women's Wing; it is a key mode of dissemination of the party's message into the innermost recesses of middle-class and lower middle-class families in Pakistan. It also helps shed light on the changes that are symbolized by the growing presence of today's women who, albeit in women-only gatherings or in burqa in the presence of males and on television, have become the party's most articulate public speakers and vehement spokespersons. Bano's discussion of the establishment of women's publishing under Hameeda Begum is supported by Umm Zubair, another contemporary of Hameeda Begum who recalls the work of an early cohort of Jamaat women. These women expanded their activities by using their pocket money to start a Jamaat women's monthly magazine, *Iffat*. Zubair's account of the publishing efforts of these early Jamaat women, their

2. This was an anticolonial and leftist movement of Indian writers, some of whose members were vehement critics of the inequalities of gender, class, and religion in Indian, including Muslim, society. For more information see Zaheer 2007.

editorial discussions over the content of the magazine and other activities of the women involved, provides a rich history of the hesitant steps of early middle-class Muslim women as they ventured into the larger sphere of public life (Zubair 1999). The account differs from, but also, in some ways, resonates with the lives of elite and English-educated middle-class women of the same era, for example, Shaista Ikramullah (1963) and Jahan Ara Shahnawaz (1971).

There is no doubt that middle-class Muslim women's lives in the past were much more circumscribed within the home and family and their activities more strictly limited to what is considered the private sphere. Zubair recalls that when Hameeda Begum began to tour different towns and cities, she made sure that she was accompanied by another worker or her mother, in deference to the word of God, as she understood it, that no woman should venture out alone and that women should return to their homes before nightfall (Zubair 1999). Indeed, it was rare for her to be out late at night even in her own town and she made sure that meetings and appointments were done before sunset. "She used to say that it is in our welfare to be aware of the wish of God in whatever we do" (Zubair 1999, 19).

In a review of Hameeda Begum's writing, Farukh Ahmed describes her essay "The Problems of Women and Their Solution" as a foundational text that epitomizes her thinking (Ahmed 1999, 218). In this piece Hameeda Begum argues that society had been unable to resolve the problems and difficulties that women face because of an inability to correctly identify their root causes. She describes the state of efforts to understand women's problems in her day:

> What is so perplexing is: why does the female victim of male abuse when given the opportunity, use the man as an instrument to abuse others of her own kind? Mother-in-law towards daughter-in-law, daughter-in-law in relation to the mother-in-law, stepmothers against stepchildren and stepdaughters against stepmothers? (quoted in Ahmed 1999, 218)

Hameeda Begum argues that contrary to popular perception, women's inability to unite across socially constructed boundaries is caused not by illiteracy but by lack of the right kind of education. Drawing on Hameeda

Begum's text, Ahmed attempts to answer these questions about women's disunity.

> If in the past women complained about their mothers- and sisters-in-law, now they have similar problems from supervisors and colleagues. In short, women's problems have not changed with education. Education, freedom and unveiling have not decreased women's problems, rather they have added to these. (Ahmed 1999, 222)

She concludes that the only viable solution to women's problems at home, within the family, and in the larger society was to inculcate true obedience to the word of Allah contained in the Quran and symbolized by the traditions of the Prophet Muhammad:

> The solution offered by Islam is for women to abandon her slavery to all these different masters and to commit herself to the obedience of just one God. . . . If women want to get rid of the abuse from their own gender and from men, then the only way is to rid themselves of all new and old forms of ignorance and to adopt a way of life that pleases their true Lord or that which [He] has permitted. (Ahmed 1999, 222)

This indicates that some Jamaat women consider engagement in religious learning and knowledge to be a mode of women's emancipation through transcendence. However, as a worker for the modern Islamic movement, Hameeda Begum firmly believed that efforts for social and cultural transformation alone would not succeed in bringing about the desired revolution in society; therefore, it was crucial for women to participate in revolutionary struggle alongside men in the political field. She herself was active in this struggle and also enlisted other women. Ahmed emphasizes this through her discussion of Hameeda Begum's political essay "God's Kingdom on Earth," where she invited women to join the arena of activism (Ahmed 1999, 222).

Of special interest to the present study is Hameeda Begum's strategy of offering dawat, or invitation to Islam, as described by Zubair (1999). According to Zubair, Hameeda Begum would first contact a neighbor, a cousin, or a class fellow and visit her while carrying some books. If the woman with whom she engaged in conversation expressed some misperception about Islam or skepticism about the applicability of its laws in the present era, she would take out a related essay or article and offer it to her to read. "She was so persuasive in offering her reading that no woman could resist the offer. And of course, once a person had read the book, they were bound to undergo some change" (Zubair 1999, 28).

Hameeda Begum would go to schools and colleges and contact educated women in the neighborhood to introduce them to the reading materials and books published by the movement. She always attended family and social events in the hope of an opportunity to start a discussion about Islam. Zubair recalls a particular incident:

> I was attending a wedding party in her family and she urged me to start a discussion [about Islam]. I said: "women are not interested, there is too much noise, how can we have a discussion in this racket?" She said: "You have to try to drown this noise with your own noise, since it is the work of *shaitan* [satan] to try to block all opportunities for a discussion about the faith." And that is exactly what happened. When I initiated a discussion about Islam with one woman, another joined in and so on. (Zubair 1999, 28)

Zubair adds that Hameeda Begum paid strict attention to the smallest detail in her objective to extend the invitation (*dawat*). This included special attention to attire so that her clothes were always spotlessly clean and appropriate for the occasion. If the occasion was dominated by young women, she would try to dress up a little bit, lest the girls should misinterpret that coming to Islam would mean giving up good clothes (Zubair 1999).

The most important testimony to Hameeda Begum's role in the Jamaat is available in a speech delivered in 1945 by Mian Tufail Mohammed, leader of Jamaat Islami India, in his annual report to the movement (Gilani 1999). According to Gilani, even as early as the mid-1940s, Jamaat leaders were cognizant of the activities of the women members in the Islamic movement and especially mentioned the activities undertaken by Hameeda

Begum (Gilani 1999). It is clear that women were regular attendees, if not participants, of the party's events, which always included the provision of a separate enclosure for wives and female relatives of the workers so that women could learn about the activities of the Islamic movement.

Gilani notes that in his report, Mian Tufail Mohammed summarized Hameeda Begum's activities by drawing on her own account of her contribution to the Jamaat's mission in the preceding year, which included such activities as teaching Quran, Farsi, and Urdu to female education officials, neighboring families, and their children. Of her experience teaching English to a neighbor's son, she said that in the process, "the entire family is becoming interested in learning more about Islam although previously they were almost indifferent to prayers, fasting and other Islamic activities." Listing another effort, she said she had helped a Hindu child in the neighborhood with her lessons, "as a result of which two Hindu women have become inspired and their prejudice seems to be reduced" (Gilani 1999, 31).

Maryam Jameelah: Embracing a Dynamic and Revolutionary Faith

While almost every Jamaat woman leader that I met mentioned Apa Hamida Begum as an important figure in the history of the Jamaat Women's Wing, they were less interested in and somewhat dismissive of Maryam Jameelah (1934–2012), an American convert and disciple of Maududi who was living in Lahore at the time of this study. Jameelah is believed to have become disillusioned with Islamic revivalism and eventually drew away from the Islamic movement because of its borrowing of ideas from the West. She has even criticized her mentor Maududi for his assimilation of modern concepts into the Jamaat's Islamic ideology.[3]

3. It may be emphasized that my intention here is not to offer an authentic account of Jameelah's life against which we can measure the truth or falsity of Maududi's claims. Rather, it is to examine what these claims may have meant to a young Muslim woman in the early days of the Jamaat and why it inspired her to propagate its ideology so

However, for a long time in the Jamaat's history, Maryam Jameelah was considered one of the most important spokespersons for the ideas of the Jamaat-e-Islami, and in Western literature on the party, she was considered to be Maulana Maududi's most ardent disciple. Jameelah was a young Jewish American living in New York until she converted to Islam in 1961. In her prolific writing she has described her life before converting to Islam, the process of her conversion, her correspondence with Maulana Maududi, her migration to Pakistan, and her life there. She has described the beginning and development of her interest in the treatment of Palestinians by Israeli authorities and her consequent interest in Islam and the writings of Maulana Maududi. Jameelah is recognized as a prominent advocate of the superiority of Islam and Islamic life against Western materialism; in addition, she has written a plethora of books, articles, and pamphlets promoting the early ideology of Maulana Maududi and the mission of the Jamaat.[4]

Jameelah was introduced to Islam through two books written by another Western convert to Islam, Allama Muhammad Asad, *The Road to Mecca* and *Islam at the Crossroads*. She began to develop her knowledge about Islam by seeking friends among Muslims in the New York area and also initiating correspondence with Muslims in other societies, which led her to embrace Islam at the Islamic Mission in New York. Jameelah became acquainted with the writings of Maududi in December 1960 and began correspondence with him (Jameelah 2000). In the spring of 1962 Maududi invited her to Pakistan to live as a member of his family. Maryam Jameelah accepted the offer, and a year later she married Mohammed Yusuf Khan, a member of the Jamaat who became the publisher of her books. She subsequently became the mother of four children and lived with her co-wife and her children in a large extended household of in-laws. She died in Lahore in 2012.

---

vociferously. For a detailed and somewhat different account of the events of the life of Jameelah, see Baker 2011. Baker has examined Jameelah's conversion to Islam, her dependence on and later disillusionment with Maulana Maududi and the Jamaat-e-Islami.

4. See Esposito and Voll 2001.

In *Why I Embraced Islam* (1976b), one of the most cited of her reflections on her own life and conversion, Jameelah describes a difficult and painful adolescence; she was an introspective teenager who abhorred cinema, dancing, and shopping, and felt ill at ease in an American consumerist society.[5] Her relocation to Muslim society in Pakistan provided relief from the oppressive pressures that led to her perceived sense of social ostracism in American society.

> From a bleak future in America, which had no place for a person like me, I escaped when I migrated to Pakistan. The happiness I have found in my new life is entirely due to the fact that just those qualities of character and temperament [that] Western society ridicules and scorns, in Islam are most keenly appreciated and esteemed. (Jameelah 1976a, 6)

In Pakistan Jameelah became an inexhaustible spokesperson for Maududi's vision, and in her ubiquitous books and pamphlets explicated the Jamaat-e-Islami's ideology in a systematic fashion. Her writing included severe criticisms of the lives of women in the West, capitalism, feminism, women's employment, and social life, and was invariably pervaded with her central concern for what she understood to be an unremitting clash between Islam and Western modernity. Her strongly articulated discursive critique and rejection of the West eventually led her away from the revivalist thought of Maududi, in which she discerned a reliance on ideas and concepts borrowed from Western intellectual thought. Ultimately she became an open critic of the Islamist revivalist project and Maududi himself for his incorporation of modern concepts into the ideology of the Jamaat-e-Islami. Referring to this reorientation in an interview with *Young Muslim Digest*, an online Islamic monthly magazine published in India, Jameelah said:

5. All of Jameelah's writings, like that of Maududi and Islahi, have been published multiple times and in many different formats, with variations in page numbers and, in some cases, the text itself. They are all easily available on a multiplicity of Internet sites devoted to dissemination of Islamist literature. The page numbers refer to the publication available to me at the time of writing.

> At the beginning in 1941 Maulana Maudoodi was concerned with cultural matters in Islam's relation with the West. Now everything is politics. Placing politics at the centre of the Islamic mission is contrary to the traditions of Islam. However, Jamat-e-Islami deserves all the credit for restraining the worst excesses of secular military dictatorships. (Abdul Qadir 2005)

She explained that her disillusionment with Maududi's politics was related to what she saw as his relinquishing of traditional Islamic thought and his "disdain for the necessity for beauty in the lives of his followers, of traditional Islamic philosophy and Islamic art and his whole-hearted acceptance of industrialism, technology and evolutionism" (Abdul Qadir 2005).

Jameelah's aversion for cultural borrowing from the West in any aspect of life is most vociferously orchestrated and passionately argued in her abundant writings on the significant role of Muslim women in the cultural struggle of Islam and the West, such as her book *Islam and the Muslim Woman Today* (1976a). In this book, Jameelah seeks to "demonstrate the inherent superiority of those Islamic teachings pertaining to women and why to tamper with them is mischief making of the first magnitude" (5). Among the issues about which she seeks to remove the misconceptions of modern society are: male guardianship of women in marriage, polygamy, divorce, and purdah or strict segregation of the sexes. Jameelah addresses not only non-Muslim and Western critics of Islamic practices relating to women but also modernizers in Muslim societies, whom she condemns for mistakenly seeking to change these practices. Condemning the Family Laws reforms undertaken by many Muslim states in the 1960s and 1970s, because of which the practice of polygamy became regulated or banned, Jameelah wrote: "It is a matter of shame and regret that the family laws are being mutilated in many Muslim countries so that the Holy Prophet, his Companions and our greatest divines, who nearly all married more than one wife, would be considered as 'criminals' under contemporary legislation!" (7).

The book further seeks to educate women about their proper role as Muslim women and offers injunctions about childrearing, cleanliness, and cooking. For example: "Under no circumstances should she [the

Muslim mother] permit 'pop' music to be heard in the house because this is the worst possible moral influence on the children" (13). Some sections are addressed more specifically to women in Pakistan: "Most Pakistani homes I have seen in Lahore, even of middle-class people are dingy and dirty" (14). Jameelah advises Pakistani Muslim women to make their homes attractive, not to be ashamed of cleaning and sweeping their houses instead of leaving it to servants and cleaners. She also urges them to avoid ostentatious decorations, especially "unnecessary furnishings like West-ern-style sofas, dressing tables and useless knick-knacks" (14).

Jameelah dedicates an entire chapter to a critique of the nineteenth-century Egyptian modernist reformer Qassim Amin (1865–1908), who is widely acknowledged as one of the champions of Muslim women's libera-tion in the Middle East.[6] Jameelah describes Amin as the first Muslim in history to wage a campaign against purdah:

> The campaign Qassim Amin waged in his book at the turn of the cen-tury against Purdah has, with the full support of Christian missionaries and Western imperialism, borne its luxuriant fruit. As a result of his efforts, in every Muslim land, a whole crop of women has sprung up like weeds, determined to destroy the true role of the Muslim woman and reform her until her way of life becomes indistinguishable from her sisters in the modern West. (20)

Jameelah denounces movements for "female emancipation" in Muslim societies and urges Muslims to recognize that it is "a malignant conspiracy to destroy the home and family and eventually wreck our entire society" (29). Her most trenchant attack is aimed at the feminist movement.

In the essay "The Feminist Movement and the Muslim Woman," Jameelah describes feminism as a movement that is "revolutionizing the whole social structure and changing the entire basis of human relation-ships" (Jameelah 1976a, 13). Jameelah deplores the visible effects of the feminist movement and Westernization in Muslim societies, for example,

---

6. For an insightful feminist scholarly discussion of Qassim Amin, see Ahmed 1992.

in Iran and Lebanon, where, in her view, elite women were spending less time in household work and more in social, professional, recreational, and philanthropic activities. She chides them for their behavior by citing her mentor, Maududi:

> What many modernized Muslim women are doing in rebelling against the traditional Muslim family structure is to rebel against fourteen centuries of Islam itself although many may not be aware of the inner forces that drive them on. It is the patriarchal nature of Islam that makes the reaction of some modernized women today so vehement. Although very limited in number, they are, in fact, more than Muslim men, thirsting for all things Western. They seek to become modernized in their dress and habits with impetuosity, which would be difficult to understand unless one considers the deep psychological factors involved. (15)[7]

Jameelah's exposition of gender relations in Islam is resonant of the accounts of contemporary Jamaat women in asserting that from the Islamic point of view, the question of the equality of men and women is meaningless, "like discussing the equality of a rose and a jasmine. Each has its own perfume, color, shape and beauty" (17). She reiterates her conviction that men and women cannot be considered equal or competing, but are complementary. She adds:

> The *Shariah* therefore envisages the role of men and women according to their nature, which is complementary. It gives the man the privilege of social and political authority and movement for which he has to pay by bearing heavy responsibilities, by protecting his family from all the forces and pressures of society, economic and otherwise. Although a master in the world at large and the head of his own family, the man acts in his home as one who recognizes the rule of his wife, in this domain and respects it. (17)[8]

7. Jameelah cites from the 1972 edition of *Purdah and the Status of Women in Islam* (Lahore: Islamic Publications).

8. Jameelah attributes this quote to Nasr 1966, 110–13.

Jameelah's determined aversion to Western modernity and the modernization of Islam accounts for her alienation from the present cohort of Jamaat-e-Islami women. Her influence, however, continues, as indicated by the ongoing dissemination of her publications and writing among transnationally connected young Muslim bloggers and cyber communities.

Imparting *Adab-e-Zindagi (Etiquettes of Living)*

I was introduced to the reformist text *Adab-e-Zindagi*[9] during a conversation with women members of the Al Khidmat Trust, a charitable organization affiliated with the Jamaat. Describing their instructional activities in the *kutchi abadis* or shantytowns of Karachi, some of the women referred to *Adab-e-Zindagi* as a text that they used to supplement the scriptural lessons from Maulana Maududi's *Tafhim ul Quran*. They considered it a key tool in demonstrating some of the practical modes of behavior that they found lacking among poor urban women and that were necessary to implement the Quranic injunctions in everyday life. *Adab-e-Zindagi* is an important part of the curriculum of the Jamaat-e-Islami in becoming a teacher or *mudarrisa* of Islam.

Majida said she found the book's prescriptions for purification and cleanliness useful in her project to offer dars to women in Karachi's shantytowns. I met Majida through an introduction by her cousin, a friend of mine who happened to be visiting Karachi from New York at the same time as I was undertaking my study. Majida was an elected member of the Karachi City Council, but my main interest in meeting her was as the director of the female wing of the Jamaat-affiliated charitable group Al Khidmat Trust.

After several attempts to fix a meeting at her house we were finally able to get together at her office in Karachi's Shaheed-e-Millat Road. While as heterogeneous as any neighborhood in Karachi, this section of the city is associated with Delhi-Punjabi Saudagran, members of trading and business communities who are believed to have migrated from Punjab to Delhi

---

9. Available in English: Islahi 1969.

in the Moghul era and back to Pakistan at or after partition. This social cultural community is considered economically equivalent to the elite or upper classes of Karachi because of its business activities, mostly small factory ownership and trading; but it is culturally closer to the upper sections of the middle class because of its social and political conservatism. The social-cultural positioning of these women in the urban political life of Karachi may be symbolized by terms such as "Urdu speaking," "religious," and "conservative."

As Majida and I met, members of her staff escorted women into the room who had come to ask Majida for help with money or materials. In the corridor leading to her office was a pile of steel trunks that Majida told me were filled with items for a *jahez*, or trousseau, to be given to needy families to help with the marriage of their daughters. Some of the women who came to see her during our meeting were mothers and aunts with recommendation letters from community notables, such as a schoolteacher, a social worker, or the local Jamaat representative, asking for a donation of jahez. In most cases a member of a family in need brings applications to the nazima of their area. Party workers, who are assigned designated neighborhoods for this purpose, then verify the need and distribute the jahez to those they deem deserving.

Among the contents of a trunk were pieces of fabric for shalwar kamiz (Pakistani attire) suits, some small electrical appliances such as an iron, sometimes a sewing machine, pots and pans, a set of crockery, some bed linen, and so on. Each bride was also given a copy of the Quran. Majida said her increasing dedication to the charitable activities of the Jamaat was the culmination of a longstanding desire to "do something meaningful."

Married to a well-to-do businessman, Majida was introduced to the poverty and problems of Karachi's poor and needy through a Quran group whose instructor was a member of the Jamaat-e-Islami, though she did not know this at the time. In response to Majida's request for something meaningful to do, the instructor encouraged her, since she could drive a car, to provide transport to another female instructor who was going to a kutchi abadi. After a period of offering this service, when her passenger was unable to go anymore, Majida took over her mission. She described her experience in the kutchi abadi:

Over there I would gather the women and have a dars. It was based on our book *Adab-e-Zindagi*. This book has small, very useful sections on a variety of matters such as rules for *wazu* (purification). Those poor women do not have any of this knowledge. I would teach them how to pray, how to clean themselves, and so on.

Adab-e-Zindagi is one of the key texts used by Jamaat women in their dars, in addition to the *Tafhim ul Quran* of Maulana Maududi. While the latter seeks to provide religious instruction and knowledge, *Adab-e-Zindagi* by Mohammed Yusuf Islahi focuses on behavioral changes/improvements by inculcating values and modes of practice needed to become a good Muslim man or woman. The book includes topics such as cleanliness and hygiene, behavior for husbands and wives, how to treat parents, proper manners and etiquette, devotion and prayers, decent living, call to religion, and sense of devotion. Matters as diverse as the proper manner to travel, how to greet each other, modes of speaking, prayer, business conduct, and dress are discussed in detail with frequent reference to Hadith. For example, a section on purity and neatness includes injunctions such as: "On waking up do not put your hand into vessels containing water before cleaning them. You can never tell where your hands lay while you were asleep" (Islahi 1969, 10). A section on proper behavior toward wives tells men to be kind and respectful to their spouses, to avoid being overly suspicious of their wives, and to be tolerant of their mistakes. It instructs women to be obedient toward their husbands, respect their wishes, and avoid leaving the house without their permission.

My interlocutors who referred to these texts also recalled the efforts needed to make them accessible to poor urban and rural women, both to motivate them toward self-improvement and to make the lesson relevant to the conditions of their lives. This was noted by Tayyeba, who had been offering dars in Karachi's kutchi abadis since 1993: "Most of the topics we address are related to people's real life." When I met her at Majida's office, Tayyeba was working in one of the numerous *baithak* (literally: sitting place), or temporary schools, run by the Jamaat Women's Wing in the kutchi abadi of Karachi's Lines Area. Tayyeba said that the people to whom she catered needed not only din but also faced basic issues of food, shelter, and clothing, and she geared her teaching to address these issues. She said:

> Dars has to be modified in accordance with the people who are listening to it—whether you go to a kutchi abadi or among educated people. It is also important to include an incident or an event that is relevant to the lives of the listeners.[10]

Tayyeba said she found that women in kutchi abadis understood a great deal more than they were given credit for, "in fact I think they understand more than educated people." Since women in kutchi abadis are expected to be engaged with pressing economic and social demands, the dars was tailored to enable them to make time for religion in their already over-stretched lives. Tayyeba said she offered her classes once a week and did not expect women to "attend regularly, like school children." Furthermore she said the lesson was designed to provide the most essential and basic education in a brief period of time. This vital education included information about how to pray and how to perform ablution or ritual cleansing for prayer. Tayyeba was indignant that many of her pupils did not even know how to recite the *Kalima* (literally: "the word" in Arabic), which is a fundamental expression and affirmation of faith in Islam; its recitation is a requisite of Muslim identity and submission to Allah.

Commenting on her experience, Tayyeba said:

> Women [in katchi abadis] do not know how to pray, how to say the kalima, how to do ablution for prayers—indeed, some women don't even know how to cleanse themselves after periods [of menstruation]. We provide them with even this kind of knowledge.

Like some other Pakistani women from the middle classes and some working-class women, Tayyeba had spent some time, over twenty years in her case, in Saudi Arabia, where her husband was employed. She had undergone five years of training in offering dars from Quran classes run

10. Interview with Tayyeba, Karachi, July 2005.

by the Jamaat-e-Islami for the non-Arab Muslim community in Saudi Arabia. Describing her induction into the learning and teaching of the Quran, Tayyeba said:

> I came into the classes because my mother died suddenly in Pakistan. . . . When I went back to my home in Saudi Arabia [after her death], I couldn't come to terms with it. My children were young at the time. Although I was there I felt as if I was not there. Believe me if I had not gone [to the Quran study group] I would have become insane.

Comparing her experience of dars classes in Saudi Arabia and Pakistan, Tayyeba said she found more conservatism in Pakistani society toward discussing bodily issues than she had witnessed in Saudi Arabia. She found the training in Saudi Arabia to be more practical and useful, since it was common for teachers to include information about rules related to behavior during menstruation, rituals for purification, and other matters that middle-class Pakistani women are not used to discussing openly. In the classes that she attended in Saudi Arabia, when Pakistani women would look away or lower their eyes from embarrassment around certain topics, the Saudi teachers would admonish them, saying: "There is no shame in Shariah. Why do you lower your gaze?" Tayyeba said she found a similar situation in Pakistan, so that women would be too embarrassed to ask about matters such as purification after menstrual periods and would remain "impure and ignorant." She used these insights and experiences as a guide for her own pedagogy among women in kutchi abadis and elsewhere in society: "There are a lot of things that people here have no knowledge about. In Saudi Arabia they kept providing us all this practical knowledge. Here we are not at all practical."

The experiences of women such as Majida and Tayyeba reflect a noteworthy aspect of the NGO-type activities of Jamaat Women's Wing, which in the last three decades has begun to reach beyond middle-class boundaries—physical and social—to impart their reformist message to rural women and women in urban shantytowns. In a process requiring serious modification of the rules of purdah as laid out by Maulana Maududi (Maududi 1939), the party now regularly organizes visits by groups of

women and girls to rural areas outside the cities or to urban shantytowns
to offer both religious instruction and tips on health, hygiene, personal
cleanliness, and other matters.[11] These women are continuing a tradition
of service and education characteristic of women's participation in the
Jamaat since its inception and are also, in very important ways, extending
this role. Such women may be seen to embody the fulfillment, disruption,
and unforeseen expansion of the idealized version of Islamic femininity
epitomized by Maulana Maududi in *Purdah and the Status of Women in
Islam.* This expansion of Jamaat women's social horizons can be understood with reference to similar education and charitable activities undertaken by women in the founding days of the movement, when women's
activities were deemed to be strictly confined to family and social events.

Imminence and Distance

Early Jamaat women's activism, it seems from their own accounts, was
circumscribed by the gendered boundaries between home and the world,
public and private, men's domain and women's, as prevalent in most of
Indian Muslim society among the middle classes and also stipulated by
the party. This may be a starting point against which to measure both
the imminence and the distance between these women and the new generation of women. It is clear from the accounts of the lives of Hameeda
Begum and Maryam Jameelah that despite the constructions of purdah
as delineating strict gender divisions between masculine and feminine
spheres, these boundaries were never precise or impervious to gendered
interruptions. For example, Maulana Maududi invited Hameeda Begum
and, regarding her as morally responsible, entrusted her with responsibilities that disrupted the accepted conceptions of men's and women's
domains.

Some aspects of the construction of present-day women's activities
of education, reform, and religious consciousness raising are resonant

---

11. Jamaat women reject the suggestion that their role in the party or in society has
entailed modification of Maududi's injunctions.

of the published descriptions about the activities of Hameeda Begum. A member of the Karachi Women's Commission highlighted the informal, religious, gender-oriented, and modest nature of the Jamaat women's movement, saying:

> In the name of God we began a movement, consolidated it, and all our activists and our organization are convinced that what we are doing is simply to establish the religion (*din*) of Allah on His land.[12]

Ayesha's explanation of the mission of the Women's Wing resonates with the understanding of early Jamaat women, who differentiated the moral and social underpinnings of their project from that of other women's movements of their era. Like their predecessors, the Jamaat women also seek to discredit the feminist project and render the women's movement as culturally alien and irrelevant to the nation. Like other Jamaat women whom I interviewed, Ayesha suggested that feminist understanding of domestic violence in Pakistan, and women's legal, political, and economic status, were fundamentally flawed and irrelevant to most women in Pakistan. She said:

> We do not doubt that other women's NGOs are Muslims but we cannot ride together because we are riding on two different boats. We are Muslims and we believe in Quran and Sunnah. They take their agenda from the UN and the guardians of the UN are Jews and Christians. So there is an ideological difference between us—the solutions that they offer may be appropriate for them but they are not appropriate for us.

This aversion to feminism by contemporary Jamaat women, while seemingly a rehearsal of the earlier discourses of Islam versus the West reflected in the writings of Maryam Jameelah, evinces a historical process of reflection, theorization, and strategy that marks off the contemporary Jamaat women's project from that of their predecessors. Even though it may be imbued with similar moral and reformist zeal, the present-day

12. Interview with Ayesha, Karachi, June 2003.

movement is much attuned to and shaped by local, national, and global politics, as is apparent in Ayesha's statement quoted above. More important, it also marks a very different conception of community than was evidenced in the texts of and about Hameeda Begum, when the Jamaat considered itself a movement for social reform of a Muslim community rather than a movement for changing the social and legal sphere of a nation. Thus, while Hameeda Begum's mission was enacted on the register of two different and disconnected enclaves, those of religious and so-called modern women, the project of contemporary Jamaat women is rehearsed on a shared and, therefore, more intensely contested terrain. This distinguishes their project from the more separatist orientation of women, such as espoused by Hameeda Begum and Maryam Jameelah.

Jameelah's writings constructed Islam's inner coherence as a sufficient and privileged counter to Western modernism and thus focused on emphasizing the difference and conflict between Islam and the West. Today's Jamaat women display awareness of the need for new modes of negotiating these boundaries, representing political-moral positions, and using rhetorical strategies for engaging with feminism. In our encounters, Jamaat women not only acknowledged the change but also considered themselves active participants in bringing about important changes in strategy. Thus Ayesha noted that one aspect of the women's organizing that has changed significantly is the recognition of the need to publicize their own presence and work to the larger public. She said that while Jamaat women previously did not pay much attention to the idea that "there is such a thing as publicity and that there are specific modes and techniques of publicizing," they were now much more active in drawing attention to their own activities.

Some of the ways in which the Jamaat has chosen to publicize its heightened interest in women and development include dedicating the party's annual international conference to the theme of women's rights, the celebration of women's events such as International Women's Day, and the initiation of social research projects and surveys modeled on the activities of NGOs in Pakistan. These are modes of acting and self-becoming that are directed toward the exigencies and demands of a modern, consumerist, and self-promoting society. Ayesha summed up the new religiously driven gendered agency in these terms:

> Now we have realized that although our initial position (regarding publicity) was correct, the demands of the world we live in are such that we should probably make known our activities. Just as the rest of society is engaged in self-promotion, our acts of goodness, too, must be publicized.

4

Vanguard of a New Modernity?

Cultural Politics in a Postcolonial State

Like members of Islamist groups involved in electoral politics and national debates elsewhere, Jamaat women are organizing groups of people and enhancing their participation in electoral and claim-making activities related to what is considered the modern public sphere.[1] I propose that these processes of social and political organizing entail particular interrogations and reconstituting of identities that fundamentally alter women's understanding of both what it means to be "religious" and where they situate themselves in the continuum of tradition and modernity. Thus, while Jamaat women see themselves as pious women and believe themselves to be acting in the cause of Islamic revival, they are also shaped by the processes of modernization and the discourses of modernity such as rights, freedoms, and democracy. Jamaat-e-Islami women describe themselves as "modern" but take care to distance their modernity from the West, and they fight for the rights of women but distinguish their activism from feminism. In contrast, they position themselves as ideally situated, being educated middle-class professional women and also "true believers," to offer a balanced solution to the Islam-versus-modernity predicament that overhangs all issues of gender, politics, and development in Pakistan (Mumtaz and Shaheed 1987; Said Khan 1994; Jamal 2005).

In addition to their efforts to construct a moral society that I discussed in chapter 3, Jamaat women's transformative project manifests

---

1. For some examples of such organizing, see Esposito and Burgat 2003.

itself socially/politically in three main aspects of their activism: prioritizing of the nation-state as the main agent for guaranteeing women's rights to live as Islamic citizen-subjects; emphasis on socioeconomic factors for safeguarding the Islamic family and resituating it in public space; and appropriation of feminist, that is, modern methods of activism and organizing, such as NGOs, workshops, consciousness raising, and advocacy groups. Jamaat women challenge the mainstream feminist movement and share with it multiple sites and spaces of interaction between citizen-subjects and the nation-state in Pakistan. In this process, Jamaat women may be said to seek a new gendered modernity that entails a reworking of the modern Muslim identity that was associated with the nation-state at its creation in the mid-twentieth century. Their self-construction marks them differently from earlier cohorts of Jamaat women who eschewed the "modern" label and from many Muslim women in Pakistan, past and present, who consider themselves to be part of national or global cultural modernity. They are significantly different from mainstream Muslim nationalist movements in South Asia, including women's movements, that advocated progressive interpretations of Islam in an attempt to construct a "Muslim modern" that could resonate with the aspirations of the region's Muslim elite and also reflect popular attitudes to Islam. They challenge both intellectual discourses of key nationalist thinkers and popular perceptions about Islam and Muslim community so as to enable the assertion and, if possible, dominance of the Jamaat's own interpretation of Islam and its vision of community. It is contemporary Jamaat women's historically specific strategies for reconciling Islam and modernity (rather than substantiating or rejecting their claims to "becoming modern") that are of interest in this discussion, and the social, cultural, and political conditions that have necessitated and enabled these discursive strategies.

In this discussion I use the terms "modern" and "modernity" with cognizance of some persuasive critiques of these concepts from postcolonial and poststructuralist scholars. For these scholars modernity invokes a process of regulating religion in public politics (Asad 2003), the disciplinary modes involved in the production of subjects through individualizing and totalizing discourses (Foucault 1982), and longstanding politics of discursive constructions of the West and its Others (Hall 1996). These critiques of modernity continue to be relevant to any discussion that deploys the terms "Islamic," "Muslim," or even "religious" as qualifying of subjectivities (Razack 2007). Reviewing some prevailing representations of Islam and gender in the context of Canadian society, Sherene Razack has argued that contemporary discourses about Muslim women are over-whelmingly cast in terms of a pre-modern/modern distinction (Razack 2007). In addition, in the context of Pakistan, and perhaps other Muslim societies and communities, notions such as "modern," "progressive," and "forward looking" serve as important euphemisms—or even rhetorical modes of the variety that Gayatri Spivak has reconceptualized as "cata-chresis," that is, a misuse of a term for which no referent may be available in the obligatory discourse—for those who cannot or may not use the word "secular" or "liberal" (Spivak 1993, 161). Thus, despite important questions about the usefulness of the concept of "modernity" in postcolonial analy-sis, I consider it appropriate for my discussion.[2] More important than the analytical usefulness of the concept "modernity" to me is the weightiness of "modern" as a folk or native category in Pakistan and more specifically for Jamaat women as they make their identity claims in relation to other women and in defining their place in the nation. For these women their self-definition as "modern" serves to both dislodge entrenched, negative understandings of "religious" in Pakistan and also signals their engage-ment with a sphere that is not religious but that they are loath to term "sec-ular." It may be pointed out that Maulana Maududi, like many exponents of Islamism in Pakistan, translated the term "secularism" as the Urdu term "ladiniat" (without religion, or antireligion), and one who is "secu-lar" would therefore be blasphemous.[3] The idea of a "gendered modern"

2. For a discussion, see Bilgrami 1994.

3. An extreme example of the negative connotations of "secular" or "secularism" in Pakistan was the 2010 assassination of the Punjab Province governor Salman Taseer, who called for modifications in the country's controversial Blasphemy Law. The ambiva-lence of some journalists and columnists and the enthusiastic support for the murderer indicated that many Pakistanis considered the circumstances extenuating because of Taseer's secular lifestyle and political orientation. See Shah 2011; and "Taseer Himself

is thus both a discursive regime for constructing particular types of citizen-subjects in a modern Islamic nation-state and a rhetorical strategy for these historically constructed subjects.[4] Thus, Jamaat women's attempt to achieve Islamization of women's status through the state is a historically specific mode of engagement with modernity implying particular processes of subject formation.

The relationship between knowledge/power and identity is germane to processes of subject formation, as developed by Inderpal Grewal and Caren Kaplan in the notion of "scattered hegemonies" (Grewal and Kaplan 1994; Grewal and Kaplan 2000). Grewal and Kaplan have attempted to bring together Foucault's insights about the disciplinary processes of subject formation with postmodern theories of culture and Marxist theories of capital to suggest ways in which we may study the "impact of global forces such as colonialism, modernization, and development on specific and historicized gendering practices that create inequalities and asymmetries" (Grewal and Kaplan 2000, 9). In contrast with representations of unitary identities and interests, this theorization asserts that human subjectivities are intersected by a plurality of interests, including class, race, and sexuality, and emphasizes the operations of various power relations in representational practices. Thus we may investigate historical conditions as not simply causative but also constitutive of subject formation, and women as multiply positioned agents interpellated by heterogeneous discourses.

Such an approach diverges from studies of politico-religious movements that investigate political, economic, and social conditions as a context in which—or against which—religious movements arise (Keddie 1998; Mumtaz 1994; Shaheed and Mumtaz 1992). While these latter projects seek causal factors for the emergence of such movements, it is

---

Responsible for Killing: JI," *The News*, January 6, 2011, http://www.thenews.com.pk/Todays-News-5-24093-Taseer-himself-responsible-for-killing-JI.

4. For a powerful discussion of discourse, subjectivity, and rhetorical agency, see Sinha 1999.

not my intention to explain the self-formation of Jamaat-e-Islami women instrumentally, as an outcome of social and political conditions without self-reflexivity. At the same time it would be untenable to attempt to understand Jamaat women as simply religious or pious subjects constituted outside of the histories of colonialism, nationalism, development, and globalization, and their attendant material and discursive aspects (e.g., Deeb 2006; Mahmood 2005). Without casting any doubt on the religious or pious character of individuals, it is possible to argue that women's subjectivities are formed through complex interrelationships of experience and knowledge that we tend to divide into the personal and physical, the religious and spiritual, the cultural, the political, the local, the global, and so on. To discuss the self-construction of a group of Muslim women, it may be necessary to draw attention to political, economic, and cultural *factors*, explicate their actions through dispositions and practices, and problematize the relationship between knowledge and identity. I approach their self-formation and their activism through the notion of *discourse*, or the rationally possible ways of knowing in a given time period, which changed the way in which women could think about Islam and modernity and thus emerge as particular kinds of gendered subjects at a particular time and place (Grewal and Kaplan 1994). An important part of such investigation is also to deploy Foucaultian insights into governmentality, or the manner in which political, legal, and economic practices identified with the state are also understood as questions of gender, self, and identity (Dean 1999; Gordon 1991).

To trace the "conditions of possibility" for a discourse and, therefore, for particular types of subjectivities that it allows or rules out, according to Foucault, is not simply to revert to the historical causes and timelines that are seen to precede a particular moment; rather, it is to examine the modes of knowing that make possible particular types of subjects at a given moment, to explicate the discursive shifts involved in this process and make visible the power relations that structure each discursive shift. For Foucault, discourse is above all the structuring of power as knowledge that enables people to make sense of events and consequently discipline themselves to act in particular ways (Foucault 1991). While Foucault associated the practices of disciplinary power with only modern secular regimes, similar practices of power/knowledge may be discerned in modern religious discourses that emerged in colonial contexts and aimed at disciplining individuals to act as particular types of moral subjects.

Drawing on the work of feminist and other postcolonial studies scholars who have deployed Foucaultian theories to understand cultural, political, and economic flows in the contemporary world, I seek to examine the historical local and global conditions that have opened the discursive space for a "gendered Islamic modern" that could sustain Jamaat women's claims for women's leadership in Pakistan. This may draw attention to some of the ways in which, despite secular or religious nationalist assertions of autonomy, the conceptual categories of colonial rule may persist in territorially independent postcolonial societies. Further, we may be able to understand Jamaat women's attempts at domesticating modernity as part of attempts to challenge the dichotomy of the religious and the secular that underlies secular and religious projects of social integration in Pakistan.

Gender and the Ambivalent Space
of the Modern Islamic Nation

Political literature in and on Pakistan has traditionally relied on an understanding of modernity as a particular notion of progress and democratization, involving a liberal attitude toward Islam, epitomized by those middle-class and upper-class subjects who profess a secular politics. This is based on an understanding of the mission of the nation's founding fathers, in particular Mohmmed Ali Jinnah, who declared in 1947 that Islam would not be considered the primary marker of identity in the political public space of the newly established nation-state. Jinnah's pronouncement in the founding days of the Pakistani nation that the new state would not be concerned with the religious beliefs of citizens is seen by some historians as a departure from colonial modes of classifying South Asian populations by their religious identity (see, for example, Bose and Jalal 1997). Tracing the anticolonial nationalism of the Muslim League, of which Jinnah was leader, Bose and Jalal argue that the emergence of religiously oriented nation-states was the outcome of the interplay of anticolonial resistance, center-province politics, British constitutional maneuvers, and social construction, rather than the culmination of Muslim nation-ness or British categorization. For these authors, Jinnah's demand for Pakistan was not so much an expression of the Muslims' longing for a separate homeland but rather the strategic tactics of a seasoned constitutionalist and lawyer.

This is supported by other evidence that has traced the roots of communal separatism in India further back to colonial structures of power in the 1920s and 1930s, which consolidated the interests of Hindus and Muslims around communal issues by granting separate electorates to the Muslims. Page, for example, considers this "one of the most crucial factors in the development of communal politics," which made it difficult for genuine Indian nationalism to develop (Page 1982, 260). He notes that before the Montagu-Chelmsford proposals and their embodiment in the Government of India Act of 1919, which introduced separate electorates for Muslims, cross-communal alliances did take place in the interest of reform at the provincial level, but with the introduction of diarchy, communal antagonism became a permanent feature of provincial politics. Because of this, the formation of all-India cross-communal alliances first became difficult, then impossible.

An important group of historians, political leaders, and activists support the contention of Jalal and Bose that despite the mobilizing of Indian Muslims around the banner of Islam, the founding fathers of the nation-state had envisioned a polity that was not dominated by religion or ethnicity (Haque 1983; Asghar Khan 1985; Mumtaz and Shaheed 1987). Jinnah's cautionary advice against divisive notions of religious identity is also widely acclaimed by Pakistani feminist and human rights groups as an egalitarian mission that, while acknowledging the primacy of Islam in Pakistan, deemed it to be irrelevant to issues of justice and equality in legal and political matters.

It is within these anticolonial and postcolonial processes of communal/community identification that we must situate the evolution of the Jamaat-e-Islami and the development of Maulana Maududi's vision for Muslim life and politics that began in 1932.

In describing the Jamaat-e-Islami as the vanguard of the Islamic Revolution, Reza Nasr argues that Maulana Maududi sought to construct a movement of Muslims in twentieth-century colonial India to challenge both British colonialism and distinguish themselves from rising Hindu nationalism (Reza Nasr 1994, 1996). The impetus for this movement that would turn it into an Islamic revolution leading to an Islamic state, Reza Nasr adds, would be neither the religiously trained Islamic scholars or ulema nor the masses of Muslim society; rather, the vanguard of the Islamic Revolution would be the middle-class Muslim man who in addition to following Islam was "a modern creature with modern social links, political aspirations, and ultimately, [a modern] cultural outlook" (Reza Nasr 1996, 51). One may locate this individual within the Indian middle class under colonial rule, which has been theorized by Partha Chatterjee (1993) as the main agent of modernity and what may be referred to as "secular" nationalism in the subcontinent.

Chatterjee has argued that, unlike the Western nation theorized by Anderson (Anderson 1991), the imagining of nationhood in postcolonial contexts was enabled by the politicizing of the private sphere rather than by the separation between a political/public and domestic/private sphere. It is in the inner sphere of the private, Chatterjee says, that nationalism launches "its most powerful, creative and historically significant project: to fashion a 'modern' national culture that is nevertheless not Western. If the nation is an imagined community, then this is where it is brought into being" (Chatterjee 1993, 6).

According to Chatterjee, middle-class subjectivity in India was produced by its consciousness of its mediating role in this nationalist formulation, since the middle class literally occupied a middle position between indigenous culture and modernity, between the colonial ruling class and the native classes. Its primary social preoccupation was with that "vital zone of belief and practice that straddles the domain of the individual and the collectivity, the private and the public, the home and the world, where the new disciplinary culture of a modernizing elite has to turn itself into an exercise of self-discipline" (Chatterjee 1993, 36). This self-disciplining of the elite became evident in new ideas and standards of behavior that shaped relations between men and women, marriage, childbearing and rearing, and the exercise of authority within the middle-class family.

Engendering Islamic Modernity

Drawing on Chatterjee's formulation of the mediating role of the middle class in anticolonial secular nationalism, Hatem suggests that Islamist discourse, which is also produced by a section of the middle class, conceives of its mediating role in a different manner (Hatem 1998). Rather than seeking to modernize the private sphere of cultural difference, it seeks to expand the expression of cultural difference into the modern (universal) arenas. In doing so it, too, seeks to discipline and normalize the relations of power between the men and women of the middle classes within and outside the nuclear family. Accordingly, it does not reject, but embraces, modern regimes of power/knowledge and the developmental project of the postcolonial state. Hatem suggests that rather than implying an end to modernity, Islamists have their own view of modernity and accept the nuclear family and modern systems of education and training as the basis of an alternative Islamic society. Thus, according to Hatem, rather than reading Islamist and secular discourses as simply enacting a struggle between tradition and modernity, we should see them as competing definitions of modernity aimed primarily at the new middle classes.

Hatem's intervention offers an important framing for a review of the Jamaat's cultural orientation in its formative phase when Maududi's main concern was colonial retreat and rising Indian national consciousness. Reza Nasr, as well as other scholars of Islam in South Asia (for example, Robinson 2000), observe that the Jamaat tended to neglect socioeconomic effects of colonial rule while privileging the cultural aspects of Western modernity. Thus Maududi did not see problems of imperialism in economic impact but rather in cultural terms. For him,

> Its evil lay in the propagation of such moral and ethical evils as women's emancipation, secularism and nationalism[,] all of which ran contrary to the teachings of Islam and had caused them to be ignored or rejected. He drew on conflicts in the Indian social context but gave them meaning in a more general framework—relations between Islam and the West. (Reza Nasr 1994, 49)

The complex gender and class implications of this Islam-modernity discourse shape contemporary Jamaat women's construction of their religious-political selves and are in turn reconfigured by their actions as historical agents. Jamaat women's entry into the space of gendered political-cultural activism has been facilitated by important changes within the movement, in the space of local and national politics, and at the transnational political-cultural level.

It is important to understand that contemporary Jamaat women's self-construction is not a negation or challenging of the Islamist movement's underlying ideology, but rather marks both a development and further cultivation of the vision of the founding father, Maulana Abul Ala Maududi, whom scholars of Islam in South Asia have described as modernist. The vision of the Islamist revolution was expanded, modified, and multiplied in its interaction with a variety of historical and cultural processes in Pakistan, to which I now turn.

Islamization: A Gendered Discourse of Citizenship

Scholars on Islam and politics in Pakistan widely agree that the military regime of General Mohammed Zia ul Haq (1977–88) marks a crucial key turning point in the relationship between Islam, nation, and identity in Pakistan (Haque 1983; Asghar Khan 1985; Weiss 1986; Mehdi 1994; Haq 1996; Shaukat Ali 1997). While Islam has always been an underlying feature of all political, legal, and social discourse in Pakistan, initial ambivalence about its exact relationship to the state had enabled modernizing leaders before General Zia to defer the issue of defining what is Islamic by simply focusing on avoidance of what could be clearly considered un-Islamic (Choudhury 1988).

Zia went much further than his predecessors in instituting a series of wide-ranging legal, political, economic, and social education measures and describing them as a state project termed "Islamization." I emphasize that we must also understand Islamization as a gendered discourse of citizenship with an effect on subjectivities that facilitated the emergence of a particular type of nation/society in a manner that institutionalized the existing inequalities of gender, class, and religion.[5] As I have argued elsewhere, central to this project was a recasting of the construct of the modern Muslim woman (Jamal 2002).

Furthermore, Pakistani political analysts and feminists like to point out that politico-religious parties, despite their ideological influence, were unable to succeed in formal politics until General Zia enabled their access to key political and military institutions (Said Khan 1994; Asghar Khan 1985; Rashid 1985). Indeed, the Jamaat-e-Islami's access to government power was enabled by General Zia's personal and political commitment to the general thrust of Maududi's ideas about the Islamic state. In addition, regional and global political conditions of the 1980s gave a great boost to General Zia's regime. A crucial event was the Afghan War during the late 1970s and 1980s and the enlistment of Zia's military government as the frontline ally of the United States in its support for the Afghan forces fighting Soviet troops.

The politico-religious parties, such as Jamaat-e-Islami, were key players in providing ideological support for government policy by legitimizing the Soviet-Afghan War as a jihad. The relationship between the Jamaat and the Zia regime was not always smooth, but there is no doubt that the Jamaat benefited politically and financially from this relationship. For the first time in its history, the Jamaat was able to gain positions in General Zia's cabinet; it expanded its ideological influence to the military and Afghan refugee groups; and it saw an increase in its national and international significance as it became an important conduit for billions of dollars in aid for Islamic activities from the Gulf Arab petro monarchies (Reza Nasr 1994). This war increased state reliance on the Jamaat because of its role in developing Islam as an ideological bulwark against communism.

---

5. Unlike some other societies such as Iran or Algeria, there was no Islamic revolution in Pakistan. While Islam was always embedded in the political, legal, and social discourses in Pakistan, the term "Islamization" is used by scholars to describe a particular project by which General Zia introduced a series of political and legal changes in Pakistan, mainly through ordinances that were supposed to implement a particular interpretation of the Shariah.

Many scholars have documented the disastrous social and political effects of the Afghan War and General Zia's role in it: the rampant spread of a drugs-and-weapons culture, the indoctrination of young men into Islamic militants, the dismantling of secular educational institutions and introduction of dogmatic syllabi in public schools, the proliferation of repressive and sectarian madressas, and so on (see, for example, Hoodbhoy 2009; Rashid 2001; Shakir 1997). The discriminatory nature of the laws enacted in the name of Islamization and their impact on women and religious minorities has been ably documented and analyzed by Pakistani feminist and progressive authors (for example, Khan 2007; Mumtaz and Shaheed 1987; Weiss 1986; Rouse 1998; Jahangir and Jilani 1990).

While women's legal and social status was systematically reduced and while public denigration of women and girls became commonplace, as many scholars have noted, I argue that these changes in women's public status were achieved through the development of new ideas about the middle-class Muslim family that resonated with many men and women of rising sections of the middle class. General Zia's blend of pragmatic modernism and religion echoed the aspirations of the present cohort of Jamaat-e-Islami women activists in Karachi and Lahore. For Zia, middle-class women's participation was crucial in national activities, though it would have to be supplementary and subordinate to that of men. He said that women could become rocket scientists provided they could also fulfill their duty of building the family (Shaukat Ali 1997). Zia's socioeconomic and cultural policies, especially in education, may be considered a key moment in shaping the subjectivities of religion-oriented middle-class women in Pakistan. Women supporters and members of the Jamaat-e-Islami were enlisted in promoting an image of *chadar*-clad, or veiled, women in the public space; some (older women) even occupied positions in Zia's nominated parliament, the Majlis-e-Shoora (Shaukat Ali 1997). The following statement of Zia resounds with the sentiments of many contemporary Jamaat activists that I encountered:

> It is a gross misconception that Islam ordains women to remain shut up within the four walls of their homes. Islam enjoins no such thing. This is one of many local taboos with no Quranic sanction to support

them. Islam allows equal rights to both men and women. When I say equal rights, I mean equal opportunities for education, work employment, effective participation in national life. We cannot immobilize a near 50 percent of our human resources, leaving them uneducated and untrained, neglected or outcast. (Zia 1979, 319)

In their attempts to acquire modern education and training while strengthening their "Islamic" obligations, Jamaat women both invoke and rework their ideological reliance on founding texts of the Jamaat, epitomized by the writings of Maulana Maududi and his well-known disciple Maryam Jameelah, who emphasized the dangers of women's public participation rather than its benefits.

Islamism and Neoliberalism:
Global Projects of Social Integration

Like many other economically strained countries of the South, Pakistan has imbibed the philosophies of global deregulation, economic liberalism, and denationalization promoted by international agencies and organizations. The incorporation of the Jamaat-e-Islami into mainstream politics coincided with the prioritizing of new development policies of the World Bank and international donors that de-emphasized the state sector and began to channel grants and aid to economically vulnerable groups through nongovernmental organizations. This privatization of the development project appealed to ordinary citizens in Pakistan as an antidote to inefficient and poorly funded public institutions and widespread corruption and exploitation at the highest levels (Hasan and Junejo 1999). The commonsense recourse to neoliberal economics was quickly embraced by the so-called citizens sector; from a few hundred NGOs in the 1970s, Pakistan at the end of the 1990s had about twenty-five thousand to thirty thousand (Hasan and Junejo 1999, 26–27). Politico-religious parties, such as the Jamaat-e-Islami, were often the most strident critics of the activities of feminist and human rights NGOs, but they also promoted the self-help and community development ideology of these groups. It resonated with their own project of dawat, or invitation to the Islamic life, as is evident from the proliferation in recent years of community-based groups aimed at improving education and health within an Islamic framework.

A key feature of the contemporary global development discourse is the enthusiastic summoning of women as neglected actors in the development and nation-building process. Women in Development (WID) programs in Pakistan, financed mostly by international agencies and Western donors since the 1970s, articulated with the state project of Islamization to produce contradictory results for women. For example, the state deferred to international pressure by creating a women's division in the government in 1979 at almost the same moment as systematic measures were enacted to reduce women's social and legal status. General Zia's take on "mainstreaming" women was his philosophy of *chadar* and *chardewari* (four walls), according to which women's independence and safety was to be secured by increased moral regulation and control of their participation in the public sphere (Shaheed and Mumtaz 1992; Mumtaz and Shaheed 1987; Shaukat Ali 1997). Pakistan hosted the First International *Seerat* (Prophet's biography) Conference of the World Union of Muslim Women in 1988, and Zia regularly presented chadars to women as part of his effort to Islamize Pakistani womanhood (Shaukat Ali 1997, 56–57). While seeking to restrain the fluid traditions of devotional Islam (e.g., by controlling funding for Sufi celebrations, referring to Sufi saints as "ulema," building mosques in sanctuaries, and discouraging women's participation in shrine-related events), Zia also propounded a vision of political, economic, and social modernization that was acceptable and even desirable for many middle-class Pakistani women (Shaukat Ali 1997).[6] Zia's mixture of neoliberal ideology and Islamism in the context of Pakistan refocused economic and social growth toward community effort rather than state responsibility, charitable and philanthropic activities instead of distributive justice, and moral regulation instead of social change. This period opened new possibilities for Jamaat-e-Islami women's projects that fused moral subject construction with social and economic development.

6. For a fuller discussion, see Jamal 2002.

The prominence of transnational Islamist movements and the growing centrality of Islam in international public discourse impelled many Pakistani women and men, particularly from the middle classes but also from the elite, to question the role of Islam in their daily lives (Weiss 1986).[7] For the vast majority of middle-class and lower middle-class women in Pakistan, much of the discussion of women's rights and their social status took place in informal sites such as Quran classes, dars, and charity and social events. It is these women who are the main subjects and agents of the Jamaat's version of Islam, which is offered as a balanced alternative to both the esoteric religiosity of Tablighi groups and the secularism of Western-educated elite groups.[8] The Jamaat's unique recruitment structure, which depends on a huge circle of supporters and sympathizers in addition to formal members, also facilitates the participation of those women who may be hesitant to enter the public space of formal politics. Many women reported that their initial association with the party was through participation in social activities centered on literacy, education, religious seminars, and women's support groups.

Gendered Changes within the Jamaat-e-Islami

Meanwhile, Jamaat women's appropriation of this space of political activism was facilitated by the changes within the movement itself that, although starting out as a religious reformist movement, fully transformed into a

---

7. A relatively less-theorized process of women's mobilization in the Jamaat is the transnational cultural exchange among Islamist movements that has enabled the imagining of a modern but Muslim identity for many middle-class women in Pakistan. This is enabled by the use of the media and Internet contacts as well as increased frequency of travel to their countries by diasporic Pakistanis who bring accounts of their own processes of adaptation to the imperatives of Western society. It is relevant to point out here that the Jamaat-e-Islami is itself a transnational movement with branches in Pakistan, India, Bangladesh, and Kashmir, as well as Britain and North America.

8. For a good introduction to the Tablighi movement, see Iqtidar 2011 as well as the substantial writings of Barbara Metcalf, in particular "'Traditionalist' Islamic Activism: Deoband, Tablighis, and Talibs," *Social Science Research Council*, January 1, 2004, http://www.ssrc.org/sept11/essays/metcalf.htm.

political party (Reza Nasr 1994; Grare 2001). Over the years, the Jamaat slowly abandoned its initial reluctance to engage in mainstream nationalist politics and undertook the compromises necessary for electoral politics. A pragmatic approach to politics gradually replaced the ideological drive of the Jamaat, until the religious movement became a political party (Reza Nasr 1994; Grare 2001). In this process membership in the party also underwent necessary alterations; political activism for both men and women was not seen as additional to, but rather as a necessary aspect of, Islamic identity in the contemporary era. The latest manifestation of what feminist scholars often term the "woman question," suggesting hegemonic debates about women's status, has occurred since the 1970s in public national and international development discourses and has influenced feminists and human rights groups within and across societies and nation-states. Its reverberations in Pakistan led politico-religious parties to direct their female supporters' activism toward this newly available discursive space.

While the positioning of the Jamaat men and women within Pakistani politics received feminist attention in Pakistan, what was less remarked on was the changed positioning of women within the politico-religious movement. Contrary to widespread feminist assumptions, women were not newcomers to Jamaat-e-Islami, since they had always complemented the political agenda and activities of the movement. However, since the 1980s there was clearly an enhanced awareness within the movement of the important cultural-political role of women, and this was evident in the proliferation of women's groups affiliated with the Jamaat and the expansion of women's activities in a variety of areas.

Among the most important events in the repositioning of Jamaat women within the party and at the national level was the Musharraf government's attempt to mainstream women in politics by reserving 33 percent seats for women in the national assembly and 50 percent in municipal councils. As I discussed in chapter 2, this impelled the Jamaat and other religious parties to set aside their long-standing reservations and support female candidates to compete in local and national elections. These women, who became city councilors and parliamentarians, actively participated in political training, capacity building, and other programs to boost women's political participation that were conducted by government and nongovernmental bodies, often with funding from the UN development agencies and other international and national donor agencies. Female politicians and public representatives of the Jamaat also became highly visible and vocal through their participation in television talk shows popularized by the flood of independent television channels that followed the deregulation of media as part of the government's compliance with international globalization imperatives.

Cultural Intersections of Local, National, and Global

Middle-class women, who form the majority of the Jamaat's female supporters, are among those who benefited most from the modern education projects of postcolonial states in many Muslim societies. For example, during Zia's time, because of the influx of international funding for infrastructure development (in return for Pakistan's support for Western interests in the Afghan War, 1979–88), record numbers of women, and men, from the middle classes entered universities and employment sites in urban centers such as Karachi. There they became exposed to the politics of Jamaat-e-Islami, which has always defined education as a key site of social political change. According to Reza Nasr, the Jamaat-e-Islami prioritizes education not simply "to rejuvenate religious observance but more to train a cadre of dedicated and pious men who would be charged with initiating, leading and subsequently protecting the Islamic revolutionary process" (Reza Nasr 1996, 77). The epitome of this ideology is the Jamaat-affiliated Islami Jamiat-e-Tulba, an Islamic organization of male students, which has been the training ground for many of the party's leaders. Reza Nasr sees parallels between the programs of fundamentalist Christian groups, such as that of Jerry Falwell in the United States and Opus Dei in Spain, and the Jamaat's emphasis on education as the means of diffusing the power structure and affecting sociopolitical developments. Education as a basis for training is so important for the Jamaat that, despite its approval of General Mohammed Zia ul Haq's Islamization program, the party withdrew its support for his regime in 1984 because of Zia's decision, as part of his antiliberal, antileft politics, to ban student unions in Pakistani universities.

The gendering of politics in general has expanded this project to women students in colleges and universities through recruitment activities of the Islami Jamiat-e-Talibat, the women student's equivalent of the Islami Jamiat-e-Tulba. The effectiveness of such recruitment was powerfully evident in the experiences of Zainab, a young lawyer, and Suriaya, both involved with a Jamaat-affiliated group, Women's Aid Trust (WAT). When we met for an interview in Karachi in June 2003, Zainab had not yet joined the Jamaat and was the only one of my interviewees without hijab or burqa. She described her initial interaction with a Jamaat woman:

> One of my acquaintances came to me and said that she was working for JI at the time I was in the university and she said she wanted to start an organization. I had my *dupatta* (scarf) around my neck, my hair was cut short [signifiers of modern womanhood in Pakistan]. I told her, "But you are from Jamaat Islami and I refuse to change myself until I feel the desire to do so from within myself. I will not change under duress so that I have a veil (niqab) on my face but continue to retain my faults." She said, "We want you the way you are. Please work with us."

Although Suraiya did not need to be persuaded in a similar way, she said she too was drawn to the movement while at Karachi University. She joined the Islami Jamiat Talibat and became politically active despite the reservations of her parents and later her husband. Suraiya said she had been able to recruit many other family members into the party:

> Initially I did face some problems from my family. My mother supported me but my father was not too keen on my involvement in politics. However I had made up my mind and later on my three other sisters also followed me in joining the Jamaat. . . .
> When I got married my husband was not very interested, but, thank God, he is now also involved in Jamaat.

The women I interviewed were holders of graduate degrees in genetics, economics, law, political science, or journalism—mostly Western social and natural sciences. None had a formal degree in the traditional madressa system, although all had been through informal processes of religious learning through individual study or in neighborhood circles organized by Jamaat women. Maulana Maududi's works, including his commentary on the Quran and his writings on women and Islam, formed a significant part of this informal learning process.

Although Maududi is widely seen as an opponent of women's participation in the public sphere, especially because of his well-known thesis that links women's emancipation and the fall of civilizations, the modern educated women of the Jamaat-e-Islami reject the counterpoising of gender segregation and gender rights in women's political and social struggles.[9] They either deny that women's exclusion from public life exemplifies the politics of Jamaat-e-Islami or argue that such policies are meant to be supportive of middle-class and lower middle-class women in a globalizing world rather than intended as a means of oppression. The Jamaat women's agenda calls for segregated workplaces and increased training opportunities and educational institutions for women to boost their economic and political role. At the same time, Jamaat women insist that Muslim women are entitled to financial support from their male relatives so that they are not forced into the workplace.

Arabization of the Pakistani Middle Classes

Some of the strongest supporters of the state's Islamization project and also of politico-religious parties are the middle-class traders and petty entrepreneurs who have gained from a variety of political realignments and socioeconomic changes related to the conditions of the past three decades. The ascendance of this class is ascribed to a number of factors including increased access to financial credit for hitherto excluded groups, the use of financial incentives to neutralize political opponents, and, most of all, a dramatic boost to Pakistan's economy by trade and labor migration to the oil-rich Arab Gulf states (Asghar Khan 1985; Haque 1983; Hussein 1997;

9. For Maududi's views on women's emancipation and gender segregation, see Reza Nasr 1996, Jameelah 1976a, and Maududi 1939.

Hoodbhoy 2009). This class of merchants and traders continue to be the major support base of the Jamaat-e-Islami.

While the political, economic, and social effects of the oil-related traffic and diaspora have received some attention, there is also an important gendered dimension of the travel of middle-class and lower middle-class workers and their families between Pakistan and the Arab Gulf states. I would argue that Gulf Arab societies, in addition to being major sources of aid for madressas and philanthropic Islamic projects, have become important cultural reference points and spaces of cultural exchange for middle-class and working-class Pakistanis. Millions of Pakistani workers returning from years of working in Arab countries have changed Pakistan's cities, towns, and villages by equipping local mosques and madressas with outsized loudspeakers to propagate puritan beliefs, bringing back Arab-style hijabs for their wives and daughters, voluntarily policing community morality, and maintaining, often violently, sectarian boundaries.

Hoodbhoy (2009) has correctly pinpointed the cultural and material effects in contemporary Pakistani society of a concerted move in religious orientation among Muslims toward the tradition of Islam that is associated mostly with Saudi Arabia. Hoodbhoy echoes the concerns of many Pakistani scholars and ordinary citizens that an intensive Arabization of society accompanied by sterner interpretations of Islam has pervaded society through the state-sponsored program that is misleadingly referred to as Islamization (Hoodbhoy 2009; Jamal 2002; also see Hussain 1997). More important, Hoodbhoy rightly emphasizes that this puritanical impulse marks a dramatic shift in the centuries-old conceptions of religion and identity in South Asia that were tied to more humanistic Persian and Turkish Islamic traditions. In "The Saudi-isation of Pakistan," published in January 2009 in the widely distributed Karachi-based English-language monthly magazine *Newsline*, Hoodbhoy dramatically calls attention to the strong cultural pressures in Pakistani society that were drawing it away from its historical South Asian traditions and toward Arabian Islam.

> Grain by grain, the desert sands of Saudi Arabia are replacing the rich soil that had nurtured a magnificent Muslim culture in India for

a thousand years. This culture produced Mughul architecture, the Taj Mahal, the poetry of Asadullah Khan Ghalib, and much more. Now a stern, unyielding version of Islam (Wahhabism) is replacing the kinder, gentler Islam of the Sufis and saints who had walked on this land for hundreds of years. (Hoodboy 2009)

The effects of Arabization are most visible in the cultural practices and cultural expressions of what Hoodbhoy described as the "lower middle" and "middle middle" sections of the middle class. While elite and upper-class women may follow the latest intellectual, social, and sartorial trends in New York or London, other classes are more interested in the lifestyles current in Dubai and Jeddah. These places have also become attractive holiday destinations for middle-class families, and several million Pakistanis, including many families, have lived in or visited the Gulf Arab states in the last thirty years.[10]

Pakistani male workers of all classes, but also women, have brought back with them new ideas about Islam that are definitely doctrinaire but in some ways more liberating for many middle-class women than prevalent notions of religion and culture in South Asia. One example is the tremendous appeal of the hijab, which appears to offer women more mobility than formal and informal observances of purdah or seclusion.[11] Through this exposure to Islam in prosperous Middle East societies, Pakistani middle-class, lower middle-class, and some working-class women have been able to experience women-only parks, shopping centers, movie houses, and beaches, and thus partake of a life available mostly to a small

10. Although the number of Pakistani workers in the Middle East has declined after the Gulf Wars, the number of visitors from Pakistan has increased because of increased consumerism among the middle and upper middle classes in Pakistan, accompanied by the relaxation of visa controls for tourism and shopping, by Dubai and other members of the United Arab Emirates.

11. This is especially true of Gulf states such as the United Arab Emirates, Bahrain, and Oman. The observations regarding Pakistani women's experiences in these societies are based on my own experience of living in the United Arab Emirates and conversations with Pakistani expatriates.

segment of upper middle-class and elite women in Pakistan. They have also witnessed firsthand the greater freedom for women to work in banks, in offices, and even as taxi drivers, and to roam unimpeded in mixed-gender malls and other places because of the mobility offered by hijab.[12]

Many of the Jamaat women I met or interviewed had either lived in Saudi Arabia or another oil-producing Gulf state as a result of their husband's work or had visited these for pilgrimage (*hajj* and *Umrah*) or tourism. Interviewees frequently pointed to the combination of Islamic and modern that they found appealing in the lives of Gulf Arab women that was enabled by a combination of state provision, personal affluence, and different interpretations of Islamic laws relating to women's inheritance, property, marriage, and divorce. The lives of Muslim Arab Gulf women offer a solution to the dilemma faced by many middle-class women in Pakistan who are obliged to enter public spaces for education and employment but feel more comfortable in gender-segregated environments.

Vanguard of a New Modernity?

Jamaat women, in my interviews with them, frequently situated themselves at the intersection of Islam and modernity and considered both to signify progress and development; in contrast they used the term "tradition" or "the traditional" to signify cultural backwardness and retrograde customary practices. They referred to a reinvolvement with Islam as triggering a questioning of their own ideas about tradition and modernity, rather than the contact with modernity necessitating a reinterpretation of Islamic injunctions, as for earlier generations of South Asian Muslim women. I asked all my interlocutors to describe the circumstances that led them to join the Jamaat-e-Islami. Many women pinpointed a moment in their lives when they came to detect a difference between "true Islamic

12. For instance, many women saw as more appealing and "more Islamic" the hijab-wearing Arab women's mobility in contrast with the custom of purdah or segregation that was prevalent among their families in South Asia, or the greater tolerance that they perceived toward divorced women in Arab Muslim society compared with the social attitudes in South Asia.

life" and the practices and traditions that they had followed all their lives as Muslims. Interestingly, these accounts were usually framed in terms of progress, improvement, and greater participation in society rather than withdrawal from social and political life.

Maria, introduced in chapter 2, was one of the Jamaat women to be elected in 2002 as a city councilor in the Karachi municipal elections. She was a former teacher of economics at an undergraduate government college. She appeared to be in her middle forties, was married to an airline pilot, and had traveled widely out of Pakistan including to the United States and East Asian countries.[13] Maria lived with her husband and two college-going sons in Nazimabad, a suburb of Karachi associated mostly with Urdu-speaking immigrants (Muhajirs) who migrated from India to Pakistan. Maria described herself as someone who had not always been interested in religion or inclined toward the Jamaat-e-Islami. She became interested in increasing her understanding of Islam when she saw her female relatives attending Quran classes or adopting the burqa. She said she began a serious study of the Quran and became introduced to the Jamaat when, at the invitation of a female relative, she started dropping in on a Quran discussion group begun in her neighborhood: "So I undertook a detailed reading of the Quran and I saw that it was all true—and then my perception changed completely."

Similarly, Fatima, who appeared to be in her thirties, had a BS in chemistry from a local college. She was a journalist and a public relations officer for the Jamaat Women's Wing in Karachi. Fatima traced her interest in the Jamaat to joining religion classes aimed at enabling women to understand the meaning of the Quran. They read the Arabic text along with its Urdu translation:

13. In deference to the tradition of purdah, my descriptions of individual Jamaat-e-Islami women I interviewed will be deliberately sketchy and minimal. When I describe a woman as "middle aged," it indicates that I classify her as being anywhere between forty and fifty years old, and "young" would be between twenty-five and thirty-five years old. The idea in including this detail is to give a sense of the political social conditions of women's personal and collective trajectories.

When I started reading for these classes, I experienced a great change in my life. I realized that Allah has not created us to be completely free but to be His appointee (*naib*) on earth, to fulfill His mission. I started reading a variety of books and literature to understand what it means to be a naib and it became evident to me that Islam is not just a religion. It is a din, a system of life. This means that your ways of working, sitting, eating, all aspects of life are governed by a set of rules. Automatically I became interested in purdah. I adopted the veil.

On the other hand, many other women traced their induction into the politics of the Jamaat to their colleges or universities, where they came into contact with the female student activists of the Islami Jamiat Talibat. However, all my interlocutors invariably recognized their entry into the Jamaat as a significant moment of internal conversion. In this they reiterated a common motif of modern Islamist movements, in particular of the teachings of Maulana Maududi, whose exegesis necessitated such a realization for the faithful to proceed toward the true Islamic struggle.[14] Reza Nasr, for example, points out that Maududi's exegesis of the Quran and his reinterpretation of the notion of din as a transcendental system of observances and beliefs instead of simply faith or piety, implies that Muslims must break with their existing or traditional understanding and practices of Islam. This would purge them of all forms of contamination of the true faith, as he saw it, in order to be able to implement the divine will, which was to establish God's dominance as a political and legal formation (Reza Nasr 1996). Many women I met elaborated on their faith in women's rights in Islam, the meaning of submission to Allah, the rights and responsibilities of a Muslim woman, her correct demeanor in public and private,

14. The notion of an "internal conversion" is key to the Islamist project; especially Maududi, who emphasized the need for Muslims to reexamine their relationship with Islam before they could change. Traditional Islamic scholars have criticized Maududi's redefinition of din (faith), in which he linked individual faith with responsibility for social implementation of the divine law. Thus for Maududi the purpose of prayer was not simply to praise God or achieve spiritual salvation but to act out one's absolute obedience to God. (Reza Nasr 1996)

and proper behavior with family and friends and community. They distinguished clearly between their own practices, which they understood to be correct, and the customary observances and practices of an ordinary middle-class Muslim woman in Pakistan. This is both an intensification and gendering of the modern process of historical consciousness that some scholars have traced in the discourses of modern Islamist reformers, particularly Maulana Maududi. His Islam is seen to mark a shift in emphasis from a traditional to a modern Islam, or to a this-worldly, disenchanted Islam from the more classical Pietist Islam that still resonates with the majority of the Muslims in South Asia.[15] Accordingly, many women noted that while they had always believed themselves to be Muslims, the meaning of what this enjoined on them as women and as believers became clear only when they understood Islam as a system rather than as individual or communal faith.[16]

This process, invariably, also intensified the need to differentiate between secular and religious, and, as a result, many women said that they also understood the place of modernity in their lives, which was not necessarily oppositional to Islam. Their accounts indicated that in the process of rejuvenating an Islamic identity, not only did their understanding of Islam increase, but their insights into the qualitative nature of progress and development, therefore of modernity, underwent changes as well. Women often described social and cultural activities, as well as religious observances, that they attributed to their misguided understanding of not just Islam but also modernity.

Jamaat women's polysemic understanding of modernity becomes clearer in the manner in which some women described their lives prior

15. For an elaboration of this modernist impulse in Islamic movements, especially with reference to the Jamaat-e-Islami, see Reza Nasr (1996) and Robinson (2000).

16. Most Muslims use the terms "din" and "mazhab" interchangeably, but Maududi and other Deobandi-leaning scholars reject "mazhab" as individual belief and uphold "din" as an all-encompassing collective system. According to Reza Nasr, Muaudidi's reconceptualizing of the term "din" and his construction of Islam as an ideology was vehemently criticized by traditional Islamic scholars. (Reza Nasr 1996, 63).

to joining the Jamaat and after the adoption of practices they described as Islamic and that, they emphasized, included veiling but also much more. My interview with Fatima is illustrative in this regard. She described her life prior to joining the Jamaat in the following terms:

> I used to be crazy about Indian movies; I could not survive without television. At weddings I used to receive special invitations to perform *luddi* and *bhangra* and other dances. I was interested in cricket, in boys. As I told you, I was a "mod" type of girl.

Similar to women in other parts of the Muslim world who described their self-transformation through Islam, Fatima referred to this past phase of her life as a period of ignorance (*daur-e-jihalat*). Fatima also described herself during this mod phase as self-centered and impulsive and given to quarreling with friends and relatives. Her engagement with Islam, she said, changed not only her outward appearance and her daily routines but also notions of selfhood. Fatima did not seem to be referring solely to an internal conversion related to the nature of her personal, individual engagement with Islam. She called attention to the training, which is part of the organizational and intellectual project of the Jamaat, out of which she developed the skills and knowledge for public and social activism. As Fatima described her personal and religious transformation, she also emphasized the role of the collective activities of the party, especially the frequent training programs that she said helped her inculcate qualities, such as patience and tolerance, that were necessary to undertake activities at the level of the community. It is this sense of the relationship between individual righteousness and social political activism that endows Jamaat women with their historical consciousness of what Cantwell Smith has described as the idea of a "community in motion," that is, of a community both based on and integral to individual faith (Smith 1957, 26). My interlocutors related this moment of individual-community connection with a recognition of their own situatedness in a movement forward that they often described in temporal, even developmental, terms. Some of this is evident in the following comment by Fatima:

What is the meaning of Islam? To go forward to leave the era of Jihalat, to move forward in a positive manner. If that is so then we are more modern [than the secular feminists]. We are moving forward in every sphere of life whether it is *muamalat* [public affairs], *ikhlaqiat* [behavior], *muasharat* [social], or *maishat* [economy]. I have presented before you a picture of my past life. . . . I will ask you a question—what do you think? Was I modern then or am I modern now?

Evidently for Fatima, the mobilizing of her faith in the historical activities of the community in the public modern sphere connotes true progress and, therefore, modernity, rather than the earlier attributes that she had associated with the modern—and this modernity suggests a way out for women from moral ignorance and subordination as well as worldly backwardness. Modernity is not rejected as simply undesirable; instead it is redefined and appropriated.

While there was a great flexibility in what was deemed to be modern or related to modernization, I suggest that there is a difference in the manner in which my women interlocutors deployed these terms from accounts provided by scholars such as Esposito (2003) and Utvik (2003) of male Islamists in Egypt and other places. According to these scholars, while male Islamists support technological development, they are far more hesitant toward modernization as a general phenomenon and would typically oppose the use of this concept to describe their goals on the grounds that it has become synonymous with Westernization. Utvik, for instance, in pointing to the modern nature of Islamist movements, argues that the relationship between Islamism and modernity needs to be grasped not from the rhetoric of Islamists about modernization but rather how their words and actions are affecting the Muslim Middle Eastern societies in which they work.

The male Islamists in Egypt may reject being identified as modern, but Jamaat women in Pakistan have no hesitation in using the concept of "modern" or "modernization" to describe their goals. I draw attention to this difference not simply to point out a gendered peculiarity of expression, but rather to emphasize the operation of what Lila Abu-Lughod has referred to as the "politics of modernity" that must underlie any discussion of gender, Islam, and modernity and that seeks to provide a nuanced account of women's lives in Islamic societies (Abu-Lughod 1998). I argue that Jamaat women's easy appropriation of the modern signals a different ordering of the place of women in the Islam-modernity relationship and an attenuation of the unease about women's public participation evident in earlier Jamaat-e-Islami discourse as exemplified by the work of Maulana Maududi and his disciple Maryam Jameelah.[17] In these earlier works, the modernizing of Muslim women functioned both as a prerequisite for the progress of the middle-class Muslim family when it concerned women's education and literacy, and as a recurring trope for the lamentable condition of Muslim society and its capitulation in the face of Western ideas of progress when it led to women's unveiling and mobility. In fact Maududi's differentiation of these two modes of becoming modern was so emphatic that his prescriptions for women's veiling and segregation and their exclusion from public spaces often ran contrary to his emphasis on literal adherence to the scriptural texts of Islam (Reza Nasr 1996, 30).

In contrast, contemporary Jamaat women embrace the idea of the modern and point to aspects of their lives, other than education, such as economic and political activities, as definitely modern. Almost all my interlocutors qualified this by emphasizing that their notion of being "modern" was different from that of other women's groups in Pakistan and the West. Their position was clearly summed up by Ayesha, a leader of the Jamaat-e-Islami Women's Commission in Karachi:

> We have no problems with modernity, such as education, driving, employment, etc., but we have to ensure that it fits into our own ideology. We are modern to the extent that is allowed to us by Allah and our difference (with secular feminists) is also simply that [in the process of modernizing women] the foundational principles of Islam should not be compromised.

Farida, a member of the Jamaat Women's Wing who had successfully been elected to the Karachi City Council, further clarified this position:

17. Maududi 1939. See, for example, Jameelah 1976a, 1976b.

There is a difference between being progressive and being Westernized. Our misfortune is that we have assumed all forms of progress to be Westernized. We have no development and no progress although our din [faith] itself is progressive.

Jamaat women reject the notion of individual autonomy in matters of religious beliefs and practices and consider the disciplining of their selves inextricable from the moral orientation of the larger community of Muslims. As I discuss later in this book, it is also here that Jamaat women tend to differ most seriously with those who define themselves as progressive, liberal, or secular feminists in Pakistan, as well as with the majority of Muslims in South Asia. Although Jamaat women accepted the notion of modernization, they continued to reject feminism as an acceptable mode of thinking, acting, or being for Muslim women.

I argue that Jamaat women's experience needs to be situated within the interacting cultural discourses of Islamism, Islamization, and Westernization, and also within the processes of postcolonial nation-state formation, integral to which is the project of construction of a bourgeois class in the subcontinent.

Gender, Class, and Islam in the Postcolonial Nation-State

Feminist scholars have drawn on Partha Chatterjee's theorization of the processes by which state interventions in the domain of the private may be understood to explain gender and class solidarities/subjectivities in postcolonial societies, including Pakistan. Women's education and employment are integral features of the state's development agenda, and modernism is a means by which existing elite and newly emerging classes attempt to rationalize their sociopolitical domination over the rest of the population (Rouse 1998). Jamaat women's engagement with notions of gendered modernity, their disengagement with development, and their subsequent re-engagement with a different notion of the modern woman are marked by these processes of gendered bourgeois subject formation in both its elite and quasi-/non-elite manifestations.

My interactions with Jamaat women suggest that they approach the modernizing processes and ideas of state and elite classes with both opposition and approbation. While opposing the modern subjectivities that they see embodied in elite women in Pakistan, Jamaat women cannot escape the valorization of the modern that dominates the consciousness of middle-class consumerist Pakistani society. Further, this specifically classed gender consciousness is mediated by the social, political, and cultural dominance of a class of so-called secular progressives, including women, that was entrenched in Pakistani society through the colonial system of education and administration in which English language ability and access to Western culture was the provenance of elite groups. It has been pointed out by some feminist scholars (Hussain 1997; Said Khan 1994) that Islamist groups such as the Jamaat-e-Islami include many economically and socially prosperous families and individuals. But it is important to understand, in postcolonial contexts such as Pakistan, the retrospective nature of the construction of an "elite" class, a term that, as discussed in the introductory chapter, is used to refer to a heterogeneous and economically disparate group of individuals who display familiarity with Western liberal political discourses and literary/cultural traditions. In such a context the description of certain ideas and modes of being as Westernized and elite situates them in particular bodily-spatial-temporal locations. It is the cultural leadership of this location that today's upwardly mobile Jamaat women must challenge, and to do so they seek to wrest away the monopoly of modernity from the current occupants of this social cultural space—the established elites.

Jamaat women's recuperation of the modern in Pakistan is a combination of their own historical social-cultural location, prevalent media depictions of the West, and commonsense understandings of what it means to be modern in Pakistan. It may be read also as a cultural strategy for appropriating the modern in Pakistan by delinking it from colonial history, failed development policies, World Bank dictates, superpower dominance, and the local elite cultural dominance.

None of my interlocutors, possessing college degrees, can be described as "traditional" or "backward" as these terms are used in official developmental discourse in Pakistan. They represent a definite change from their mothers' generation of middle- and lower middle-class women in Pakistan who did not have similar access to university or college education; these women are also able to see themselves as progressive compared with the vast majority of women in Pakistan who belong to the urban or rural poor and have no access to education at all. Like their self-identified secular feminist counterparts, the majority of the Jamaat women I interviewed belong to a generation of women in Pakistan who have benefited from the development and modernization project of the state, especially the state's accommodations to the international focus on gender in development projects during the 1970s and 1980s.

Being holders of degrees and training in social sciences, technology, and natural sciences, they have reason to see themselves as modern and, therefore, equal to elite and upper-class women in education and skills and, in many cases, in economic and income levels. However, they face a barrier at the cultural level, since unlike the elite classes most of them are distanced from Western culture through language. All the women that I met preferred to converse in Urdu, even those who had been to "English-speaking" colleges such as Kinnaird, Lahore, or St. Joseph's, Karachi. Their sense of cultural marginalization is accentuated by their experiences of secular-elite dominated governments in Pakistan, which have established a dismal record in achieving social and economic justice.[18] These middle-class Jamaat women challenge the claims of the modernizing elite women to cultural and social dominance.

My interlocutors' disdain for short hair and Western dress and attitudes to the body were undoubtedly meant to signify the adoption of an Islamic self, but it also indicated rejection of class-specific signifiers of modernity that are associated with the elite, upper-class position in Pakistan. This challenging of the elite cultural status resonates with the discursive strategies of Islamist groups in other previously colonized societies where these groups appropriate their middle-class position in an attempt

18. For some failures of development policies in Pakistan, see Eqbal Ahmad (2000); Khurshid Ahmad (1998); Ishtiaq Ahmed (2002); and Asghar Khan (1985).

to mediate cultural struggles in the public sphere (Hatem 1998). Accordingly, Islamist movements do not reject but rather emphasize the centrality of the nuclear middle-class heterosexual family and the systems of education and training that are key to the disciplinary processes of modern society (Hatem 1998). This accounts for the emergence and increasing visibility of young modern secular educated women in today's Islamist movements. A profound gendering of political-religious movements has resulted from the interaction of Islamist and state discourses on gender, women, family, and sexualities in societies as dispersed and culturally disparate as Egypt, Pakistan, Iran, and Indonesia (Rinaldo 2008; Stivens 2000; Najmabadi 1998).

Like their gendered counterparts elsewhere, Jamaat women, too, insist on gendered expressions of Islamic identity in the public sphere of Pakistani society. However, their discursive constructions of the relationship of Islam and modernity, as, for example, expressed by my interlocutors, Farida and Ayesha, suggest not simply an assertion of difference but also a sustained questioning of Western universalism. Drawing on the insight of Sayyid (2000), it may be pointed out that Islamist discourse should be understood not through a dichotomous framework of universalism-versus-cultural particularity, but rather as an attempt to dislodge one version of universality associated with the West with another kind of universalism in the name of Islam.

Jamaat women's engagement with modernity and their appropriation of feminist discourse that I have highlighted in this discussion supports the contentions of scholars such as Mino Moallem (1999) and Lila Abu-Lughod (1998). These scholars suggest that both feminism and fundamentalism include a plurality of discourses that prohibit their classification as uniquely religious or secular phenomena. They need to be understood within the problematic of modernity as competing attempts at cultural representation and, therefore, in the shaping of individual and communal identities. This struggle appears to have infused the traditional mission of women in the Jamaat-e-Islami with a new orientation toward modernity. Take, for example, the observation by Samina that the new present leadership of the Jamaat was interested in pursuing a kind of politics based on tolerance for (at least) the practices of other Muslims. As proof, she pointed out: "For instance our present MMA coalition is comprised of individuals who once considered each other to be *kafirs*, who wouldn't agree to pray with each other." As a testimony to their more open outlook, it is noteworthy that at no time did any of my interlocutors admonish me on my appearance or dress, as has been recorded by other researchers on the Jamaat (Shehabuddin 2008, 23–24).

I conclude that it is a mistake to see the struggle in civil society in Pakistan as being a struggle between religious conservatism and secular modernity. On the contrary, it is the terrain of modernity itself that has become the major battleground in the cultural and political representation of Pakistani women. By seeking to shape the discourses of modernity in Pakistan, middle-class women are attempting to overturn the terms of the debate through which were framed thus far the leadership claims of modernizing nationalist elite and feminist activists. Jamaat women are able to use not simply Islam but also ideas about citizenship, women's rights, and progress to challenge the modernizers' claims to represent national interest and national development in Pakistan.

Some recent analyses of the Jamaat-e-Islami's more flexible position on women's roles within the party in South Asia understand this to be a concession from the male leaders of the party as a bid to expand the party's appeal to larger groups of women or to survive the forces of modernization (Shehabuddin 2008; Ahmad 2008). For example, based on her in-depth interviews with Jamaat-e-Islami women in rural areas of Bangladesh, Shehabuddin notes that "the mobilization of impoverished uneducated women who are increasingly vocal about their specific needs is compelling the party to make changes to its rhetoric and strategies" (Shehabuddin 2008, 220). She observes that the Jamaat has modified its policies on some issues of interest to women and has relaxed its traditional opposition to women's employment, education, and voting rights. Similarly Ahmad (2008) has observed a significant flexibility toward women's dress and their public participation among male Islamist ideologues of the Jamaat-e-Islami in India since the 1970s. He describes this as an internal critique by these male leaders who have begun to question some key tenets of Maududi's position toward women's role within the family and society (560–69). Such analyses may overlook the agentive role of women themselves, who are in fact bringing about important changes within the party and its position in the larger society. In other words, it is not simply a political strategy of the Jamaat to embrace more women-friendly Islamist politics, but it is the modern Islamist women who may be playing a constitutive role in the nature of Islamist politics.

The appropriation of the modern universal public sphere by women, and the modes of thinking associated with it, have expedited the gendering of political Islam, which in turn has become the necessary condition for securing the Islamization project in Pakistan.

5

Gender and Development and Its Discontents

Jamaat Women and the "Woman Question" in Pakistan

The West has raised the alarm about women's rights in Pakistan, although the [poor] status of women in Western societies becomes obvious to even a casual visitor to any of those societies. There is no doubt that women in our country are being victimized, and for the protection of women and to restore the dignity of their status Jamaat-e-Islami has prepared a Women's Rights Charter. This calls for education and training for women and the restoration of their social status. Towards this aim the Jamaat-e-Islami has set up a Women's Commission which comprises capable and qualified women in the country.
—**Qazi Hussein Ahmed,** Jamaat-e-Islami President
(Ahmed 2002, 144)

The British . . . divided our society into feudal classes and others by handing out jagirs [land] to some, who then ruled over others. Take any of the important jagirdar [landowning] families of today, you will find that they go back to the history of British rule; the British gave out titles to those who were loyal to them, they made them leaders, they made them administrators, and they gave them land and power. So, what we call today the "war of the sexes" is not really the war between men and women—it is a war between justice and injustice, it is a war of the powerful and the weak, it is an issue of those who believe in Allah and those who have wandered away.
—**Atiya Nisar,** Jamaat-e-Islami Women's Commission

I request my sisters—no matter what stage of life they are in, whatever their area of work, whatever responsibilities they are required to carry—to stop and reflect on the new world order which is presented to us as a new event that is shrinking the world and transforming it

into a global village. If we think a bit more deeply we will realize that long before the United States made its claim to be a superpower with the right to impose its writ over the whole world, Allah the Creator who made you and me, and His Prophet, offered us a similar concept of supreme leadership—that there is only one power which dominates the whole world. And that power is Allah, the Lord of the worlds. You can either become a servant of God or a servant of the worldly power.
—**Rehana Afroze**, Jamaat-e-Islami city councilor

The Jamaat women leaders cited here were addressing a public event that I attended in Karachi on International Women's Day in March 2005 organized by the Women's Commission of the Jamaat-e-Islami. The themes reiterated were not extraordinary for a women's event in Pakistan: violence against women, the complicity of the police and law enforcement bodies, the low social and economic status of women in Pakistan, and the deprivation of their rights by social and political authorities.

What made this event noteworthy for me was its uncanny resonance with another International Women's Day event that I had attended in the same city a few weeks earlier. This previous event was organized by the Women's Action Forum (WAF), the Human Rights Commission of Pakistan (HRCP), and several other civil society groups, all of which are members of the Joint Action Committee for People's Rights (JAC), a coalition of Pakistan-based NGOs operating in the human rights field. Representatives from Pakistan's women's movements, directors of feminist NGOs, and speakers from human rights groups at the meeting vociferously condemned the lack of progress on women's social and economic status, the increasing violence against women in Karachi exacerbated by the complicity of the police, and the lack of commitment by the state to improve women's citizenship rights.

While the JAC event attributed women's declining position to the Islamization of laws, especially the Hudood Ordinance and its effects, the Jamaat women's event blamed women's low legal, social, and economic status on the insufficient expansion of the Islamization of laws into society. The two events, with not surprisingly divergent ideologies but highly corresponding concerns, are illustrative of a newly emerging, intensely intimate, highly variegated, conflicted, and complex space of women's activism that is shared by feminist and Islamist women in contemporary Pakistan.

Like many other Muslim majority states Pakistan is a signatory to a number of international agreements related to women's rights, most notably the Convention on the Political Rights of Women, the Convention on the Rights of the Child (CRC), and the Convention on the Elimination of All Forms of Discrimination Against Women (CEDAW). As in numerous other Muslim societies, many of the problems afflicting the state's unsatisfactory implementation of its developmental projects, and the psychic, cultural, economic, and social dislocations associated with these projects, are represented in oppositional terms as religious-cultural backwardness against modern progress. National development projects, often initiated in response to demands by women's groups for removal of discriminatory practices or alleviating glaring gender disparities, are most vehemently and vociferously opposed by men who position themselves as representatives of Islam. Parties such as the Jamaat-e-Islami frequently accuse NGOs and feminists of undermining Muslim culture and local customs, promoting Western cultural and political agendas, destroying traditional social structures, and corrupting women and girls (Hussain 1997, 220–23). In extreme cases *mullahs* (religious leaders) have sanctioned the kidnapping of NGO activists by local men on charges of "corrupting their women," hurled abuses against them in media and public lectures, called for state action against them, and, on occasion, even inflicted death threats on women's rights and human rights activists.[1] These highly publicized

---

1. The accusation of blasphemy and the declaration of someone as *kafir* (unbeliever) has emerged as a common strategy of twenty-first-century politico-religious groups seeking to delegitimize feminist and human rights politics in Muslim societies. See Aisha Ghaus Pasha, Hafiz A. Pasha, and Muhammad Asif Iqbal, *Nonprofit Sector in Pakistan: Government Policy and Future Issues*, Working Paper of SPDC No. 2 (Karachi: Social Policy and Development Center, 2002) 7; and Ahmed 2002. One of the most horrific examples of this violence was the public murder of Salman Taseer, the governor of Punjab province, in January 2011 for opposing Pakistan's controversial Blasphemy Laws, under which Asiya Bibi, a

discourses often elide understanding of the multiple ways in which politico-religious movements, such as the Jamaat in the present era, rather than
simply resisting global development agendas, are also significantly influencing the direction of these projects.

It is no coincidence that modernization and development are seen
as not only religious questions but also extremely gendered issues, since
the revitalization and modernization of Muslim society has always been
entangled with "the Muslim woman question," the code name for a set
of colonial discourses about the poor conditions of women in colonized
Muslim societies (Abu-Lughod 1998; Ahmed 1992; Haddad 1998). Emerging as an issue of public interest and as an instantiation of culturally
imposed oppression, the social and economic status of Muslim women
in South Asia remains perennially constrained within this detrimental
framing. The banner of modernizing and revitalizing Muslim society in
nineteenth-century India was taken up first by elite modernizing men and
then women of the elite classes (Mumtaz and Shaheed 1991). With the
intensification of anticolonial nationalist movements in the 1940s, such
as the Muslim League in India, the woman question, now further convoluted in terms of Islamic-versus-Westernized, preoccupied the terrain of
Muslim nationalism.[2] In the postcolonial state of Pakistan, modernizing
elite Muslim men and women considered women's development and progress a testimony to their own modern credentials. Their main opponents
were deemed to be those traditionalist Muslims, mostly in the persona
of male religious leaders, who construed any type of cultural or social
change in Muslim societies as capitulation to the West. While elite women
were highly visible in the nationalist modernizing discourses, women supporters of the Islamist parties, mostly middle-class women, were implicitly considered to be the desiring but silenced objects of state-sponsored
development projects aimed at increasing women's economic and political

---

Christian mother of four, was sentenced to death. The Jamaat-e-Islami was one of the most
vocal supporters of the Blasphemy Laws and death penalty for Asiya Bibi.

2. For a theorization of the relationship of colonialism, nationalism, and gender in
Muslim societies, see Ahmed 1992.

participation (Gardezi 1997; Haq 1996; Mumtaz and Shaheed 1987). This sterile construction has historically overshadowed all struggles involving women in Pakistan and has inflected the new terrains of Women in Development (WID) and Gender and Development (GAD).[3]

Reverberating beyond the issues of modernization and development, the polarization of Pakistani society into liberal, secular, progressives versus conservative, religious Islamists threatens the very possibility of civil society—which has resurged in the post–Cold War era as a desired goal of feminists and human rights forces in Pakistan. In recent years, NGOs, feminist groups, and political activists in Pakistan have coalesced around the idea of civil society as a project for the expression of liberal, progressive, leftist, and secular ideas (e.g., Asghar Khan 2001; Hasan and Junejo 1999). In fact, this civil society is a highly contested terrain because of the convergence of ethnic affiliations, tribal authorities, media, social movements, local and global political, cultural, and economic interests, and religious groups. Furthermore, a significant proportion of civil society comprises those who have entered the terrain of advocacy and activism with the aim of challenging, limiting, altering, or regulating the state's developmental projects rather than promoting them. This character of Pakistani "civil society" is often conceptualized as an "unresolved struggle between the practices and values of pre-capitalist society and new modes of social life, between authoritarian legacies, and democratic aspirations" (Asian Development Bank 2009, 3). In its report on civil society in Pakistan, the Asian Development Bank (ADB) pointed to an evolutionary trend in which older forms of social authority such as councils of elders, neighborhood associations, and shrines are being challenged by

---

3. Following global discourses of the World Bank and United Nations both government officials and feminist groups enthusiastically adopted WID and GAD philosophies in Pakistan. WID refers to attempts to include Women in Development programs, while GAD seeks to rethink development theory and practice through a gendered lens. In recent years both the state and feminist groups have adopted the more contemporary GAD in their discourses, although this does not necessarily reflect a significant change in development directions.

newer groups emergent from capitalist development. Thus the authors of the report observed: "Such are the dynamics of an evolving civil society, caught between the throes of a dying social order and the birth pangs of a new one" (ADB 2009, 3). This understanding of civil society as a teleological project that will eventually lead to the attainment of human freedom and a better life for all ignores the possibility that while some older social or cultural arrangements may indeed be waning in the face of capitalist modernity, others may transform or even transmogrify into different forms capable of surviving, displacing, or co-opting capitalist development.

As noted earlier, the Jamaat's penetration into state processes intensified during the 1980s when the military dictator General Mohammed Zia ul Haq initiated an aggressive state program of Islamization and introduced legal and political changes that a range of Pakistani scholars consider to be detrimental to women's status, human rights, and fundamental rights of citizens (Mumtaz and Shaheed 1991; Jahangir and Jilani 1990; Asghar Khan 1985; Khan 2007; Shakir 1997). The configuration of local, regional, and international imperatives shaped during the 1980s to the late 1990s continues to influence gender and development issues even when military regimes have been replaced by popularly elected leaders or conservative governments by more liberal ones. From the perspective of women's rights and human rights, the transnational framework developed in opposition to Zia and continued through the adoption of UN discourses on women's rights as human rights enabled Pakistani women, who were involved in it, to build alliances with women's groups in other societies, organize with Muslim women transnationally, and build a strong regional South Asian presence that could culturally challenge Arabized Islamization. It also enlarged the scope of women's struggles and impelled the bourgeois women's groups to engage, to some degree, with the larger struggles of workers and peasants, religious minorities, and oppressed nationalities. However, it remains true that the global and transnational framing of women's issues allows Pakistani feminist struggles to be appropriated in the interest of dominant geopolitical agendas, neoliberal restructuring of national economies, hegemonic culturalism, and even militarism.[4] Furthermore, the implicated relationship of national and international and its shifts and turns in the past three decades worked to transform economic, political, and social structures as well as individual and collective subjectivities. Increasing rural to urban migration, appropriation of higher education by men and women of the middle classes, the entry of middle-class groups into local and national politics, the access of these groups to modern technology, new avenues for business and overseas employment, as well as the interpellation of middle-class women and men by national/global discourses of community development and NGO-ization, have radically shifted the terrain of developmental and civil society politics in Pakistan. The result is that the representative national position, which was identified with elite groups and hence with secularism, developmental economics, and liberal politics, has been infiltrated by other groups that were previously excluded in decision making on matters of national progress (Asghar Khan 1985; Iqtidar 2011; Said Khan 1994; Weiss 1986; Weiss and Gilani 2001). An adequate conceptualization of the large-scale and complex mobilization of Jamaat women at various social sites and the significance of this mobilization for feminism in Pakistan enjoins us to interrogate and resituate the Muslim woman question in ways that dislodge the intractable framing of Islam-versus-modernity or mullahs against Pakistani women.

Because of their highly visible and publicly orchestrated opposition to Women's Rights as Human Rights and their "anti-West" stance, women leaders of the Jamaat-e-Islami are noticeably vocal in all matters related to women, gender, and development. Jamaat-e-Islami women oppose the gender and development agenda of the modernizing elites and NGOs for three main reasons: they see them as part of the ongoing practices of colonial domination of Muslim societies implemented through Westernization, secularization, and marginalization of Islam in social life; they oppose the notion of women's equality and autonomy as being disruptive of the

---

4. For a good discussion of the problems of transnational frameworks such as Women's Rights as Human Rights, see Razack 2005; Said Khan 2002; Spivak 2005; and Grewal 1999.

"Muslim family" and therefore of the Islamic social order; and they argue that the gynocentrism of the development agenda not only threatens the Muslim family but also draws attention away from the social inequalities based on class and feudal structures in Pakistani society.

In this chapter I offer an account of the complex relationship of Jamaat women to the projects of gender and development in Pakistan. I draw attention to their negotiations with the development projects of the mainstream feminist movements and their commitment to the implementation of what they consider to be correct Islamic principles. In this process Jamaat women engage in an alternative reconceptualizing of Muslim women's needs and interests that draws them into the discourses of citizenship, nation building, migration, Muslim capitalism, NGO-ization, and transnational feminism. This process also entails the expansion of women's role within the party in ways that intensify Jamaat women's investment in the project of gender and development that they wish to disavow. Thus in their attempts to challenge the liberal notions of civil society and its attendant ideas of individual autonomy and freedom instead of human subservience to divine law, Jamaat women are drawn deeper into the hegemonic project of civil society.

Before continuing to discuss Jamaat women's position vis-à-vis development and the feminist project, it is necessary to sketch out the development of feminist nongovernmental organizations, or the "NGO sector," and its entangled history with what is deemed to constitute civil society in present-day Pakistan.

The Shifting Space of Women and Development in Pakistan

A prominent Pakistani feminist has observed that there is now a new forum for debate between two polarized groups in society that she terms the "Western progressives" and the "religious elite" (Said Khan 1994, 87). Said Khan's argument is situated within her discussion of the social and political effects of the state-imposed project of Islamization from 1977 to 1988, undertaken by the military dictator General Mohammed Zia ul Haq.

Said Khan points to the attempts of Islamist parties to incorporate notions of modernity and Western capitalism into an Islamic framework.

According to Said Khan, the social and political project of Islamization enabled politico-religious parties to enter political life from which they had hitherto been denied through democratic and popular processes. She declares, "I would argue that the debate or the conflict between these two groups is a debate within the elite, and further that the religious fundamentalists are more of an imposition on the people, and more elitist than Westernized progressives" (Said Khan 1994, 87).

Elaborating on and intensifying the new discursive space recognized by Said Khan, I would add to her analysis the global discourses of gender and development, which have multiplied the opportunities for interaction between the two groups of women who are deemed to be secular feminists on the one side and their religious opponents on the other (Mumtaz 1994; Mumtaz and Shaheed 1987). This space remains undertheorized in the recent accounts by Pakistani scholars of the NGO-ization of the women's movement and analyses of the relationship between civil society and the state (Bari and Gul Khattak 2001; Weiss and Gilani 2001; Said Khan 2005).

From a few hundred nonprofit organizations in the 1970s, the number of NGOs in Pakistan was estimated to have increased to forty-five thousand in 2009 (ADB 2009; Hasan and Junejo 1999). This sector, which ranges from small neighborhood groups to massive institutions, engages over six million members and employs a quarter million people in an array of projects including education, sports, emergency services, civic amenities, vocation and training, advocacy and organizing (ADB 2009; Hasan and Junejo 1999). According to a survey, nearly half (46 percent) of Pakistan's nonprofit organizations cite education as their main activity, followed by advocacy (18 percent), social services (8 percent), religious activity (5 percent), and health (6 percent).

It is pertinent to point out that the dramatic NGO-ization of social service delivery and political development that marks the present moment was a reversal of a trend that was ascendant in Pakistan in the 1970s. At that time the government of Zulfiqar Ali Bhutto (1971–77), under his declared policy of Islamic socialism, implemented a large-scale nationalization of industries and the strengthening of trade unions (Hasan and Junejo 1999). This period of increased political awareness fostered unionized politics and advocacy groups including those focusing on women's issues (Ghaus-Pasha and Asif Iqbal 2003; Hasan and Junejo 1999).

The shift in Pakistan's national development policy during the 1980s, away from state-led to privatized or community-based development, is related to a number of changes at the local, national, and global levels, notably the post-Soviet Union global predominance of neoliberal economic theories and strategies for social development. There was a change in development discourse away from the welfare state concept and toward a search for alternative, cost-effective solutions to social and economic problems. This global neoliberal agenda was experienced in Pakistan in the form of pressure from international aid agencies and donors to privatize service delivery and farm out larger development projects to the citizen sector (Ghaus-Pasha and Asif Iqbal 2003; Hasan and Junejo 1999, 26). In a report prepared for the Karachi-based NGO Resource Center (NGORC) Hasan and Junejo (1999) underline the aggressive adoption of the global economic politics of neoliberalism by successive governments in Pakistan during the 1980s.[5] In the report, titled "The State of the Citizen Sector," they note that in addition to the retrenchment of the public sector, the concept of "institutional development" became the dominant discourse according to which development began to be defined not as the work of government and its institutions but as the "participation of people at all levels of society in a coordinated and institutionalized form" (Hasan and Junejo 1999, 26). They emphasize that the increase in NGO activity has significantly shaped the reconceptualization of the development project in Pakistan.

The neoliberal interpellation of citizens to become self-reliant instead of state-directed held an undeniable appeal for a Pakistani society perennially plagued by failures of successive governments to provide basic social

5. NGORC was set up by the Aga Khan Foundation in 1990 with the aim of enhancing the effectiveness of NGOs in Pakistan and centralizing gender-sensitive participatory approaches to social and economic development in the country. For more information see the Center's website, http://www.ngorc.org.pk/index.htm.

and civic amenities to people. In addition to long periods of military rule by General Zia (1977–88) and General Musharraf (1999–2008), Pakistanis have elected several governments, many of whom were not able to complete their term in office because of political maneuvering by the army, and all have displayed corruption and inefficiency.[6] The turn toward privatization of a variety of government responsibilities appealed to Pakistani citizens who are weary of ineffective and poorly run public institutions and the lack of funding to vitalize these public institutions. There is rampant corruption and exploitation at the highest level of bureaucracy as well as in both civilian and military democracies and dictatorships. Pakistan has experienced explosive population growth and migration to urban centers, which increased the gap between service availability and people's needs (Ghaus-Pasha and Asif Iqbal 2003; Hasan and Junejo 1999). Reflecting a common refrain of neoliberal restructuring in the contemporary era, the NGORC report states: "There simply weren't enough resources to adequately equip and manage public services and utilities" (Hasan and Junejo 1999, 26).

Another transnational discourse that changed the development space in Pakistan in the past three decades was the international interest in and increased support for WID programs by the industrially advanced countries due to the ongoing agenda of the United Nations Decade for Women (1976–85).[7] These UN initiatives augmented the availability of donor funding to WID projects. The government of Zulfiqar Ali Bhutto introduced its WID program in 1973; the new constitution provided equal rights for both sexes and prohibited gender discrimination. In addition, ten seats in the National Assembly and five seats in provincial assemblies

6. In May 2013, for the first time in Pakistan's history, an elected government completed its five-year term and handed over power to another democratically elected government. The defeat of the outgoing party was widely attributed to corruption and inefficiency in its government.

7. The United Nations declared 1976 to 1985 the "UN Decade for Women," during which all signatory states were expected to implement the UN conventions aimed at improving women's political, economic, social, and cultural status throughout the world.

were reserved for women until 1983.[8] Since then successive governments in Pakistan, despite their professed differences in ideological positions with regard to women, have diligently displayed a commitment to the United Nations WID agenda. This has continued even when they were introducing measures seen to be detrimental to women's status. For example, General Zia ul Haq, whose top-down Islamization program substantially diminished women's legal and political status through the Hudood Ordinance, enhanced the existing Women's Division into the Federal Ministry of Women Development, Social Welfare, and Special Education (MOWD) purportedly to improve women's social and economic position. An unanticipated but pro-feminist event at this time was that many existing women's and human rights NGOs became politicized and organized themselves into effective coalitions—for example, the Women's Action Forum and the Pakistan Institute of Labor, Education, and Research—in response to General Zia's oppressive measures for women, workers, and religious minorities. The intense opposition of religious groups and politico-religious parties to the advocacy and political work of these women and labor groups against the Hudood Ordinance and in relation to workers' rights and reproductive health issues has since intensified the secular versus religious tensions in the nonprofit sector (Ghaus-Pasha and Asif Iqbal 2003).

The significance of transnational relations in transactions between the state and NGO sector cannot be overemphasized; as the NGORC points out, the single most important factor for the dramatic increase in the NGO sector and the NGO movement in Pakistan during Zia and afterward is the "influx of international donors and funding" (Hasan and Junejo 1999, 27). The Pakistani state's involvement in the Afghan War was rewarded with a generous volume of humanitarian and military funding to support Afghan refugees inside Pakistan and to boost the country's war efforts in favor of the United States against the Soviet Union. For example, the government created the Trust for Voluntary Organizations in 1988

8. This provision was allowed to lapse until it was revived in 2002 by the government of President Pervez Musharraf.

specifically to disburse a huge endowment by US Agency for International Development (USAID) to the citizen sector in Pakistan. According to the NGORC, over two hundred organizations became involved in service provision to Afghan refugees in Pakistan. At the same time Pakistani nonprofit groups, especially those affiliated with politico-religious parties, also became an important conduit for foreign assistance to the Afghan groups fighting Soviet troops (Hasan and Junejo 1999).

At the local political level, the nonprofit sector suffers from the patronage and denial politics of political leaders, bureaucracy, government, and the military. The NGORC draws attention to local problems of the NGO sector that grew out of the attempts of General Zia to strengthen his rule. In 1985 General Zia declared the end of martial law, announced a return to a parliamentary system of government, and ordered elections on a nonparty basis. The NGORC report notes that measures taken by the government to support this setup, such as allocation of development targets and funds and employment quotas to politicians to develop their constituencies on a nonpolitical basis, were "widely misused" since "a spate of new social welfare organizations seem to have been expressly created to absorb the special funds" (Hasan and Junejo 1999, 23). Thus in the spirit of self-help, rural and poor urban communities were made dependent on political handouts rather than state-initiated social and economic development.

Furthermore, new government regulations requiring representatives of elected provincial and national assemblies to prove themselves to be "social workers" led to an increase in political opportunism (Hasan and Junejo 1999, 23). This enabled the recasting, reinterpretation, and appropriation of the identity and social relations embedded in the category "social worker" by various groups in society. The NGORC also traces the increase in community organizations to the concept of "partyless" elections. Since there was no political party to rally around, representatives began to develop their own vote banks from within their local area or ethnic group. Community-based organizations (CBOs) were set up by individuals to build these banks.

General Zia's partyless elections dispersed many individuals and groups belonging to the elite and upper middle classes who were affiliated with nationalist or leftist parties and whose political ambitions were muzzled by the government policy. According to the NGORC, "Many of the [NGO] organizations that emerged during this time were created by individuals whose political ambitions were thwarted or unrealized" (Hasan and Junejo 1999, 23).

By the early 1990s the assumed superiority of NGOs over state bodies in delivering essential social and economic services was widely acknowledged in society and at the government level. It became customary for governments in Pakistan to include NGOs in policymaking and five-year development plans. The government also set up social welfare councils at the national, provincial, district, and subdivisional levels to provide assistance and grants to the voluntary sector. In 1984 the Companies Act was amended to allow NGOs to register as nonprofits, and many NGOs registered under this act (Hasan and Junejo 1999, 30–32). By the time of the seventh Five-Year Plan, the NGOs were considered key players in social service delivery and were urged to work closely with the government to implement the objectives of the plan. Commenting on this, the NGORC report states: "There has also been a growing trend of involving NGOs in policy discussion to the point where their participation and input have become a regular feature" (Hasan and Junejo 1999, 32).

It is important to emphasize, as do Hasan and Junejo, that despite their reliance on NGOs, Pakistani governments perceive them not as agents for development and change but rather as vehicles for the delivery and implementation of social welfare. There is an ongoing struggle to further co-opt NGOs by the government and counter efforts by NGOs to expand their focus from development to advocacy, lobbying, and policy research. Governments may sometimes join anti-NGO forces in condemning their role in society and casting aspersions on them as agents of the West. In one instance, the Punjab government, in its attempt to curb NGO activity in community mobilizing against the political system, attacked NGOs by categorizing them variously as "anti-government, anti-Islam and anti-state" (Hasan and Junejo 1999, 34).

From the point of view of the project of civil society and its gendered dimensions, it is generally acknowledged that a key moment was the emergence of a robust women's movement in the 1980s that was vocal in challenging the controversial and oppressive Hudood Ordinance. One could argue that the open challenging of Hudood Ordinance by women's groups opened a new space for nonparty-based politics in Pakistan. The banning of mainstream political parties and politicians created a different forum for organizing by women than the usual service and welfare mode. The spectacular emergence of a women's front directly challenging the government in the absence of political activity by mainstream political parties came to be viewed as a legitimate mode of organizing by other groups, who were concerned about particular needs at the local level but were left without leadership from traditional sources such as political parties and trade unions. Indeed, as I have argued earlier in this book, the expansion of gendered politics and the awareness of "women's issues" have profoundly increased the significance of women as political actors in many sites including the spaces of the Jamaat-e-Islami.

The Jamaat Women's Wing has undoubtedly participated in the conditions of Pakistani society and been shaped by the prevailing discourses. In the past three decades, the Jamaat's Women's Wing and its female student's party have been complemented and strengthened by a series of affiliated women's groups catering to women of the lower middle classes. These organizations are run by professional, university-educated, middle-class women, mostly in their thirties and forties, who have benefited from the national and international emphasis on women-centered development, the transnational Islamic movements, and international neoliberalism. Similar to the traditional NGOs, many of these women's groups have evolved from the institutionalization of activities that were previously informal and voluntary and philanthropic. Unlike the charitable and welfare groups from which these new organizations have emerged, the latter position themselves as working for the public interest and benefit, in addition to being voluntary, independent, and nonprofit. There is little question that the emergence of these religiously identified groups and their appeal among middle-class urban women is related to the mainstreaming of gender by successive governments and increasing induction of women's movement activists into state-established policymaking groups (Said

Khan 2002).[9] At least one of my interlocutors mentioned her involvement in official WID projects, and some of the other women became involved in implementing this agenda following their election to municipal and local bodies.

Samina, a member of the Jamaat Women's Wing, was previously involved in mainstream women's movements and had founded an NGO in the 1990s. She said she had been active in the WID network and, through it, was in frequent interaction with UN agencies, women's groups, and feminist NGOs such as the Aurat Foundation. She had also participated in the Beijing Follow-up Group, which was established by the Pakistan government of the period, although the Women's Wing did not send any representative to the Beijing Conference in 1995, as the party decided to boycott this meeting. Describing her WID experience with other women's NGOs, Samina said: "I am proud that at that time over there we were able to cooperate on the basis of 'Jiyo aur jine do' [live and let live]." However, the ideological differences between the feminist-oriented NGO network and the Jamaat soon became overwhelming and she decided to quit participating:

> I realized that in that platform there were a number of issues that were common to all women that I too believed in; indeed, women were being deprived of certain rights that were granted by Islam. But there were other areas with which I was in strong disagreement, such as the demands for women's unlimited freedom that would lead to the destruction of the family unit, our culture, and our religion.

Despite the expansive political-cultural rift between feminists and Jamaat women, the two groups of women are forced to interact, and even

---

9. Said Khan argues that there has been a complete surrender of the women activists to the state; this became evident when many women's groups joined the illegal military regime of General Pervez Musharraf in celebrating International Women's Day at a conference and demonstration in Islamabad in 2000. This, she declares, is an example of "mainstreaming or 'working from within' carried to its logical and repugnant outcome" (Said Khan 2002, 43).

cooperate, around women's issues at the local level; for example, the shelter set up by the Women's Action Forum (WAF) Panah often seeks the services of the more organized and established shelter, Gosha-e-Afiyat, operated by the Jamaat women. Women from both sides of the feminism-fundamentalism divide are also compelled to dialogue in elected bodies in which they are members, and some of them have participated in UNDP-funded programs for training women parliamentarians. On at least one occasion Jamaat women joined the WAF to highlight issues of violence against women, following the rape of nurses at a hostel in Sindh province. Both groups of women have also influenced each other in the ambiguous and ambivalent manner in which they frame their demands for women's rights.

Gender and Development Discourses of Jamaat Women

Asked to elaborate on the Jamaat Women's Wing's understanding of the status of women in Pakistan, Samina responded:

> Our Pakistani woman is at a crossroads—and she is also doubly oppressed. On the one hand she is deprived of the rights that she has been given by Islam, her Prophet, and by Allah. On the other hand she is also suffering because of her pursuit of the ideals of equality and freedom and all the evils of Western society.

Like other middle-class and elite women activists in Pakistan, Samina and other Jamaat women acknowledge the low social, economic, political, and cultural status of women in Pakistan. Jamaat women also consider women's rights groups to be implicated in many of these problems, which they tend to frame in culturalist terms. According to Ayesha:

> The present situation is such that on the one hand, the rights granted by Islam are out of women's reach, and on the other hand, women's rights activists, supported by the media, are trying to fire women's imaginations. In attempts to overcome their helplessness and to improve the lot of their children, women have needlessly come out of their homes or are trying to muster the courage to come out.

Ayesha shared with me the findings of a survey undertaken by the Women's Commission to support her argument that women's economic independence is not the unmitigated freedom that feminists have represented to Pakistani women. She said the respondents comprised professional and working women in Sindh province and the study was meant to elicit women's experiences in paid work. Ayesha said that the survey indicated that the majority of women were working out of economic necessity and that 80 percent of them would leave their jobs if their husbands were obliged to provide for them. These results, Ayesha said, led her to conclude that women's economic independence was not the solution to their problems:

> The solution to women's problems lies only in following the directives of her Creator. Islam gives a woman the right to fulfill all her needs and desires while staying in her home. Her husband, father, brother, and son are responsible to provide for her. And in case of their absence, the state must be her economic guardian. But if a woman wants to go out and work then it is the responsibility of the state to ensure that she can maintain her dignity.

In contrast to the feminist notion of women's autonomy, Jamaat women uphold the idea of *kafalat*, which may be translated as "security" or "responsibility" in the context of Muslim women's economic, social, and political status. Referring to the Quranic Surah Al Nisa, Ayesha related it to the concept of "collective responsibility" for community construction as defined by the Egyptian Islamist theorist Sayyed Qutb (1906–1966). Islamist movements have, following Qutb, translated this idea of collective responsibility into the concept of the modern Islamic nation-state. The idea of *kafalat* or protection of women is necessary to maintain the gendered separation of responsibility and reduce social interaction between men and women that was emphasized by Maulana Maududi as the cornerstone of an Islamic social system (Maududi 1939). Thus the Jamaat women demand that the political and legal authority of the state should, rather than promote women's economic, political, or social rights, enhance men's ability to offer political, social, and economic support to women of all classes.

Violence against Women

In our discussions, women repeatedly expressed disapproval for multiple forms of violence against women including violence within the home and community. However, they vehemently opposed the feminist struggle for women's rights as human rights and the demands for gender equality through political, legal, and economic measures. In particular, Jamaat women leaders declare that women's struggle should not be a fight for autonomy and freedom, since, they argue, the desire for these has led women in Western societies to become isolated from their families. Indeed, their main critique of the mainstream feminist movement and state-led gender and development projects was related to their misgivings about the global dominance of Eurocentric ideas in the sphere of women and development. These ideas, they argued, have been adopted uncritically by Pakistani feminists and NGOs. Elaborating on this, Ayesha said: "This issue of the oppression of Pakistani women was initiated outside [in the West] and then it was conveyed to us—through NGOs. Now we are told that the Pakistani woman is oppressed, so we want to decide once and for all what are women's problems."

Ayesha said that middle-class and lower-income women were being misled by slogans and campaigns of NGOs and feminist groups, which highlight gender oppression as the main problem of women in Pakistani society. She asked me to consider some slogans and songs used by feminist groups, particularly the Aurat Foundation, to create awareness among women about gender inequality and violence against women within the family and home. She said these were in fact misleading Pakistani women:

> Their songs and plays proclaim that a woman is shackled by her jewelry, her nose ring is a lock, her bangles are likened to handcuffs, and women's freedom is seen to lie only in the idea that she should get a job. If her husband seeks sex with her against her will then it is considered violence against her.

The feminist focus on gendered oppression, according to Ayesha, indicated that feminists and NGOs had uncritically adopted the global discourses and projects of women's development instead of undertaking a serious analysis of the problems of women in Pakistan. Because of this, Ayesha believed, their conceptualization of Muslim women's issues and their understanding of the sources of women's oppression is limited and prevents feminists from making headway in their struggle for women's rights and well-being. Instead, she argued, Muslim women should look within their own religion for concepts of freedom and rights. She expressed concern that Muslims were becoming more alienated from a "true" understanding of Islam because of the greater involvement of Western nations in Muslim societies and communities after the events of 9/11 and the "war on terror." At a meeting with Ayesha and Shahida, another member of the Women's Wing, in Karachi in July 2005, the two women related the Pakistani state's support for the US-led "war on terror" to a wider discourse about development, progress, human rights, and women's rights, saying: "There is a trend among Muslims to look for the true representation of Islam in the light of the United Nations agenda rather than in the light of the Quran." Insisting that these representations were interrelated with feminist struggles in Pakistan, Ayesha continued:

> What is happening is that there is one representation of Islam by the United Nations, the United States, and feminists and their supporters; there is another representation in the Quran. The trend is to see as the enlightened version only the one that is legitimated by the United Nations and United States; so that even the questions of religion are going to be decided by the United States. Who is the United States to decide what is enlightened Islam and what is not?

Critique of WID and GAD

We may understand Jamaat women's perception of gender and development through the ideological framing of global development philosophy by the well-known Islamic economist Professor Khurshid Ahmad, who is also the Jamaat-e-Islami *naib amir* (vice president) and editor of *Tarjuman-ul-Quran*, a monthly organ of Jamaat-e-Islami.[10] Like some crit-

---

10. Dr. Khurshid Ahmad was a senator in the government of Pakistan (March 2006–12). He held the portfolio of the Federal Minister of Planning and Development

ics of modernization and development theory (for example, Escobar 1995; Tucker 1999; Grewal 1988), Ahmad has deemed contemporary global developmental discourses advanced by the World Bank, World Trade Organization, and the United Nations to be permeated with cultural imperialism, paternalism, and Eurocentrism.

For the most part, the thrust of Ahmad's philosophy of Islamic economics and development is a critique of modernizing Muslim leaders who adopted Western-initiated development projects. These leaders, whether capitalist or socialist, according to Ahmad, have failed to provide adequate answers to the problems of non-Western societies in the post–World War II era (Ahmad 2000, 6–8). Evaluating the entire global developmental exercise of the past fifty years as superficial and counterproductive, Ahmad has argued that Western developmental institutions have failed to become an integral part of the societies in which they have been transplanted. In the article "Islamic Approach to Development," Ahmad deplored the possibility that economically rich and politically triumphant countries of the West, as well as the poverty-stricken and newly independent countries of the ex-colonial empires in Asia and Africa, have been misled in their devotion to the guiding principles that dominated international development in the postwar period. Ahmad blamed the North-South disparities and the worsening relations between countries of these regions on the deleterious effects of the global agenda. Referring to figures reported by the United Nations Human Development Fund, Ahmad pointed out that three decades of Western-led development efforts had only led the rich to become richer and the poor to become poorer (Ahmad 2000, 6). Ahmad criticized the postcolonial nation-states' unquestioning adoption of Western-offered solutions such as industrialization, transfer of Western technology and foreign aid, import-substitution, export-promotion strategies, and so on (7). In particular he blamed the conditions of poor countries

---

and became Deputy Chairman of the Planning Commission (1978–79) during the government of General Zia ul Haq. For his contribution to theories of Islamic economics and finance, Professor Ahmad has received many prestigious awards from the Kingdom of Saudi Arabia and has been a visiting professor at the King Abdul Aziz University.

on "the Third World's western-educated elite, who had been brought up in the cradle of colonialism and had inherited power from the departing masters" (8). Terming this an "alliance of convenience between the West and the new power-elite of the Third World," Ahmad emphasized that this agenda was being seriously challenged by indigenous—that is, Islamist—forces (8).

Ahmad's strongest criticism of global development discourse is that it promotes an imitative mentality among Muslims that "aggravates the trends towards moral decay in [the] society but also perpetuates the hegemony of western culture on Muslim lands" (Ahmad 2000, 10). Furthermore, Ahmad points out development discourse alienates the elite from the rest of the population and encourages their cultural and material collusion with and dependence on the West. He draws attention to the effects of Western-dominant development on the consumption habits of the modern sector, which has created economic and social dualism in society and encouraged the imposition on the mass of people of a highly consumption-oriented, privileged society that erodes indigenous values and traditions. "This is alienating the allegedly developing sections of the society from the rest. Symbols of modernization are becoming targets of hatred" (11).

Postcolonial feminists cannot dismiss Ahmad's analysis of colonialism and his insightful critique of political conditions in postcolonial societies, nor can they argue with his contention that the development philosophy that dominates global thinking has "proved to be highly divisive in Muslim society, splitting it up into modern and traditional, liberal and conservative, urban and rural, rich and poor and so on" (Ahmad 2000, 11). Indeed, many Muslims would agree with Ahmad that "Islam wants to transform human society and restructure its socio-economic life according to the values of justice and fair play. It also seeks to weld the moral and material approaches into a unified and integrated approach to life and its problems" (10).

While many postcolonial feminists may concur with Ahmad's analysis that dominant global development projects have led to wasteful patterns of consumption and production, the prioritizing of hedonistic individualism over national economic goals, and instituting the artificial separation of material, cultural, and value systems, it is harder to embrace Ahmad's unitary and culturalist solution for these problems. For Ahmad the problem of global development projects is ultimately linked to a timeless conception of "man" and "Muslim society" and a utopian notion of "the Muslim world" that are all imbued with a unique cultural and social essence different from other societies. Significantly, Ahmad's vision of development emphasizes "the inculcation of correct attitudes and aspirations," in addition to the production of skills and knowledge for participatory activities (Ahmad 2000, 20). For Ahmad these attitudes and aspirations inevitably entail the restructuring of society along the lines of what the party has determined to be Islamic and its narrow interpretations of acceptable and unacceptable activities. Ahmed states:

> This [Islamic development] calls for a high priority to be given to the expansion and Islamisation of education, the overall moral orientation of the people and the evolution of a new structure of relationships based on cooperation, sharing and co-participation. (20)

Further, Ahmad calls for "a truly Islamic framework" of production in which "the production of all those things whose use is forbidden in Islam would not be allowed; the production of those whose use is discouraged would be discouraged, and all that is essential and useful would be given priority and encouragement" (21). Elaborating, Ahmad deems that *halal* (permissible) and *haram* (forbidden) are "clearly spelled out," and in doing so indicates that a particular vision of Islamic Sunni society will prevail in which the Jamaat's ideologues would determine what is permissible and forbidden, although these are contested and variously understood by different Muslim sects and groups. Indeed, many Muslims in Pakistan, including feminists and human rights groups, contest the definitions and interpretations of Islamic and un-Islamic by political and religious forces that selectively privilege some scriptural or oral traditions over others.

Finally, Ahmad's understanding of the world as split between Muslims and non-Muslims reflects a Manichean outlook and speaks to the party's own ideological project rather than a realistic account of the political, social, economic, and cultural heterogeneity that underlies the Muslim *ummah* (community). Ahmad declares that investment and production in Pakistan should be restructured to meet the "priorities of Islam and the needs of the ummah" (Ahmad 2000, 21). Many Pakistanis who have experienced firsthand the unequal conditions of life and employment as immigrant workers in prosperous Muslim societies would be skeptical of Ahmad's appeals for reducing "national dependence on the outside world and greater integration within the Muslim world" (21). Furthermore, the post–Gulf War (1990–91), the divergent politics of Muslim states after 9/11, and the rise of sectarianism within Pakistan have weakened the idea of a seamless "Muslim world" even as these events have heightened many Muslims' realization of their historical and political differences with "the West." The crux of Ahmad's arguments is to uphold the Jamaat's singular understanding of Islam and the party's discriminatory conception of a Muslim community as the only approach that would ensure economic and social justice in Muslim societies.

Resonating with Ahmad's analysis, Jamaat women argue that the notion of a "gender gap" was initiated in the West and appropriated and sustained by the discursive strategies of NGOs and feminist groups that have consequently brought into public discourse questions addressing issues such as women's (lesser) share in inheritance, the lower value of a woman's testimony, women's right to solemnize marriage ceremonies, and demands for 50 percent quota for women in political representation.

Implementing the Din

As illuminated by Ahmad, the objective of development for my interlocutors was not economic development or individual or group rights, but rather to institutionalize the din in every aspect of social and political life, including gender relations. Elaborating on this ideology, Ayesha said the Women's Commission did not ignore the issue of violence against women and it was definitely a part of the Jamaat's charter, which the party was obliged to implement. She added, however, that the Jamaat's solution was not economic independence but rather economic protection or kifalat, a key demand of the Women's Commission and discussed later in this chapter. Jamaat women argue that feminists fail to improve women's status when they focus on women's rights instead of on improving the family and society through Islamic teaching. In this regard Ayesha's comments are illustrative:

> You propose that [women are abused] because of a lack of education, because of lack of access to employment. We argue that these are not the reasons—you have not provided the correct training/guidance. We believe that when one is able to establish a relationship with Allah, then in the darkness of the night the man knows and the woman knows that they have to answer only to Allah for their deeds.

In response to the remark that violence against women is an issue even in countries where there is an Islamic state, such as Saudi Arabia and Iran, Ayesha responded: "A true Islamic state has not been achieved anywhere—in Saudi Arabia it is partial, since there are some Islamic laws but there is also kingdom." She implied that the monarchical setup had resulted in inaccurate application of Islamic laws, for example, the cutting off of a thief's hand for stealing. She said Islam does not allow this unless such an individual has first been provided adequate clothing and food by the state and society.

Hadia, another interlocutor and one of the most respected women leaders in the party and in the Women's Commission, summed up the Jamaat's position on women's rights: "Normally the relationship between men and women is described as a relationship based on oppression or necessity. I disagree that it is either of these. I believe this relationship is a responsibility that we are trying to fulfill in accordance with the framework of Islam."[11]

Hadia said that Islam's teachings were not simply related to the obligations that all human beings, male and female, owe to Allah, but also involve a responsibility to other individuals and human beings. She interpreted this to mean that "every Muslim man and woman has the social and religious responsibility to undertake this task [to improve society in accordance with Islamic prescriptions]."

11. Interview with Hadia, Karachi, May 2004.

It is the Jamaat women's project to implement the din on the individual and social level as well as through the machinery of the state that brings them into direct conflict with the project of civil society being constructed by feminist and human rights advocates. At the crux of this project is the separation of religion from politics in order to open a space in civil society for debate and social transformation. My interlocutors argued that the call to separate (private) faith from (public) politics was the most dangerous and also the least advised course of political action for Muslim women. This was repeatedly emphasized as a problem inherent to dominant notions of development being promoted globally by Western agencies. While this argument is commonly understood as Jamaat women's anti-Western orientation, it is also at the crux of the reformist understanding of Islam promoted by the teachings of Maulana Maududi and a radical departure from conventional notions of Islam as practiced in the Indian subcontinent, which I will discuss in the next chapter. Many of my interlocutors reiterated their understanding of din as a unified and total system rather than individual faith or belief open to diverse interpretation. Furthermore, following Maududi they consider the implementation of din to be an individual as well as collective (state) responsibility. Thus, Jamaat women vociferously oppose any attempt to repeal the Hudood Ordinance and argue that any modification in laws imposed in the name of Islamization should be undertaken only to bring them into greater conformity with the Shariah in order to erase oppressive indigenous customs and traditions.

The Women's Commission: Embodying the Development/Religion Crossroads

Jamaat women consider themselves to be ideally suited, because of their knowledge of the world and of din, to offer a balanced solution to the contentious issue of gender and development in Pakistan. When asked to elaborate, my interlocutors invariably turned to the area of gender relations within the family as evidence of their own successful balancing of private and public, religious adherence and worldly progress, domestic responsibility and national duty. However, their idealized balance has required a greater engagement with and deeper insertion into a discursive space in Pakistani society, opened mainly by the women-centered demands of the mainstream women's groups, where problems and solutions for issues of women and gender are introduced, debated, opposed, and mainstreamed. Despite its disavowal of the significance of gender as an analytical frame for approaching or resolving women's problems in Pakistan, the party's reorientation to women and gender is evinced in the setting up of the Women's Commission.

The establishment of the Women's Commission in 1998, as a nation-wide advocacy and policy group focused solely on women's issues, marks an important moment of the insertion of Jamaat women into the discursive arena of gender and development in Pakistan. Perhaps no greater indication of the growing importance of the new concept of "gender" to the Jamaat-e-Islami is available than the Conference for the Protection of Women's Rights organized by the Women's Commission in October 2005 in Peshawar as a key event of the Jamaat-e-Islami's annual international congress of members, supporters, and affiliates. The Commission conducts social research in some of the areas prioritized as "women's issues" by feminist groups and NGOs—violence, employment, education, reproductive rights, and health. Using mainstream social sciences methodologies including surveys, interviews, and focus groups, it has generated a substantial literature on women's rights and status from an Islamic perspective, mainly designed to counter the contentions of feminist groups.

Jamaat women frequently reiterated that the party's rationale for establishing the Women's Commission was the failure of mainstream feminists and women's groups to understand the problems of poor urban and rural women in Pakistan. My interlocutors argued that leading feminist groups tended to underplay the class, gender, and electoral politics that were implicated in the prevailing constructions of women's oppression in Pakistan. Furthermore Jamaat women, justifiably, situated Pakistani feminist leaders in a different social class and cultural location from themselves and the mass of Pakistani society, and therefore questioned their ability to seriously understand the problems of nonelite women in society. In contrast, assuming a seamless connection between class and religious identity, Jamaat women argue that their own, more correct relationship with Islam automatically connects them with poor urban and rural women and their problems. In fact, despite their commitment to a singular understanding of Islam and their "Urdu-medium," that is, nonelite cultural positioning, my interlocutors' understanding of women's issues and their solutions reflected a range of subjectivities indicative of distinctive blends of socioeconomic levels, ethnolinguistic groups, regional location, professional abilities, family connections, and personal disposition. For example, they evinced differences in their attention to and understanding of the interrelationship of gendered oppression with feudalism, Islamism, and electoral politics in Pakistan. The critique of feudal interests in politics was most vociferous among those who were operating in the middle-class, urban city-burbs of Karachi, which are populated by Urdu-speaking mohajirs or migrants from India who have negligible connections with farming or agricultural income. It was somewhat ambivalent for women located in other parts of the country where feudal and religious power are less clearly delineated. More important, Jamaat women's strategies and solutions for Pakistani women reflected their conceptualizing of different groups of women as differently constituted by class, education, economic needs, social status, and urban or rural location. These differences in focus and interest may be evinced from the discussion of problems and solutions for peasant women in Sindh and for urban middle-class women in Lahore offered by two leaders of the Women Commission in Karachi and Lahore.

Ayesha, Karachi, June 2003

Explaining the "genuine" problems of Pakistani women—in contrast to feminist misperception of these problems—Ayesha recounted for me her experience in Larkana, a small town in Sindh, where she went to meet a group of *hari* (landless peasant) women. She said many of the women had bare feet and arrived on donkey-driven carts. During the discussion, Ayesha asked the hari women how they felt about the fact that they were deprived of their rights. According to her, the women answered: "Get my husband his rights and I will get mine too." After relating this incident, Ayesha asked me:

Now you tell me, her husband is beaten up every day (by a feudal master) and he beats her when he comes home. Meanwhile it is declared [by feminists] that "the hari woman is being beaten," but there is no awareness of the oppression of the man who is being beaten up by the landlord and who has to witness the desecration of his [sic] women. The woman is victimized and this should be protested, but what about the man whose woman was victimized in this way? And what about her brothers?

Ayesha charged NGOs and the feminist movement as being dominated by women from the feudal and wealthy classes who were presenting themselves as champions of women's rights, when, she argued, it was a fact that many of the problems of women in Pakistan were due to the feudal and economic exploitation system. Being somewhat removed from the provinces, Khyber Pakhtoon Khwa and the Punjab, where Jamaat-e-Islami and its allies are implicated in feudal networks, Ayesha declared that in supporting the Pakistan People's Party (PPP) or the Muslim League, feminists help support the feudal system:

The women of this feudal system have come out as the representatives of Pakistani women. But these are the same women whose houses contain jails where the poor peasants are victimized. Then how can we say that men as a class are exploiters? If you want to fight for women, why not stand up against this class?

Elaborating the Jamaat Women Commission's position on women and the economy, Ayesha gave me a transcript of a public talk on "Women and the Economy" by the convener of the Jamaat Women's Commission in Karachi, Atiya Nisar.[12] In this document Nisar argued that the feminist ideas about women's rights do not reflect the "realities on the ground" in Pakistan. Her main focus was the demands of the women's groups for equal political and social rights and gender equality in economic and political participation. Both, she said, were irrelevant to the majority of

---

12. Atiya Nisar, "Women and the Economy," unpublished paper in Urdu given to the author by the Jamaat Women's Commission, Karachi, 2004.

urban and rural poor women. Nisar exclaimed that if women's employment was the route to their economic and social independence, then in our society it would be:

> the *masis* [poorly paid part-time domestic workers] who should be the most contented. The reality is that their men are either unemployed or idle. . . . After toiling the whole day when she reaches home even her meager earnings are confiscated by her husband. And refusal to give them to him may result in violence against her.

In another public talk by Nisar in Karachi in 2004, the Women's Commission identified the feudal and landowning elite classes and their cultural domination as responsible for the social and cultural exploitation of women. Drawing on this document, Ayesha said:

> Our feudal and landowning classes use any excuse to disallow the marriage of their daughters outside the family in order to retain the property within the family. In the province of Sindh this tendency has acquired a grotesque practice of so-called marriage to the Quran, which is a way of making a girl give up her right to marriage and pledging to remain single for the rest of her life. Following the example of these feudals and landlords, ordinary people have also started excluding daughters and sisters from birthright. Brothers tell women that if you want to maintain a relationship with us you must forego the idea of a share in inheritance. For fear of losing their kin women are compelled to declare that they have willingly foregone their rights.[13]

Sadia, Lahore, March 2005

In contrast to Ayesha's concentration on rural and urban poor women in Sind, there was a markedly different group of women who were the focus of the remarks of Sadia, a leader of the Women's Commission in

---

13. Atiya Nisar, "Women's Economic Self-Sufficiency," transcript of a talk by Nisar provided by the Jamaat Women's Commission, Karachi, 2004.

Lahore. Like Ayesha, Sadia reiterated that it was incorrect to relate Muslim women's problems to gender oppression: "I believe 100 percent that the Quran gives us equal status (with men)." She also emphasized that the Women's Commission was created because it was perceived by the party that women were being "made into an issue" both globally and locally. The aim of the Women's Commission was to proceed beyond legal and policy matters and examine where and in what ways women were being oppressed and suggest solutions.

A graduate in psychology and political science, Sadia told me she had studied and read various social and philosophical texts, including Western social and political thought (including discussions about socialism), until she came to understand Islamic thought: "I realized then that the other ideas are not practically applicable." Since gender relations are the key focus of the Women's Commission, Sadia spent some time explaining her vision of gender equality. She dwelt on her own supportive and affirming relationship with her husband, a cardiologist, saying: "I strongly believe that there is a very smooth gender equality within the natural order—I am dominant in some matters and he is dominant in some matters. This means equality, doesn't it?"

This notion of equality, which hinges on a reconceptualization of gender relations within the heterosexual middle-class Muslim family as companionate and egalitarian rather than hierarchical and patriarchal, was a recurrent theme in my more affluent and professionally educated interlocutors' description of their own experiences within their families. It is also indicative of Jamaat women's conviction about a perceived imbalance in the lives of both elite women who are deemed to be victims of runaway modernization and poor working-class women who are too far behind. This was usually followed by elaboration, as from Sadia, that although egalitarian, the family is an institution that needs to be managed "like any other" and in which men have "some priority" in decision making. It was an attempt to embody the Islam/development nexus in the most intimate spaces of their experiences.

Sadia, who like other Jamaat women members has a hectic schedule of public social, cultural, and political activities, in addition to her domestic responsibilities, elaborated on the appropriate role for women in contemporary Pakistani society:

> Take your wristwatch, for example. Its rightful position is on your wrist, but you can place it anywhere on your body and it will still work. You could even put it up on the wall if necessity calls for that. But it is only when it returns to your wrist that we will say it is now in the right place and that is where it looks the best.

Sadia's elaboration of the Women's Commission's stance on women's participation in politics, education, and employment appeared to be in line with the traditional ideology of the party outlined by Maududi: Muslim women have complete freedom of mobility but the best place for them is where they are designed by Allah to perform their optimum role. If women stay within the place designed for them by their creator, that "place is the best."

I asked Sadia whether the Women's Commission was aware of the negative impact of the Hudood Ordinance on the lives of women and girls within the family. In particular, I asked her to comment on the problem of punishing family members in cases of women killed by their husbands, fathers, or brothers because of the prevalence of the law of *Diyat* and *Qisas*. This law enables any of the heirs of a victim to forgive the murderer and is freely used by families and communities to acquit murderers who are in most cases close relatives of women killed for alleged sexual transgressions or to settle disputes.[14] Sadia reiterated the Jamaat's official position that staunchly opposes any attempt to change the laws that were established in the name of Islam. She said the problem was not the laws but rather the training of individuals engaged in their implementation and the creation of the moral environment by the state. Like the main party, the women leaders of the Jamaat evince a vanguardist orientation toward social transformation, according to which only

---

14. For a discussion of the law of Qisas and Diyat and its implication in the murders of women, see Warraich 2005 and Khan 2007.

certain morally adequate individuals or groups are deemed qualified to implement change.

I pressed Sadia to explain her vision of a moral environment and whether it would entail strict gender segregation and imposition of purdah or burqa through the use of legal force. She argued that neither the Quran nor the Jamaat had forced anyone to wear a burqa and emphasized that there would never be a law in Pakistan requiring women to wear a veil.[15] However, she added that the party would continue its efforts to create an environment where women would be encouraged to wear veils. And this would be done through inculcating a moral sensibility in society such that individuals would consider it their collective responsibility to normalize the veil and women would embrace the veil willingly. She explained:

> You have to collectively believe that when a woman wears burqa the society does not become tighter but expands for her. I too wear burqa but I do not want to be the only one—I do not want to be an abnormality. I want a society where a woman in purdah is fully accepted and comfortable—not through force but through choice.

This is interesting since the Jamaat-led coalition Muttaheda Majlis-e-Amal (MMA), during its government in two provinces (2002–8), instituted head and body covering for school girls. Suggesting that the burqa or purdah is a choice also runs contrary to the stated position of the Jamaat-e-Islami as articulated by its founder Maulana Maududi and reiterated by Jamaat representatives in provincial assemblies.[16] The noticeable ambivalence in some of my interlocutors' remarks about the private/public gendered divide constructed and upheld by the party's (male and female) ideologues speaks to the tortuous strategies of contemporary Jamaat women to expand the

15. It may be noted here that the MMA in 2012 called on the Baluchistan provincial assembly to impose burqa for school girls in the province. The measure has not received majority support.

16. See Baluchistan dossier, "Pakistan Military Operation and Human Rights Violations in Balochistan," Baluchistan National Party, 2006, http://www.bsona.org/files/Balochistan_Dossier1.pdf.

boundaries of the space of women's public participation while retaining an inner space of women's activity. Thus Sadia emphasized that the Women's Commission was also concerned with issues outside the family where women were being denied access to their rights. She said women were equally entitled to fundamental rights of citizens in Pakistan: "So we want to struggle, from our own platform, to raise consciousness among women of the rights that they do have as well as those that are denied to them."

Ultimately, Sadia emphasized, the Islamic society desired by the Jamaat would be achieved through education, reiterating the significance given by Maulana Maududi and the party's agenda to disseminate Islamic knowledge and raise awareness in society through not simply elimination of illiteracy but also popularizing of dini [relating to the din] knowledge:

> Individual and state/society must share equal responsibility for social change and personal change. . . . If an individual is good but society is not good, it forces the individual to commit acts that are wrong—and this is what creates conflict. We want to bring about transformation at the level of the individual and at the level of society, and we want the state to create the conditions that enable the individual, as a human being and as a Muslim, to live her life and facilitate the creation of a healthy society for the world to see.

The conditions that Jamaat women consider necessary for a morally healthy society have impelled them to reconceptualize their project in the light of changing social, economic, and cultural conditions of Pakistani society and the shaping of middle-class women's needs/desire by the discourses of capitalism, neoliberalism, and feminism. Even though they emphasize their commitment to Maududi's original prescriptions for women and understand their mission to be the moral transformation of Muslim women according to these precepts, the women leaders of the Jamaat understand the competition posed to their project from a variety of social forces including feminism and heightened consciousness of women' rights among middle-class women, consumerism, social mobility, and increased reach of the mass media. In response they tend to mitigate the hard-line party position against women's insertion into public life by acknowledging a diversity of reasons that could induce different women to participate in social, economic, and, recently, political life. In a significant shift from the party line, Jamaat women also sanctioned paid work for women who may, regardless of economic need, desire to work outside the home for personal fulfillment. Many of the women repeated this new thinking in different ways and on different occasions. Ayesha encapsulated this perspective succinctly:

> We must convince society that, although women's primary responsibility is the household, if a woman for some reason has no domestic responsibilities or has less responsibilities, or if a woman has the capability to take on work in addition to her domestic role, or additionally if a woman has skills and wants to utilize them, then she must have permission to do so. Islam must not be used to place unnecessary restrictions on women.

This stance toward women's employment enables the Women's Commission to appropriate the opportunities and spaces opened by neoliberal development and enfold them into what they consider to be the Islamic ideal.

Islamizing Gender and Development

Jamaat women's engagement with gender and development discourse is too complex to be defined as simply an antidevelopment position. It is, in many ways, an effort to navigate the knotty developmental terrain with the Jamaat's ideological and philosophical compass, the latter exemplified by Ahmad's analysis of international development. In this process, Jamaat women's engagement is as developmentalist, state-oriented, and permeated with class and other social inequalities as the mainstream feminist project. Both projects developed in the context of local and global political, economic, and cultural changes that have shaped Pakistan since the 1970s and 1980s: neoliberal economic and political restructuring, intensified Islamization in law and society, and proliferating global discourses of community-based development, with women as important actors for change. The present cohort of Jamaat women is both shaped by these conditions and one of its agents of change.

Like the secular progressive feminists, Jamaat women have imbibed the main thesis of the global women-and-development agenda that has permeated Pakistani society. This has enabled the emergence of a new space of social and political interaction and contestation between the two groups of women. Jamaat women's position, I have proposed, situates them not outside of or in opposition to women and development. They are deeply implicated in the discursive struggles by which elite and middle-class Pakistani women's groups have been able to bring a gendered argument to issues that were never before discussed as women's issues in Pakistan, such as honor killing, forced marriages, political representation, and employment. At the same time this "women-centered" terrain of civil society activism has enabled Jamaat women to compete with feminism-oriented women's groups on the issues of employment, marriage, divorce, and political representation by claiming to offer a grassroots perspective that distracts attention from the oppressive ideologies of male-led parties with which these groups are affiliated. Thus they can frame their language in terms of NGOs but also suggest that they are in a position to offer a middle ground between the male-centered extremist religious voices that would deny the average woman any access to the benefits of modernity and feminist champions of women's rights, whom they construct as unable or incapable of avoiding the pitfalls of uncontrolled modernization demonstrated in Western societies.

Like the women activists who describe themselves as feminist, Jamaat women voice a commitment to fighting violence against women and ending the exploitation of women in marriage, divorce, and the workplace. But they strongly disapprove of women's struggle for equality with men under the agenda of women's rights as universal human rights since the Jamaat is ideologically committed to men's superior status as providers of sustenance (*kifalat*) for women.[17] Like all women's NGOs in Pakistan, Jamaat

---

17. Jamaat women's ideas about kifalat were spelled out in Nisar, "Women's Economic Self-Sufficiency."

women believe that expanding education opportunities for women and the poor is the only way out of the country's social and economic quandary; however, unlike feminist groups they argue that Western scientific and humanist education by itself is not enough. The moralizing logic of religious education they believe is equally necessary since, they argue, it is also the educated Westernized upper classes who engage in outdated, oppressive, and backward practices that subordinate women.

There is little doubt that Jamaat women's projects are permeated by the women and development discourse and their activism seems more and more shaped by this direction. Indeed the pervasive effects of WID and GAD are noticeable in the ambiguity evident in my interlocutors' responses about the direction toward which they expected or hoped to see Pakistani middle-class women moving. It was clear that, without expressing obvious disagreement, not all women shared the idealized notion of a Muslim woman content to remain permanently confined to the home and family while being provided for by a supportive and moral Muslim man who would represent her in economic and political life. From an absolute insistence on women's employment as permissible only in cases of dire necessity, the Jamaat women's position now accords this permission to middle-class women who want to use their talents and capabilities to work outside the home, with a provision that they must balance work and home. While this was repeated in different ways by many of my interlocutors, it was best elaborated by Farida in June 2003 in her comment on women's economic participation:

> Look, women just have to be mobile, there is no question about it. And for Muslim women it is a responsibility and a mission to improve the world. And so we cannot have an aimless life.

Farida went further to propose that many middle-class women were leading aimless lives that did not benefit themselves or their children. Restating the party's prescription for women to devote themselves to the education and training of children, Farida adapted it to the current social and economic aspirations of upwardly mobile middle-class women, saying: "It is important that women should not simply abandon their children to *ayahs* (nannies). By all means get support but also be personally involved."

Locally and globally circulated notions of gender mediated by class, cultural, and social and economic changes intersect with ideas about "Islamic" to inflect Islamist women's aspirations for the direction of women's progress. Middle-class women of the Jamaat-e-Islami, interpellated simultaneously by global discourses of women and development, nationalist conceptions of modernization, and the culturalist solutions of Islamist ideologues, like middle-class women anywhere, must negotiate their needs, interests, and desires through the assorted hegemonies that configure their lives.

6

To Forbid Evil and Enjoin Virtue

Creating Moral Citizens

Many contemporary Islamic reform and renewal movements derive legitimacy for their community-building projects from the Quranic injunction, *"amr bil maruf wa nahin anil munkir"* (to enjoin good and forbid evil), a verse of the Surah Al Imran.[1] The relationship between the individual and community at the heart of this injunction is also central to many debates about individual versus community, feminism versus Islamism, and religious versus secular state that have emerged in many Muslim-majority societies, including Pakistan. Often deteriorating into vigilantism by Muslims against fellow Muslims and religious minorities, the sentiment of self and collective moral regulation reflects longstanding debates about the interrelationship of the pious subject, religious community, and modern nation-state. Since Sunni Islam does not legitimate the authority of the ulema or religious leaders as obligatory, a central issue in Pakistan is whether the construction of a pious self is incumbent primarily on the individual believer and whether moral regulation is a responsibility of the Muslim political collectivity, presently crystallized in the postcolonial nation-state.[2] Furthermore, unlike Shia Islam, which has a

---

1. The Quran, Sura Al Imran, ch. 3, verse 110.

2. An important difference between the two main Muslim schools is that Shias believe in the Imamate or the rightful leadership by Prophet Mohammed's descendants and the guidance of the clergy. Within Shia Islam there are many differences over the role and nature of clerical authority. Among Sunnis there is no formally defined justification

clearly defined chain of religious authority from the Prophet Muhammad and his descendants, Sunni Islam abounds in debates about the nature of religious authority and its modes of transmission, including, for example, whether religious or moral authority flows through rational legal institutions or affective mystical channels. In the context of South Asia, Maulana Maududi's unique interpretation of the Quranic verses related to the issue of religious authority have led individuals and groups of Muslims to bring together religious subjectivity, local notions of morality, and modern ideas about citizenship for the purpose of disciplining fellow Muslims and fellow citizens in public life (Maududi 1968). For women participants in the Jamaat-e-Islami, the understanding of *amr bil maruf wa nahin anil munkir* as a state responsibility and also as a key process of community construction has been significant. It has allowed them to bridge the gap between piety and politics and fuse their individual/private projects of moral self-formation with the modernizing politics of nation building and political community construction.

Furthermore, because of the lack of success in mustering the popular support needed for significant electoral gains, Jamaat women's projects of righteous self and community construction slide into—indeed, are predicated on—their ability to harness the violent potential of the state embedded in its policies, laws, and discourses. Holding the nation-state responsible for a collective responsibility to implement the din (faith), they demand governmental disciplining of citizens through education policy, media policy, national culture, gender and development, and, if needed, force. Thus, even though involvement in the Jamaat's politico-religious and social-cultural projects has enabled many women from hitherto marginalized middle classes to carve out new kinds of social mandates for themselves, it has also opened up new discursive possibilities for them to erode the social space claimed by others. Jamaat women organize to defend or modify legal and political stipulations for their own salvation and their

---

for the religious authority of the ulema and the Imam, a term signifying religious leader in Shia Islam, is simply someone who gives the call for prayer or is a prayer leader. For a discussion, see Ayoob 2008.

assumed responsibility for the moral regulation of others. Many of these laws impinge on the rights of other citizens, such as religious minorities, non-Sunni Muslims, feminists, poor women and men, and nonhetero-sexuals. This seriously undermines Jamaat women's claims to represent women's interests in Pakistan and enervates their moral authority.

In our discussions, Jamaat women linked their emergent modern identities and modes of existence with the fulfillment of both citizenship rights and other obligations that they believed were enjoined on a (middle-class) Muslim woman by the Quran and the Hadith. As more Jamaat women become active in the public sphere of national politics, their self-positioning brings them into direct and often acrimonious debates with those whom one may describe as liberals, seculars, or progressives in Pakistan. While the Jamaat-e-Islami is committed to establishing what its leaders conceptualize as an Islamic state in Pakistan through electoral politics, Pakistan's liberal/secular forces argue that democracy, based on equal rights for religious minorities, women's rights, and human rights, may be achieved in the society only by a formal if not actual separation of religion and politics that would limit religious authority to the private or personal sphere.[3] These contested ideas about religious agency and Muslim subjectivity emerge as "irreconcilable differences" between feminism and fundamentalism at particular historical moments, overwhelming the public sphere of national assembly debates, street protests, and media programs. Despite these publicly contentious religious-versus-secular positions, both sides support their representational claims by invoking a diversity of discourses that cannot be strictly deemed to be either "Islamic" or "secular." Just as the Jamaat draws support from universalist traditions of citizenship rights, rule of law, and democracy, in addition to Islamic texts and traditions, liberal/secular proponents of universal rights and freedoms also invoke some Islamic traditions and Quranic verses that

---

3. As I have shown elsewhere, this is neither simple nor unproblematic, since the definition of "personal" and "public" is contested. Furthermore, the notion of "private" and "public" are very different in Islam, and therefore for Islamists, than in the Western liberal tradition, which is often invoked by self-defined progressives in Muslim societies. For a discussion, see Cook 2000.

have been historically salient in South Asia, such as: "*La Ikraha Fi Al Din*," meaning: "There shall be no compulsion in religion" (Quran, ch. 2, verse 256.)

To understand the complexities of the clash of gendered secular and religious politics in Pakistan it is important to link these to historical transformations and discursive shifts in how Muslims came to see one another as religious and secular, pious and less so. It has been established that Maududi's modernist appropriations of Islam were deeply influenced by the historical, social, and political conditions of colonial India in the early twentieth century (Reza Nasr 1996, 1994; Robinson 2000; Jalal 2002, 2008). It is also widely accepted that his formulations about the nature of din (faith), his tying of religion to politics, his definition of a *momin* (believer), and the relationship between the individual and religious community ran against the historically existing and widely accepted conceptions of religious agency in South Asia (Reza Nasr 1996, 1994; Robinson 2000). These discriminatory discourses continue to form the underlying assumptions of Jamaat women's projects, especially those related to moral regulation of citizen-subjects in the public sphere, even though these women seem to be modifying Maududi's restrictive ideas about women's economic and political participation. It is therefore worthwhile to situate the historical production of the Jamaat's founding ideology within the discursive traditions of Islam in South Asia, its geopolitical dislocations and its heterogeneous appropriations by Muslim men and women at different times and different contexts.

One may begin by examining how Islamic discourses and traditions, such as *amr bil maruf*, were translocated by Islamist modernists from early exegetical contexts of the Hanbali communities of Iraq and Syria to a present-day Hanafi-majority society in Pakistan.[4] It is important to

---

4. The four schools of Sunni Islamic jurisprudence are Hanafi, Shafai, Hanbali, and Maliki, named after each jurist. The majority of South Asian Muslims who are Sunnis follow the Hanafi school. This is not to demonstrate that Hanafis are more tolerant or egalitarian compared with other schools, since Muslim feminists find many points of contention within Hanafi theology and law, but to argue that Islamism in Pakistan represents a shift in beliefs and practices of Islam developed over centuries in South Asia.

trace the various ways in which traditions of self and collectivity, public and private, have been theorized and invoked by Sunni Muslim movements at other moments in South Asia and elsewhere, and, in doing so, to address the implications of normalizing a transcendent Islamic subjectivity and agency, which these movements seek to accomplish. Such a genealogy may be helpful in explicating how contemporary Jamaat women in Pakistan have been enabled to invoke a historically specific understanding of religious subjectivity and agentive action (*amr bil maruf wa nahin anil munkir*) as a mode of self- and community formation instead of other enactments of Islamic traditions that have tended to prevail in South Asian Islamic texts, practices, and affects.

Islamic South Asia

As I have argued in this book, the overstated nature of Islamism as represented by the Jamaat-e-Islami can be illuminated only in the particular context of the history of Islam in South Asia, which, as Metcalf has emphasized, is theoretically and epistemologically unique, and which cannot be simply deduced from the history of Islam in Arab contexts (Metcalf 2005, 2–3). Indeed, Metcalf has rejected the tendency of historians to study Muslim experiences in South Asia through the idea of syncretism in order to account for the humanistic, pantheistic, and mystical proclivities of Islam in South Asia. As Metcalf points out, among the chief conceptual weaknesses of this analysis is the underlying assumption that certain items, acts, and practices could be defined as exclusively Hindu or Muslim and consequently be considered to be syncretically combined. Another important insight that Metcalf offers, based on a review of recent work on Islam in South Asia, is the vacuity of attempts that tend to privilege either texts or practices in the search for the more indigenous or authentic (6–8). Instead, she considers the privileging of Islam's humanist traditions to be an ethical strategy of Muslim theologians and philosophers that emerged in a context where Muslims as both ruler and ruled interacted with a large population of non-Muslims over long periods of time. One may infer, then, that any attempt to "correct" local practices or knowledge by recourse to a transcendent Islamic tradition or authoritative discourses may be considered to be motivated and thus not pious but rather worldly and secular.

In relating contemporary Jamaat women's project to the hegemonic processes of the postcolonial state as well as the classical and modern history of Islam in South Asia, I heed Metcalf's advice that "if at some point, some Muslims choose to claim an authoritative stance that labels others as deviant, that must be taken as part of the ethnographic data, not as some 'scientific' labeling—whether it be done by the state, other Muslims, or the academy" (Metcalf 2005, 7). In its South Asian subjectivities, the relationship between and among Islamic agents is much more provisional and complex than can be simply accessed through categories of pious and nonpious Muslims or practicing and nonpracticing Muslims. Going further, I argue that processes of moral discrimination and purification were not simply directed internally at the collectivity, as Metcalf suggests, but also became important tendencies of communal discrimination, as Islamism became enmeshed with colonial and local political conditions. Thus particular notions about the religious and secular related to specific sites outside the subcontinent, and transposed there, may work to obfuscate rather than expand and deepen understanding of the desires, dispositions, passions, and bodily enactments as these pertain to the vast majority of Muslims of the world who live in South Asia and who are often subsumed in the discursively constructed Islam of Arab and, more recently, Western contexts.[5]

In this chapter I examine some of the discriminatory and restrictive notions that were constitutive of the discourses of the twentieth-century Islamist project in South Asia and probe the ways in which these suffuse contemporary Jamaat women's claims to represent more authentic and correct Muslim women's subjectivities than either elite or poor Pakistani Muslim women. Since the opposition between religious and secular in Muslim societies also serves to undermine mainstream *feminist* positions as un-Islamic or inauthentic, I emphasize the importance of contextually

---

5. South Asian Muslim families in Toronto, for example, find it easier to impart Islamic knowledge and training to their children through Salafist tracts and ritualized practices than intuitive and nondiscursive modes of "being Muslim."

specific and historically nuanced accounts of both feminism and Islamism as modes of women's self-construction. To this end, I explicate some aspects of the unique development of the Islamist project in South Asia by situating the founding discourses of the Jamaat-e-Islami, and Maulana Maududi's novel interpretation of *amr bil maruf*, within the historically ascendant Islamic traditions in South Asia. I map how Islamist women's selective appropriation of Islamic traditions shapes their imagining of the Muslim community in the localized form of the nation-state, sustains differences between Muslim women's "religious" and "secular" agency, and even enjoins them to act in ways that seem to infringe on the rights and freedoms claimed by other groups in society.

I scrutinize Jamaat women's politico-religious project of self- and community construction by revisiting their remarks in relation to an act to regulate morality and religious practices that was proposed by the Jamaat-led provincial government in Pakistan's Khyber Pakhtunkhwa, KPK Province (formerly North-West Frontier Province, NWFP). This proposed legislation, known as the Hisba Act of 2005 and popularly referred to in Pakistan as the Hasba Act,[6] elicited a raucous public debate, including media programs and street protests by both its supporters and detractors. The Hasba Act is significant for our understanding of the Jamaat-e-Islami's project in Pakistan since it marks the only instance when politico-religious parties were enabled to act as a democratically elected provincial government with the power to legislate and enforce compliance with laws. This augments analyses of their conventional role as a pressure or allied group of the existing leaders or as alleged supporters of militant and extremist agendas. Outside of formal power, the policies and actions of the politico-religious parties are reflective of modes of "governmentality," or the construction of modern citizens through moral regulation and disciplining, which are constituent elements of the practices of power in modern societies conceptualized in the form of a nation-state. Excluded from legal, political, and military authority, Pakistan's politico-religious

6. The act relates to the term *hisba*, or *hasba*, derived from the words *hisb* and *hisab* (accountability).

parties, with the complicity of many forces, have appropriated the moral disciplinary powers that are associated with the modern nation-state in its secular forms, for example, in Western societies. In return they ignore, and at times support, the immoral use of the state's violent and militaristic mechanisms for nationalist and culturalist interests.

Theory/Politics/Islamic Identities

In making this argument my project diverges from, but also complements, other authoritative accounts that locate the practices of modern state power or "governmentality" in secular formations such as the nation-state in its imperialist and postcolonial modes and reference it with the global dominance of Western secularism.[7] Indeed, since the events of September 11, 2001, it has become almost customary for postcolonial and poststructuralist critiques of state power in secular Western or Muslim-majority societies to cite Islamist subjectivities and Muslim women's practices as examples of resistance to the normalizing techniques of secular power (Asad 2003; Mahmood 2005; Deeb 2006; Chatterjee 2004; Razack 2007). More notably, some scholars emphasize that the agentive actions of "pious" citizen-subjects such as modern-day Islamists may not be intelligible through contemporary philosophical and sociological frameworks— for example, Foucaultian accounts of subjectification—that are otherwise useful for studying the formation of modern citizens through practices of the nation-state (Asad 2003; Mahmood 2005). They focus on the need to understand these "pious" Muslims as embodying modes of rejecting or resisting secularism by cultivating different kinds of selves through the discursive resources of Islamic tradition that inhabit a different time-space (for example, eschatological, not teleological) than secular modernity.

7. Many scholars of the state have discussed the role of its regulatory practices, notably those informed by Michel Foucault's insights about governmentality as the processes by which power is exercised in the modern nation-state by disciplining and regulating subjects. However, I believe a discussion of these theories of "the state" will be an unnecessary digression here. Some literature with which I have engaged includes: Gordon 1991; Grewal and Kaplan 1994; Dean 1999; and Chatterjee 2004.

In contrast, the need for scholarly attempts to locate historically and analyze the powerful discourses and practices of Muslims themselves, which normatively construct only particular types of Muslim subjects as "pious," is supported by the work of important scholars of Islam in South Asia (Jalal 2002, 2007; Alam 2004; Esposito 2003; Reza Nasr 1994; Robinson 1999). These scholars explicate the historical ways in which narrowly defined projects of reconceptualized religion have mediated local understandings of piety and faith to build discriminatory concepts of self and community in South Asia that are articulated through class, gender, and religion. In particular, Ayesha Jalal's monumental studies of the relationship of nation, state, and ummah are an ineluctable resource for understanding the paradoxes of Muslim politico-religious subjectivity in the context of modern citizenship. By her careful study of Muslim self-projections of identity and history and her insightful analyses of Muslim nationalist politics, Jalal dissolves the argument that Muslim nationalist discourse, Islamist or otherwise, stands outside constructions of nationalism borrowed from European models of the nation-state. Jalal rejects the conventional arguments about the Muslim self that overemphasize communitarian aspects of Muslim self-construction and history. Jalal's studies of Muslim subjectivity in South Asia are integral to understanding the politico-religious agency of contemporary Islamists in Pakistan, since these groups have now become fully integrated into the nationalist project, which, according to Jalal, deployed both an Islamic conception of the polity and liberal ideas about territoriality to construct citizenship in their demands for a separate nation-state for Muslims of India (Jalal 2001).

The problem of the competing claims of Islamism and secularism in organizing identities and mobilizing politics in diverse contexts cannot be resolved simply by disengaging theoretical inquiry from the demands of political strategic action. It may be productive for Muslim women to demonstrate that some conceptions of women's emancipation are a public fiction of secularism, as are overarching conceptions of "virtuous" women, a class-imbued private fiction derived from certain constructions of "the ummah." As a scholarly project, postcolonial feminists in South Asia may—in addition to destabilizing the powers of secular modernity—construct genealogies that bring to light the conditions of possibility that have enabled particular types of Islamism to move from a marginal position to a normative definition of Islamic subjectivity in contemporary scholarship on Islam.

Furthermore, many Muslims might share the sentiments of a contemporary scholar of South Asian culture, history, and religion, who declares that "one might be a critic simultaneously of such Western liberal notions as the rational public sphere and the counter universals of Islamism" (Mufti 2000, 90–91). Mufti is referring to Asad's well-founded argument that even when liberal spokespersons acknowledge the significant role of religion in modern life, they tend to reinscribe a dichotomy between good (and therefore publicly compatible) and bad (thus incompatible) forms of religiosity (Asad 2003). While agreeing with Asad's critique of liberalism, Mufti suggests that Asad has overlooked the undemocratic/inegalitarian impulses that tend to characterize many Islamist movements (9–12). While it is true, as Asad emphasizes, that the public sphere in Western societies as a universalist concept is dominated by liberal ideologies, such important critiques of secularism and liberal hegemony do not need the fiction of a universally egalitarian impulse underlying Islamist movements everywhere. Not only does this sustain monopolistic claims to religious authenticity, but it may also encourage the untenable idea that so-called secular or nonpious Muslims are somehow uncritical of the West's dominance and imposed projects of modernity. On the other hand, Islamism as constructed by the Jamaat-e-Islami and elaborated by Jamaat women has drawn freely on multiple Western traditions and political conceptions including fascism, liberalism, and Leninism to promote a particular vision of Islam. Our projects for challenging colonialist constructions of Islam may be strengthened, not diminished, by paying more attention to how certain orientations that constituted a minor discourse in the Islamic tradition have come in contemporary global contexts to stand in for Islam itself or as the normative version of Islam. In this process, I argue that discourses of secular modernity were constitutive of, rather than simply points of conflict for, projects of Islamism. The contemporary Islamists such as the Jamaat-e-Islami in Pakistan are arguably not unbrokenly linked to an Islamic past but are, as some scholars insist (Mufti 2000; Esposito and Burgat 2003; Robinson 2000), part of another modern formation, Islamism or political Islam.

Furthermore, to address the scholarly tension between genealogy as an account of the history of discursive power, and tradition as the discursive authority of the past, it is necessary to bring together a critical examination of Islam's disjunctured localities and its globality as a tradition. My objective is to illustrate a particular mode of engaging with tradition that may not be read as simply engagement, invention, acceptance, or resistance, but rather may be termed a kind of "betrayal" of Islam's intellectual and legal resources, and that had lasting effects on contemporary Muslim communities (Lumbard 2004). For example, Qadri (2012) has traced some of the deleterious changes in Muslim legal doctrine to the invalidation of centuries of Islamic legal scholarship by some of the forbears of Islamism; he points to the legitimizing of the use of torture for exhorting confessions, which ran contrary to the majority consensus that alleged sinners/criminals were entitled to remain silent. Furthermore, as some scholars have noted, and many ordinary Muslims know, Islam's intellectual resources exceed the limits of a transmitted or discursive tradition; they also hinge on the idea of a transcendent and immanent source of knowledge that can be obtained "without intermediary of instruction and which is necessary in order to fully understand the knowledge contained in the transmitted sciences . . ." (Lumbard 2004, 66). This understanding was integral to Muslim subjectivities and also to Islamic intellectual and political discourse until the middle of the nineteenth century (Lumbard 2004, 65–66). Many scholars of the Islamic tradition therefore decry the attempts of both modern puritanical and liberal secular reform movements to expel from Islamic heritage the tradition of *ihsan* or "doing the beautiful" (Lumbard 2004, 60–68). The project of Jamaat-e-Islami women, even as it opens new possibilities for Muslim women, becomes an alienating discourse for many female Muslim publics when it inclines to sever itself from what Lumbard has referred to as other types of knowledge that are understood to be part of the Islamic tradition in South Asia, such as intuitive and inner knowledges, but not as its discursively transmitted aspects (Lumbard 2004, 70).

I propose that the liberal/secular versus Islamic conflicts that have become a feature of life in Pakistan tend to reduce the multiply located and heterogeneous historical understandings of piety and freedom, especially among Muslims in South Asia. Thus, the seemingly conflictual forces of Islamism and secularism may inadvertently collaborate to create and sustain a discursive normativity according to which "Islamism" is seen as a correct or totalizing religious identity, and other Muslim subjectivities—those that do not publicly claim the position of "Islamic" or those that differ ideologically from mainstream Sunni Islamism—are seen as deviant or contaminated practices and beliefs. This chapter therefore also signals toward some of the gendered "betrayals" of Islamic tradition in the South Asian context that mar the experiences of both religion and politics in Pakistan.

Differing Notions of Self/Community among South Asian Muslims

It was due to this abundant generosity of Islam that Arabs, despite being at its center, and birthplace, had no special position. The new Muslim races that came from far and distant lands, excelled themselves in every branch of skill and learning so much so that Arabs had to make place for them in their midst, to the extent that if you were to look at the learned works of the times, there would be few indeed on which the non-Arab races have not left their mark.

The point is that, just like the Love of God, the stintless favour of Islam was so universal that neither descent and nationality nor color and family played any role whatsoever.

So too does the overflowing source of Divine Bounty remain on the lookout for those thirsting for Love: it has no business with lineage and nationality, with race or heredity. (Maulana Abul Kalam Azad, 1910)[8]

The marked disdain for cultural arrogance and egotistical piety that are evident in the passage cited above, and in all of the theological, exegetical, journalistic, and literary writings of Maulana Abul Kalam Azad

---

8. As translated in Azad 2006.

(1888–1958), may be situated at the heart of the best tradition of Islam in South Asia.[9] In this tradition the concept of self-righteous discrimination as a public enactment either through voluntary organizations or through state machinery has never elicited much support from ulema, Sufis, poets, and ordinary Muslims. Islam, as it has prevailed in South Asia since at least the thirteenth (Islam's seventh) century, is a complex formation rooted in the study and interpretation of Islam's founding texts, Islamic doctrines of Gnostic mysticism, variants of Sufi thought, and heterogeneous hermeneutical and interpretative traditions. At the lived level this has translated for centuries for Muslims of South Asia into the tension between love/knowledge of God and obedience to God, the relationship of infinite mercy to eschatological judgment.[10] I maintain that it is the systematic undermining of these tendencies that must be exposed to critical scrutiny and genealogically related to the contemporary religious politics that is framed as Islamic secularism versus Islamic fundamentalism in Pakistan. Many of the devout Muslims and ulema who joined the anticolonial struggle in British India in the 1940s and the secular nationalist movement for the creation of Pakistan were motivated by a vision of a Muslim state that would realize their long-held understanding of Islam. The dominant nationalist ideology and politics in the Muslim homeland they were seeking, they imagined, would be rooted in the concept

9. Maulana Abul Kalam Muhiyuddin Ahmed Azad was a scholar and a senior political leader of the anticolonial movement for India's independence from Britain. Azad, who became India's first education minister after independence, was a staunch advocate of Hindu-Muslim unity and state secularism, and opposed the partition of India on a communal basis. One of his most read books, *India Wins Freedom*, first published by Orient Longman, Hyderabad, India, in 1959, was reprinted by the same publisher in 1989, in accordance with Azad's instructions to reveal some parts of the text thirty years after his death. The book challenges dominant accounts of the anticolonial nationalist struggles in India in the early twentieth century. A journalist and also a classical Islamic scholar, Azad wrote and published numerous articles on politics and some highly regarded commentaries on the Quran. Maulana Azad's views on theological matters are reflected in his magnum opus, *Tarjuman al-Quran*, which has been published in four volumes.

10. For a useful account of Islam's history in South Asia that privileges its mystical dimensions, see Schimmel 2003.

of *Allah-Ar-Rahman-ar-Rahim* rather than *Khuda-e-Zul-Jalal*—divine mercy, not divine fury.[11] This egalitarian vision has, of course, failed to realize because of the collaborative and independent actions of secular nationalist elites, religious political elites, and the military establishment. As a result, the average Pakistani citizen, male, female, or transgendered, religious or not, Muslim or otherwise, has experienced a polity in which Islam, as nation or state, has routinely been invoked as divine fury but never in the name of divine mercy. Therefore we continue to witness in Pakistan what appears to be a contradictory situation: The monumental success of religious parties to mobilize masses of people in the name of Islam countered by the monumental defeat of the same parties to win popular support as political representatives of the nation. The obdurate framing of all aspects of social life into secular and religious enables the unitary identification of "Islam" with politico-religious parties and boosts their ability to mobilize Muslims under the banner of "defending Islam." However, these same "masses" refuse to vote for the politico-religious parties since they expect little from them in terms of social or distributive justice or empathy for their human desires and frailties.[12]

Islamism, Community, and Communality

Despite the pervasive assumptions of Islamic-versus-secular/liberal underlying political discourse in contemporary Pakistan, authoritative scholars of Islamic reformism in South Asia evince a markedly different understanding of subject formation and community discrimination than a simple juxtaposition or variance between Islamism and liberalism or secularism. A distinctive characteristic in accounts of Islamic subject

11. I am grateful to my father, Maulana Jamal Mian of Firangi Mahal, a veteran of the anticolonial nationalist struggle, for clarifying to me his vision and this important orientation to Islam, which animated his own involvement in the "Pakistan Movement" as well as that of many other devout Muslims and ulema like him.

12. Despite the post-9/11 global representations of Pakistan as a hotbed of Islamic radicalism, it is pertinent to emphasize that the majority of Muslims in Pakistan have not been proven to be advocates of militancy in religion.

formation in the context of South Asia is the tendency to read Islamic discourses in relation to Western secularism *and* in relation to the multiple modes of interpretation and religious authority construction among Muslims in the region. Such analyses emphasize the innovative character of Islamic revivalism in comparison with religious practices and discursive traditions of Islam in South Asia, explicate its role in the shaping of gendered and classed subjectivities among Indian Muslims, and point to the deployment of moral discrimination and virtuous disciplining as processes of cultural nationalism in the communal politics of colonial India (Alam 2004; Jalal 2002; Smith 1957; Robinson 2000; Reza Nasr 1996, 1994; Metcalf 1999).

Bose and Jalal have discussed some enterprises of the British colonial state in India that encouraged processes of community redefinition and social mobility, in particular constitutional identification of groups as majority and minority on the basis of religious enumeration. While cautioning that Muslim social identities were not only a colonial artifact, they emphasize that there was a significant link between the emergence of these identities and the constitutional politics of British rule in India. Although religiously informed identity was not instrumental in the rise of twentieth-century communalism and separatism, since Muslims continued to be divided by language, region, and class, Muslim social identity informed by religion appears to be a significant factor in the cultural nationalist project of the two-nation theory that constructed the Muslims as a distinct nation in India (Bose and Jalal 1997). Thus Bose and Jalal advance arguments to emphasize that anticolonial Indian nationalism and its bifurcation into Hindu and Muslim communitarian identities in the nineteenth century were multifarious and contested processes involving intense traffic between the religious, the cultural, the political, and the economic. Many of the Muslims of nineteenth-century India, more so than many other contexts in which Muslims had to contend with colonialism and Western modernity, felt a challenge to assert a nationalist identity against the colonial power and also to uphold and police the boundaries of communal difference against other local modes of identity construction. Thus among the significant factors in the fashioning of Muslim political identities in the subcontinent were the responses by Muslims to the nascent discourse on Indian (predominantly Hindu) nationalism in the subcontinent during the nineteenth and twentieth centuries (Alam 2004; Jalal 2002). Jalal has pointed to the differing weight given to the construction of social/communal difference by Muslim reformers as they attempted to reformulate local knowledge of Islam. This process enabled the fashioning of religious, cultural, and linguistic identities that could participate in the emerging discourse on the Indian nation (Jalal 2002).

Recognizing the discursive context of the Islamist tracts of Maulana Maududi, which were formulated at a time of colonial retreat and the rise of Indian national consciousness, is important to accounting for the exclusionary concept of community evident in the ideology of the Jamaat-e-Islami. Reza Nasr, in his authoritative study of the Jamaat-e-Islami, has emphasized that Maududi's discourse of Islam was aimed at the revival of its religious values, but not solely. He argues that Islamic revivalism is not simply a cultural rejection of the West; rather, it is closely tied to questions of communal politics and its impact on identity formation, discourses of power in plural societies, and nationalism. Maududi's discourse, though aimed at the West, was motivated by Muslim-Hindu competition for power in British India. His aim, according to Reza Nasr, was to put forth a view of Islam whose invigorated, pristine, and uncompromising outlook would galvanize Muslims into an ideologically uniform and, hence, politically indivisible community. In time, this view developed a life of its own and evolved into an all-encompassing perspective on society and politics, and has been a notable force in South Asia and Muslim life and thought across the Muslim world (Reza Nasr 1996, 5–6).

These reformulative/reformative processes articulated with other changes—in education, technology, employment, attire, health, and social interactions—that affected Indians with the development of colonial power in the nineteenth and twentieth centuries. The experience of colonization led to self-examination among Muslims of both their cultural-religious identity and their disempowered existence in this world. This is encapsulated, for example, in the poetry of the satirist Akbar Allahabadi (1846–1921), who laments the capitulation of Muslim culture to colonial modernity and the dilemmas of coping with the altered realities of social life that split the Indian Muslim subject between religion and modernity:

Gharaz dugana azab ast jan-e majnun ra/bala-e suhbat-e laila wa furqat-e- laila [Thus is the lover of Laila doubly doomed/To succumb to Laila's wiles or forever live without Laila].

Reza Nasr notes that Maududi's redefinition of Muslim identity was intended both to "remove them from the colonial normative order and distinguish them from the emerging Indian one" (Reza Nasr 1996, 50). His aim was to transform Muslim morality for the purpose of building a communalist identity that would preclude a secular Indian identity. As a result, his formulations produced a "rationalized and systematic view of the faith directed at shaping politics and society" (63). Reza Nasr explicates Maududi's systematization of Islam as an "Islamic view of modernity" rather than a presentation of the fundamentals of the faith. "The religious underpinnings of Maududi's views camouflaged his subliminal modernization of thought and practice, which often worked in ways that were not readily visible" (63).

Constructing Islam and Difference

Jalal has drawn attention to some of the effects of what she has identified as the projects of cultivating a Sunni orthodoxy in the subcontinent dating back to the seventeenth century. She asserts that discriminatory tendencies in Muslim reformism affected ideas about Muslim self and community and that Islamic reformers may have sacrificed the quintessential nature of Islamic thought in their efforts to develop a distinct Muslim identity. According to Jalal, Sunni reformers of the seventeenth and eighteenth centuries, such as Sheikh Ahmad Sirhindi (1564–1624) and Shah Waliullah of Delhi (1703–1762), sought to counter "the world denying tendencies of an Indian Sufism" by reinstating "the world-affirming teachings of the Sharia[h]" (Jalal 2002). In so doing, Jalal contends, Shah Waliullah's major text, *Hujjut al-Balagha* (literally: The conclusive argument from God), appears not only to underscore religion as a demarcator of difference, but also promotes particular ideas about what constitutes religion as faith, thus transforming Indian Muslim approaches to the Shariah. She declares that some of the categorical assertions made in the text "betray Waliullah's own spatio-temporal location in predominantly non-Muslim India rather than anything remotely connected with the spirit of the Quranic message."

Indeed, Jalal argues, in the process of upholding Islam as primarily a social demarcator rather than a faith, Shah Waliullah may have compromised certain Quranic principles. Among these are the emphasis on individual responsibility for good and evil, the rejection of intermediaries between the individual and God, and the idea of collective repentance (Jalal 2002). According to Jalal, Shah Waliullah's directives were motivated by the shock experienced by Muslims due to the establishment of British colonial rule and the loss of Muslim political power in India. In support of her contentions, Jalal recalls a similar critique of Shah Waliullah by the Pakistani Islamist modernist Fazlur Rahman, who had interpreted it as contradicting the democratic impulse of the Quran (Jalal 2002).

Other historians of Islam in South Asia have also observed important ruptures created in Muslim subjectivity as the traditions of mysticism and devotional Islam were undermined by the modernizing forces of colonialism and Islamic modernism (Alam 2004; Reza Nasr 1996; Robinson 2000; Smith 1957; Zaman 2002). For example, Robinson declares:

> The great event of Islamic history over the past two hundred years has been the attack by the movement of revival and reform on all ideas of saintly intercession for humankind with God and the new emphasis on this worldly dimension of the faith. The main movements of Islamic assertion have been, and are impelled by the consciousness to act in this world to achieve salvation. (Robinson 2000, 133)

Robinson and Reza Nasr emphasize that the Islamic reformist project since the nineteenth century was reinforced by new approaches to Islamic mysticism. Some of these, such as the forbidding of any thought of intercession at the shrines of Islamic saints, marked a major departure from the devotional and mystical dimensions of Islam that had prevailed in many regions, including South Asia, since at least the thirteenth century, and that continue to hold the imagination of the vast majority of Muslims in this region. According to Metcalf, a common element of the different Islamist reformers was the cultivation of a "new orientation of the subject."

This encouraged participants to "set themselves apart from the common religious practices' dependence on the mediatory powers of saints and their blessed tombs, in particular from pilgrimage and customary ceremonies of propitiation and intercession" (Metcalf 1999, 220).

The disdain for intercessionary Islamic practices was, of course, part of the development of a new understanding of Islam in South Asia in which, as noted earlier, Islam became seen as an object that might be analyzed, conceptualized, and even presented as a system (Robinson 2000). According to Robinson and Reza Nasr, it is these processes of analysis and reconceptualization that led to a distinctive reordering of Islam in the twentieth century, as by Maulana Abul Ala Maududi through his structuralist construction of din (Reza Nasr 1996). According to Reza Nasr, traditional Islamic scholars have severely criticized Maududi's redefinition of din (faith) and accused him of tampering with the "very foundation of the Islamic faith" (65). Indeed, Reza Nasr and Robinson point out that Maududi's mixing of religion with political action was not widely welcomed among the ulema of his time, but was seen as a drastic departure from the prevailing belief in Islam as a message from God to the human individual (Robinson 2000, 90–91; Reza Nasr 1996, 65).[13] Furthermore, most contemporary reform movements, which fall under the broad label of "Islamist," such as Jamaat-e-Islami, are concerned with the transmission and preservation of textual authorities rather than the cultivation of the intellect, that would enable one to aver the truth through one's own experience and consciousness (Lumbard 2004, 41–43). Lumbard lambasts both modernists and puritanical reformists for denying "the efficacy of our speculative, intuitive and imaginal faculties" (41). This tendency is evident from Islamists' emphasis on correct practice, bodily regulation, and modes of interaction, which have the ultimate aim of promoting narrowly constructed faith or din. Other modes of Islamic practice and interpretation, including those that have been salient in South Asia, balance faith and intellect with the development of speculative and intuitive capabilities (Lumbard 2004, 43). While many of those reformers who

13. See Nadwi 1980.

are considered scriptural literalists were also Sufis, the resolve to curtail the influence of mystical and rational knowledges was particularly strong among later Islamist reformers, such as Muhammed Abduh, the Wahabis, and Maududi (Lumbard 2004, 53–54). In their reformist zeal, these leaders of Muslims in the modern world sought to return to the Quran and Sunnah, and in the process disregarded thirteen centuries of Islamic intellectual history, legal thought, and knowledges (Lumbard 2004; Robinson 2000; Smith 1957; Alam 2004; Qadri 2012). This approach, as Lumbard points out, tends to deprive people of the traditional modes of channeling religious passions toward the divine (Lumbard 2004, 67–68). In South Asia devotion to Sufi shrines and their rituals are important modes of channeling passions of Muslim subjects.

The marginalization of Islamic mystical orientations was intensified by the coming together of Islamic modernism with modern systems of education and colonial methods of community categorization and classification in India. Processes of self-disciplining and communal reform fused with communalist sentiments constructed ontological, and not only religious/cultural, differences with Hindus and other religious groups (Jalal 2002, Alam 2004). For our discussion, it is important that scholarship on South Asian Islamic modernism invariably emphasizes deep changes that were wrought in the very understanding of Islam among those who became the exponents of these movements (Smith 1957; Robinson 2000; Reza Nasr 1996; Metcalf 1999).

It is this multifaceted interaction of colonial modernity and Islamic modernism that became entrenched in the projects of politico-Islamist parties in Pakistan and is reflected through their modes of monitoring and controlling deviationist tendencies within individuals and fellow religionists, especially those of non-Sunni minority Muslim sects.

Reformulations of Gender and Family

The gendered and class-specific dimensions of these processes of reformism, self-questioning, and self-construction are important for our discussion, since they imposed new social and religious standards on middle-class women's identity in Muslim India. An important concern of Muslims in the face of colonial modernity was the cultural and social survival of the middle-class family evinced in growing debates about domestic matters, in particular the role of women in public space (Robinson 2000; Smith 1957; Metcalf 1999). These reformulations of the family included an Islamic discourse that focused on the qualities of the Prophet Muhammad as a perfect human being to be emulated by the middle-class family. The weight of newly refashioned identities for Muslim women and the new responsibilities assigned to them have been amply illustrated by Metcalf (2004) and Minault (1998) in their discussions of the copious literature that had emerged in the colonial period aimed at reformulating Muslim women's subjectivities. Men and women of the Muslim elite and upper classes were interpellated in gendered ways toward salvation, affirmation of individual autonomy, quotidian practices of religious self-building, reflexivity, and self-consciousness.

Scholars of Islamic modernism, such as Metcalf and Robinson, point out that the responses of nineteenth-century Indian Muslim reformers to the challenge of colonial modernity (and one may add, the responses of modern-day Jamaat women) need not necessarily be understood as simply capitulation to colonial/Western modernity but also as religious adaptations within the Islamic tradition. While historians of Islam have noted a discursive shift in Islamic ideology in twentieth-century South Asia, and theorized it as a change in orientation from an otherworldly oriented Islam to this-worldly Islam (for example, Robinson 2000), there is a need for closer study of the gendered and class implications of such changes for gendered Muslim subjectivities in South Asia and their relevance for the contemporary interface of Islamism and feminism.

The impact of these shifting understandings of Islam and family on the constructs of the Muslim individual, in particular the Muslim woman, are yet to be explicated and linked to contemporary subjectivities and political agencies. I contend that in the case of Jamaat-e-Islami women, the relationship between the secular "individual" and religious "subject" may not be forced into a coherent narrative of Islamic or modern but needs to be theorized, in the words of Spivak, as a "constitutive contradiction" (Spivak 1988, 274). In other words, they are not only pious subjects who must exist in conditions of secular modernity; modernity and Islam are both constitutive elements of their selfhood. Like all individuals, within themselves and as who they are, women may occupy multiple subject positions, produced by "scattered hegemonies" (Grewal 1994, 7), which may instantiate contending discourses and contradictory desires.

Amr Bil Maruf: A Religious Duty and a Doctrine

In his groundbreaking work, *Commanding Right and Forbidding Wrong in Islamic Thought* (2000), Michael Cook aptly describes this Quranic injunction as a humanist impulse rather than a discriminatory or disciplinary practice. Using the Hanafi translation of a verse of the Surah Al Imran, *amr bil maruf wa nahi anil munkir* (commanding right and forbidding wrong), Cook discusses its significance both as a religious duty and as a doctrinal issue for Islamic scholars.

What is of interest to this study is that Cook successfully conveys the heterogeneity of Islamic expression and understanding in a variety of historical, temporal, and geographical contexts without prioritizing some over others.[14] Cook amply demonstrates that *amr bil maruf* is not simply a Quranic duty but also a doctrine that involves many varying accounts and is far from uniform. "It varies with time and place, from sect to sect, from school to school, and from scholar to scholar" (Cook 2000, xi).

The most important of the issues that Cook addresses is the attempt to understand whether the injunction to command good and forbid wrong is amenable to interpretation by human reasoning or whether it must be approached as the immutable and self-evident words of God. Some of the issues Cook brings to light are debates among Islamic exegetes and jurists: whether the duty is meant for individuals and what types of subjects are expected to comply; the eligibility of different groups and individuals such as men, those in power, women, and slaves to perform the duty,

---

14. Cook offers a substantial account of the treatment of amr bil maruf by Shia/ Imami scholars, which is relevant for Islam and politics in the contemporary world. However, I do not engage with this discussion, as the present study is focused on the Jamaat-e-Islami, which defines Muslim identity and Islam exclusively in terms of the Sunni tradition.

and whether it is to be undertaken by individuals or groups; the modes in which it may be performed; the role of the state; and the conditions under which the duty may lapse. For example, he notes that many debates were concerned with alcohol, music, and sex, the varying definitions of private and public space in which moral admonishment of fellow Muslims was to be undertaken, and the clarification of wrong and right down the ages. Cook's work explicates the ambiguity that marked the discussions around the relational responsibilities of individuals and the state and the elaborations of public and private realms: "At one edge of this territory, a thin line separates forbidding wrong from culpable subversion. At the outer edge, the frontier between forbidding wrong and the invasion of privacy is no thicker" (Cook 2000, 12).

Hanbali Theology

Cook demonstrates that while both Shia and Sunni sources refer to eschatological traditions related to the duty of forbidding wrong, the only case of its enactment on a day-to-day basis is the milieu in which Hanbalism took shape. According to Cook, this marks not a norm but rather a "conspicuous exception" to the absence of historical accounts of the enactment of this tradition. Much of the Hanbali theology of commanding right is available in the form of concrete and specific responses to questions that were addressed to Ibn Hanbal (d. 241/855). Cook examines a key text of this tradition, the compilation of Ibn Hanbal's responses by Abu Bakr al-Khallal (d. 311/923), who dedicated his life to this project. The text was republished in 1975 in Cairo, amid the revival and renewal processes that are termed Islamism (Cook 2000, 90).

Cook's voluminous study underlines that the tradition of *amr bil maruf* is not a significant aspect of Islamic practice among the major Sunni schools that are followed by the majority of Muslims outside the Arab region. It is a tradition of importance mostly for followers of Ibn Hanbal or Hanbalis. Cook's discussion of early Hanbalism situates the duty of forbidding wrong in the geographical, political, and social contexts of early Hanbalism in the very different environments of Baghdad and Damascus. The situation of the Hanbalites as a political constituency, the nature of the community, the style of the individual preachers in each city and at different periods, as well as the condition of the caliphate at a particular historical moment all contribute to the understanding of the tradition. Cook provides a rich account of the kinds of issues and matters that concerned Muslims and the responses of Ibn Hanbal to these concerns. For instance, one case put to Ibn Hanbal is that of a woman whose husband fails to pray. "She orders him to do so, but without effect. Ibn Hanbal's reply is that she should seek divorce" (Cook 2000, 95).

Of particular interest for my discussion are the insights provided by Cook that help us understand the significance of modern state power to the Islamists' project of building a moral community in contemporary Muslim majority societies such as Pakistan. Not surprisingly, Cook explicates in some detail the interpretation and elaboration of this Hanbali tradition by the thirteenth-century jurist, Ibn Taymiyya, who may be described as the main intellectual and spiritual fount for many present-day Sunni Islamist groups, including the Jamaat-e-Islami in South Asia and the Muslim Brotherhood in Egypt. According to Cook, although Ibn Taymiyya considered the forbidding of wrong to be incumbent on every Muslim, he emphasized that it was a collective obligation whose burden lay most on those who were in authoritative positions, since they were most likely to enjoy the power to implement it (Cook 2000, 155). Ibn Taymiyya recommended that it be performed in the three modes specified in the Prophetic tradition by those who possess the knowledge of right and wrong. These specified modes comprise, in order of priority, physical action, verbal admonishment, and silent condemnation. Thus although Ibn Taymiyya was known to have an ambivalent relationship with the state of his time, he placed the onus of responsibility for performance of the duty on constituted authority (Cook 2000, 157). Thus, Cook argues, Ibn Taymiyya parted from the traditional Hanbali position in his unequivocal legitimizing of political power to achieve moral aims (157).

Furthermore, unlike Ibn Hanbal, Ibn Taymiyya did not follow the quietist variety of moralism and linked moral performance to social action, such as unilateral destruction or removal of an offending object like alcohol or a musical instrument. This set the trend for the later incorporation of his doctrine into Saudi society because of the influence of the eighteenth-century reformer Muhammed ibn Abdul Wahab-al Tamini (1703–1792) and his alliance with the Saudi clan. Though discernable among some Islamic reform movements, particularly the Jamaat-e-Islami, Ibn Taymiyyah's influence became profoundly evident in South Asian Muslim societies after the 1970s because of the expansion of the power and religious ideology of the oil-enriched Saudi kingdom over the Muslim world. Pakistani women have experienced, and feminist scholars have lamented, many significant changes in the relationship between the gendered or non-Muslim individual, the community and the state, as a result of the pervasiveness of Wahabi-influenced morality and religiosity in the society (Saeed and Khan 2000; Shaheed and Mumtaz 1987; Hood-bhoy 2009).

Ibn Taymiyya's interpretation of forbidding wrong, as evident from Cook's study, received further glossing from later scholars linked with Sunni Islamist movements such as Muhammed Abduh of Egypt (d. 1323/1905) and Sayyed Qutb (1906–1966), who demonstrated a concern for solidarity and organization that was not evident in classical sources. These modern Muslim scholars shifted the focus from personal duty to reprove fellow Muslims to a "systematic and organized propagation of Islamic values both within and outside the community" (Cook 2000, 515). For these scholars, until a moral Islamic community was in place, individual believers were not obligated to correct other Muslims; thus forbidding wrong is not applicable in many societies, including Muslim majority states that are not deemed to be "truly Islamic."

Maududi's View

In the case of the Jamaat-e-Islami, Maulana Maududi specifically authorized a connection between individual action and collective performance. In *Tafhim ul Quran*, Maududi seeks to adjudicate a widespread disagreement among Muslim scholars about whether the injunction to command good and forbid evil is meant for each momin (believer) and "whether it is by action, or words or, at the very least, in one's heart" (Maududi 1968, 145–55). Maududi reflects a particular strain of modernist reformers in twentieth-century anticolonial India who challenged the monopoly of the ulema over commanding good and forbidding wrong and, in a bid to mobilize Muslims politically, emphasized that it is incumbent on all Muslims. A traditional source of confusion for Muslim scholars has been an apparently contradictory injunction in the same Sura, which says: "Let there arise from among you one group that is willing to invite all people to what is good and forbidding what is wrong." Maududi argues that this verse (Al Quran, Sura Al Imran, verse 11) should not be understood to mean that the duty of commanding right and forbidding wrong is limited to a select group (for example the ulema) and thus as absolving the individual believer. He insists that the requirement for there to be one group is a minimum one, which does not contradict the injunction as applicable to all (Maududi 1968, 145–55).

Writing against the backdrop of colonial South Asia, where Muslims were a religious and political minority, Maududi also reframed the question of who was to lead the performance of forbidding wrong and building a moral collectivity so that the mantle of authority could be taken up by a select group of believers, that is, the Jamaat-e-Islami. Maududi's argument is particularly noteworthy since, as Cook (2000) suggests, it reflects a modernizing tendency in the discourse, and thus, it may be argued, paved the way for the conceptualizing of the modern Islamic nation-state in Pakistan. Maududi's interpretation is also important because it opens the way for individual action and vigilantism among those who deem themselves to be the moral leaders of the community. Indeed the Jamaat-e-Islami, despite my interlocutors' protestations to the contrary, has been severely criticized for its patronage of religiously motivated attacks by individual or groups of Muslims against what they deem to be un-Islamic or anti-Islamic acts or practices.

An outspoken detractor of the Jamaat's current politics is the Islamic scholar Jawed Ahmed Ghamdi, himself a Salafi, who left the Jamaat-e-Islami in protest over the party's narrow and doctrinal prescriptions of Islam. Ghamdi and his colleagues in the Al Mawrid project seek to promote interpretations that resonate with the humanist and pluralist traditions of Hanafi Islam in an attempt to counter the increasing sectarian violence in Pakistani society that tends to be explicitly or implicitly endorsed by the politico-religious parties. Ghamdi, who was once a follower of Maulana

Maududi, argues that Maududi's interpretation of the duty of imposing Islam on fellow Muslims, in the absence of political power, has deteriorated into vigilantism against fellow Muslims and non-Muslims (Ghamdi 2011). According to Ghamdi, Maududi and other Islamists mistakenly believe that they are enjoined to use all means to fulfill the Quran's apocalyptic verses describing Muslims as the best community and Islam as the best faith, which were destined to hold sway over all of humanity. Indeed Ghamdi has accused Maududi of advocating a dictatorship of the pious. He suggests that Muslims have strayed from the principles of Islam and have therefore lost their position, which could be redeemed not through force but by internal reform and revitalization and influencing others through their practices. They could then hope to achieve political and moral ascendance—which ultimately was to come from Allah rather than by political or military means. Ghamdi emphasizes that individual and groups of Muslims are instructed to promote Islam only through dawah and example. While agreeing that the Muslim collectivity is enshrined in a democratically elected state, Ghamdi differs from the Jamaat by emphasizing consensus on ways to accomplish Islamic behaviors and practices and whether to call for jihad (Ghamdi 2011).

Jamaat leaders deny that the Jamaat endorses violence even as they lament that power in Pakistan is controlled by nonreligious forces (Rahman, Sabibzada, and Ahmed 1999, 49). They publicly reiterate that the responsibility of commanding good and forbidding wrong lies ultimately with a collective authority that embodies Islamic principles, a modern Islamic state, and that individuals may not take it upon themselves to force religious compliance on others (Murad 1999, 51–53).

On the whole the Jamaat-e-Islami's invoking of "forbidding wrong" may be said to be characterized by ambivalence and political expediency, since the leaders of the party have harnessed this argument to different political strategies at different times. They emphasize self and community renewal for the sake of righteous recompense but also for the goal of the restoration of Islamic power and the reestablishment of Islamic systems of justice and government in this world within a particular nation or state (Ahmad 2000). The reform of the individual and society is oriented not simply toward the Day of Judgment but also for restoration of Islamic power and for the success of the Muslim nation-state in worldly politics. In contemporary Pakistani society the Jamaat emphasizes dawah and training over armed revolt but refuses to condemn violent acts of individuals when undertaken in the name of Islam, such as the assassination of leaders who publicly oppose blasphemy and other "Islamic" laws.

For a fuller grasp of the significance of the Jamaat-e-Islami's unique mixture of politics and religion and to discursively situate Jamaat women's subjectivity within the history of Islam in South Asia, I will turn to Cook's discussion of the Hanafi school.[15]

The Hanafi View: Collective, Not Individual

The majority of Muslims in South Asia follow the Hanafi school, which originated in Iraq and has been prominent in the Islamic world since the fifth century of Islam or eleventh century of the Christian calendar. Cook emphasizes the marked absence of a systematic discussion of *amr bil maruf* in Hanafi law books or in their theology, including the thought of Abu Hanifa (d. 150/767). He notes that Abu Hanifa, in response to a question of whether the duty may be invoked in support of rebellion against unjust rule, agrees that it is divinely imposed duty, but he discourages its practice as an individual action. Further, Abu Hanifa proposes emigration from an immoral environment and also legal compensation for the offending person. Thus "if someone breaks a mandolin—presumably in the course of forbidding wrong—then he owes compensation for it" (Cook 2000, 309). Among the Hanafis, Cook notes a quietist and ambivalent view of the duty marked by the inclusion of saints in the category of scholars and theologians. Hanafis did not develop their own theology or legal discussion but instead based their discussion on non-Hanafi sources such as the Shafai Sufi scholar Imam Ghazzali. In doing so they invariably toned down the

---

15. Cook (2000) presents a thorough discussion of "commanding right" and "forbidding wrong" by Shia as well as Sunni scholars. I focus on the Hanafi Sunni tradition, since this has been the majority one in South Asia and since the Jamaat-e-Islami is a Sunni movement.

performance of the duty, dissuaded against the use of violence, and tended
to equate forbidding wrong with the exercise of censorship (hisba) (326).
On the whole, Cook notes that forbidding wrong has normally taken the
form of a verbal admonishment among Hanafi scholars who tend to favor
the verses *La ikraha fi 'l-din*/No compulsion is there in religion (326).

While the Sufis do not reject outright the forbidding of wrong, Cook
points out that the engagement of well-known Sufis such as Ghazzali or
the mystic Muhyi uddin Ibn al Arabi (d. 648/1240) with this tradition is an
exceptional rather than a normal discussion. When Hanafi scholars take
up this injunction it is in the form of a critique of the historical condition
of Muslims in their milieu who need to be reformed through commanding right or who are seen to have deteriorated because of neglect of this
duty. Cook's observations coincide to a great extent with the work of well-
known scholars of Islam in South Asia such as Robinson, Metcalf, and
Reza Nasr, who have studied the historical reform and renewal efforts of
Muslim scholars in South Asia.

One may conclude from Cook's monumental work that in all the
Islamic traditions the concept of *amr bil maruf wa nahin anil munkir*
is used by Muslims specifically for other Muslims who are seen to have
strayed or are considered incompetent in the proper practice of religion.
It is a mode of including and strengthening community, not a way of dif-
ferentiating Muslims or delineating a community identity as taken up by
the Jamaat. Furthermore, it is clear that the duty of *amr bil maruf* belongs,
in the first instance, to the public space of Muslim society that exists in
between the state and its institutions, on one side, and private households
of individual Muslims, on the other. Discussion of privacy displays a
clash of two values; while it is a good thing to stop wrongdoing, it is a bad
thing to violate privacy (Cook 2000). In contrast to the Hanbali focus on
actions to prevent wrongdoing, Hanafi discourses are typically concerned
with abhorrence for spying or raiding of private homes, since, for Hanafi
scholars, admonishment of fellow believers is tantamount to censorship.
Instead the Hanafi tradition tends to rein in reformist zeal by drawing
attention to the Prophetic injunction not to disclose the shameful aspects
of the lives of outwardly respectable Muslims, and to rebuke offenders in

private. This tradition was severely tested when a Jamaat-led provincial government attempted to implement measures for the moral disciplining of citizens.

Jamaat Women and the Hasba Act:
To Enjoin What Is Good and Forbid What Is Evil

Whereas implementation of Islamic way of life revolves around Amr-Bil-Maruf and Nahi-Anil-Munkir and to achieve this objective it is necessary, apart from other steps, to establish an institution of account-ability, which could keep a watch on securing legitimate rights of vari-ous classes of the society, including females, minorities and children and to protect them from emerging evils and injustices in the society. (Excerpt from the Preamble to the Hisba Bill passed on July 14, 2005 by the Provincial Assembly of Khyber Pakhtunkhwa, KPK)[16]

In July 2005, the government in Khyber Pakhtunkhwa province (then North-West Frontier Province NWFP) of Pakistan passed (by a sixty-eight to thirty-four majority) legislation that came to be known as the Hisba Bill. The provincial government at that time was led by the Mut-tahida Majlis Amal (MMA), a coalition of religiously defined parties led by the Jamaat-e-Islami.[17] The bill was seen as part of the coalition's mandate to implement the stipulations of the provincial Shariah Act of 2003 and promote the processes of Islamization. From 2003 to 2005 the act had been the subject of a fervent national debate over the relationship between personal and public, religious duties versus fundamental rights of citizens, obscurantism versus progress, and so on. The Joint Action Committee (JAC), a forum of civil society groups, led the political cam-paign against the Shariah Act, especially its provisions relating to hasba

16. "Text of the Hasba Bill," *Dawn.com*, July 16, 2005, http://archives.dawn.com/2005/07/16/nat18.htm.
17. The MMA, which came into power in Khyber Pakhtunkhwa, was voted out in elections in February 2008.

or moral censorship, stating that these reflected the MMA government's "fascist desires to forcefully impose its own nefarious wishes on people in the name of Islam."[18] Among the most vocal members of the JAC was the Human Rights Commission of Pakistan.

In response to the widespread objections by human rights activists, religious minority groups, and feminists, Pakistani President Pervez Musharraf (who at the time was the author of a project to introduce "enlightened moderation" among Muslims internationally), acted quickly to prevent the bill from being signed by the provincial governor in July 2005. Musharraf made a presidential reference to the Supreme Court of Pakistan seeking advice as to the constitutionality of the bill and whether the governor was obliged to sign it into law. Eventually on August 4, 2005, the Supreme Court ruled several clauses of the Hasba Bill, especially the one relating to the powers of a moral ombudsman, to be contrary to the constitution. The court advised the NWFP governor not to assent to the bill.[19] The Hasba Bill was thus defeated amid protests by politico-religious groups including the Jamaat-e-Islami.

It may be noted that this was not the first time in Pakistan's recent history that the use of the Islamic tradition of *amr bil maruf* to expand state control over the individual and personal morality of citizens was rejected by Pakistan's lawmaking bodies. The wide-ranging Islamization measures proposed by the provincial government in Khyber Pakhtunkhwa built on at least two failed attempts at the federal level in Pakistan since the 1990s to constitutionalize the moral guidance of citizens as an explicit function of the state. The most recent move at the national level, known as the Shariat Bill or the Fifteenth Constitutional Amendment, in 1985 sought to empower the government of Prime Minister Nawaz Sharif to enforce Shariah, by prescribing what it considered to be right and prohibiting what it considered to be wrong for a Muslim society.

18. "Peshawar: Civil Society Groups Reject Proposed Shariah, Hasba Acts," Dawn Bureau Report, Dawn.com, June 1, 2003.

19. Nasir Iqbal, "Hasba Clauses Ruled Contrary to Constitution: NWFP Governor May Not Assent to Law: SC," Dawn.com, August 5, 2005.

Contestations of Secular and Religious

I discussed the events related to the Hasba Act of Khyber Pakhtunkhwa shortly before its defeat, in a meeting with two women leaders of the Jamaat-e-Islami Women's Commission, Ayesha and Shahida, on July 12, 2005, in Karachi. I focused my questions around the longstanding objections about the Hasba Bill of 2003 by the Human Rights Commission of Pakistan (HRCP) as expressed in an op-ed feature by its chairperson, I. A. Rehman, in a Pakistani English-language daily (Rehman 2003). Rehman explained the organization's critique of the bill in terms of three major objections. First, he questioned the real intentions of those proposing the bill, which he believed were not made explicit in its stated objectives. Second, he questioned whether there was any authoritative tradition according to which Islamic injunctions could be enforced by the state. Third, Rehman argued that areas included in the bill's statement of objectives would impinge on the state's jurisdiction. "An unavoidable question," he said, "is whether the proposed legislation is a bid to supplant the Constitution."

Other issues raised by Rehman included the relationship between federal and provincial powers, matters relating to the rights of women and religious and sectarian minorities, questions of the contravening of fundamental rights of citizens, and the Islamic history and rights of the state versus citizen relationships in Islam. The most provocative feature of the Hasba Bill for the HRCP was its appointment of a state official, "the Mohtasib," who would oversee the establishment of morality, and a special force of religious police who would ensure the cultivation of virtue in public, including individual behavior, acts, comportment, and dress.

> Giving the Hisba force or the police the power to prevent what is bad can be extremely dangerous. There are people who believe that women have no right to move about freely and they cannot cut their hair. Vigilantes have tried to cut women's hair in open streets and harassed them for walking bareheaded. Fatwas have been issued to prohibit the Sunnis' attendance at the funerals of Shias or the burial of Ahmadis. Girl students at a university have been ordered to sit in cafeterias at a distance from male students.

Rehman, who is considered a vocal critic of global imperialism, the militarization of the region, local forms and regional forms of sectarianism, and persecution of minorities in Pakistan, ended on an apocalyptic note: "Let nobody forget the lesson of history that many religious communities brought themselves and their religions to grief by committing excesses in the name of belief."

I asked Ayesha and Shahida whether the legislation had, as the HRCP feared, aimed to supplant the constitution. Rehman refers to some twenty-seven items listed under the Mohtasib's special powers. These include enforcing Islamic moral values at public places; discouraging extravagance, beggary, employment of small children, and un-Islamic social norms; prevention of indecent behavior at public places; prevention of un-Islamic practices that affect women's rights, such as honor killing, "swara" custom, or denial of inheritance; prevention of bribery in government offices; holding to account people who disobey their parents; securing compromise in cases of murder or situations of conflict between parties and tribes. Ayesha and Shahida contextualized their support for Hasba within the requirements of not only an Islamic society or an Islamic polity but also as an effective means to address some of the issues faced by the modern postcolonial nation-state in Pakistan. Their account resonated with a more general need to develop a modern public sphere where order would be maintained by the fulfilling of different responsibilities of the state, citizen, and legal system.

The Jamaat women emphasized that the Mohtasib would ensure the implementation of the laws of the land in situations that required legal redress because of the inadequacies of Pakistan's existing legal system. One example they cited was that of cases where families of a victim or injured person cannot take the matter to court because of lack of funds or fear of reprisal. According to Ayesha and Shahida, while in most instances the heirs of a murdered person approach the police or a court that is investigating the murder, there are a substantial number of "uninvestigated murders" in which the aggrieved, because of intimidation or lack of resources, are unable to demand justice. Ayesha pointed out: "Since there is no existing law under which the authorities could initiative investigation into such cases, this is where the Mohtasib can come into action." Thus they envisioned the Mohtasib's role as one of acting on his own cognizance to remedy an injustice; this is in direct contrast to the fears of human rights groups that a moral police would play an intrusive role in society, which would drastically undermine the rights of citizens. The possibility of a moral police force acting to promote rather than hamper justice is also not supported by the experiences of Pakistani women, religious minorities, and sexual minorities.

Since the main objections of human rights groups to Hasba concerned the relationship between the individual and the collective, and the problems of defining the individual citizen's constitutional rights and freedoms versus the specifically defined "public" space of an Islamic national community, I asked Ayesha and Shahida about the knotty question of defining private space and public space. In her response, Shahida repeated an oft-cited Islamic parable:

> Let me recall for you the incident relating to Hazrath Usman, the third Caliph, who once heard loud music and dancing coming from a house. He climbed the wall, and seeing that there were dancing girls, alcohol, and music, Hazrath Usman arrested the homeowner.[20]
>
> The homeowner challenged Hazrath Usman, saying: "While it is true that I have committed one offence, you have committed three un-Islamic acts—you have spied on me, you trespassed, and invaded my privacy. These are all sins in Islam." The Caliph asked for forgiveness and set him free. So if a person does any sin in their home, then they will not be caught by spying on them. This is a part of our history—and we respect it.[21]

20. Usman was the third of four Caliphs ("Khalifa" in Arabic) who led the Muslim community after the death of the Prophet Muhammad, from 632 to 661 AC. Muslims believe that these four men were true followers of the example of the Prophet Muhammad and refer to them as "the rightly guided Caliphs (Khulafa-e-Rahideen)."

21. Both women are associated with the Women's Commission, a nationwide organization set up by the Jamaat-e-Islami in 1998 to research women's issues and develop policy. The objective was to offset the gains of the Pakistan feminist women by proposing alternative strategies, deemed to be more Islamic, for addressing the social, political, and economic issues of Pakistan women.

I interpreted this as Ayesha and Shahida's way of soothing my feminist anxieties about Islamist ambitions for tighter regulation of the private and public lives of citizens—especially women—that we had witnessed in neighboring Afghanistan. Definitions of public and private, also contested and complex in the Western liberal tradition, become even more convoluted when transported in their entirety from Western legal forms by secular modernizers, or when ahistorically applied by Islamists in matters of religious guidance. Secular-progressive demands in Pakistan, as articulated by postcolonial leftists, anti-establishment feminists, or individual/collective modernists keen to preserve the status quo, range from the individual's right to protection from sexual and bodily violence to more social-status related demands for the "right" to organize balls and fashion shows, or to celebrate Valentine's Day and New Year's Eve.[22] Some groups acting in the name of Islam, including youth groups associated with Jamaat-e-Islami, have sought to disrupt privately organized New Year's Eve celebrations and threatened violence against women's groups for holding a walkathon in Lahore.

It is important to point out that rather than a spatialized or discursive demarcation, the Islamic tradition of "private" and "public" refers to more contingent forms, so that every matter or act may be deemed "private" as far as it is unknown or hidden from the public/community.[23] Conversely, a statement or act of an individual may become public by virtue of its becoming public knowledge even if performed in a privately owned space. This led Rehman to ask: "What is meant by 'enforcement of Islamic values at public places'? What is the definition of a public place? Will it not cover the bazaar, debating halls, theatres, clubs and cinema halls?" (Rehman 2003). Here Rehman drew attention to the larger-scale political-social implications of the bill, which would not simply censor individual

22. Demands for the right to celebrate New Year's or Valentine's Day are frequently expressed through op-ed opinion pieces or letters to the editor of English-language dailies catering to the English-speaking middle class. For a Pakistani feminist analysis of such discussions, see the critique in Zia 2009.

23. For a good discussion of "private" and "public" in Islam as related to hisba, see Cook 2000.

acts in government-owned sites, but would also apply in privately owned clubs, halls, theaters, shops, and even homes. The Hisba Bill, as upheld by the Jamaat, could refer to a conception of public as including all that comes into public knowledge. Jamaat women, who concede that wrongdoing in private should be an issue between the believer and Allah, argue that "private" acts of individuals or groups may become the business of the community. They invoke this notion in demanding restrictions on cable television, advertising billboards, wireless telephones, and gender segregation in markets, malls, and other publicly accessible places that affect the moral sensibilities of "pious" men and women. Indeed a major concern among my interlocutors, which I encountered several times in this study, was the proliferation of wireless telephone companies offering extended hours or free calls at affordable rates, since these could encourage interactions and romantic relations among young men and women.

The complexities of defining the fundamental rights of a private citizen in a modern nation-state became more acute in the issue of applying hisba to a Muslim male who is seen not to respond to the call for prayers, or a woman who dresses in a manner that is deemed to be un-Islamic. I asked my interlocutors to explain the apparent contradiction between their frequent reassurances to me that they were committed to the Quranic injunction that "there is no compulsion in din" and their vocal calls for the enforcement, if need be by force, of ritual prayers on all Muslim men through the institution of the Mohtasib. Shahida explained:

> This should not be seen as coercion—there is no ambiguity among Muslims about the obligation to pray. Therefore the enforcement of prayers in our society, an Islamic society, cannot be considered as oppression. And it applies only to those who identify as Muslims.
>
> JAMAL: Is it not compulsion to enforce prayers on Muslims?
>
> SHAHIDA: Let us be clear, there is no compulsion to join the "din" (faith)—but once you enter the "din," then it becomes an obligation to obey all its rules, just like any organization. You are not compelled to join, but once you do you have to obey its rules. Implementation of the obligation to perform prayers is a responsibility of the state—"amr bil maruf wa nahi anil munkir." Prayer is a duty that must be enjoined on Muslims. It will not be forced on non-Muslims, of course.

In this understanding of the private-public relationship, an individual who is conspicuously not seen to be performing religious obligation while claiming to be a Muslim is engaged in a public act of violation. My interlocutors rejected the suggestion, commonly voiced by some feminist and human rights groups as well as political leaders, that increasing the state's jurisdiction over the daily minutiae of individual lives and the performance of faith among Muslims would lead to the "talibanization" of Pakistani society, since in their view religious observance and morality were not voluntary. I also referred to Rehman's argument that the need for an intermediary to oblige the Muslim believer to obey the Quranic duties "has never been satisfactorily established" in Islamic historical tradition. It is noteworthy that Ayesha framed her response not in the context of Islamic discursive tradition but within the milieu of the modern nation-state. She said:

> Everywhere, in every state, all citizens are subject to a set of laws. Laws begin where the rights of the individual end. And individual freedom ends when it begins to affect the freedom of another individual. We all obey this, especially those of us who live in a state that also names itself an Islamic state.

Islamists subscribe to a set of what they consider divinely obligated responsibilities aimed at the salvation of the individual and the group. Ayesha's statement indicates that they also see themselves as belonging to a public realm that deems them to be individuals who are contractually related to other individuals through the laws enshrined in the modern nation-state. As self-described "religious" subjects, Jamaat women's moral agency emphasizes not individual fulfillment but rather the promotion of morality and virtue through the disciplinary powers of a constituted authority. In contemporary society their ethical moral project can acquire force only if they understand themselves as sovereign citizens and tie their project to the nation-state and its discourses of representative democracy, citizenship, law and order, and civil liberties.

It is evident that even as they disavow liberal conceptions of rights and freedom, Jamaat women become drawn into these discourses in order to fuse religious and secular agency in a productive manner. To my suggestion that their politics envisioned a singular understanding of Muslim identity that would be oppressive to Pakistani citizens, Ayesha and Shahida cited instances of feminist or state action that they regard as a violation of their democratic rights. For example, they pointed to their much-voiced antipathy to the universalist strategies for Muslim women's empowerment promoted by the United Nations through the state and modernizing elites.

> AYESHA: I ask you, how come it never occurs to you that we too are imposed on? Is it not an imposition that 33 percent of all local bodies' representatives must be women? Did it not compel us (Jamaat women) to compete for these seats instead of choosing whether we should be represented by males or females of our party?

Responding in unison, Ayesha and Shahida jointly outlined a series of measures designed to increase women's political and economic representation that were introduced by the Pakistani government in compliance with the United Nations Convention on the Elimination of All Forms of Discrimination against Women (CEDAW). The measures resulted in bringing hundreds of women, including large numbers of Jamaat women, into political bodies in the local and national elections of 2002.

The point they were making was that these measures were encroaching on the preference, indeed conviction, of many women, including even those who had been elected to political positions through involvement in politico-religious parties, to nominate men to represent their interests. Jamaat women oppose setting quotas for women in political bodies and workplaces since, in Maududi's view, Islam commands men to be the providers for women and discourages women from venturing out of the home except in cases of necessity. It is important to note that they were not lamenting the absence of a mechanism for women to opt out of public participation, since many middle-class women in Pakistan tend not to engage in political, cultural, or economic activities that require them to venture outside their family or community. It is clear that these women understood the endorsement of women's legal and political autonomy as an infringement of the abstract concept of a private Muslim woman, and thus their own rights. This concern, which is the mirror opposite of some ethnocentric positions of liberals in many contemporary Western societies, was about the development of a kind of state and society that conflicted with the Jamaat's cherished vision of Islamic community. Thus Ayesha said that by ignoring Jamaat women's opposition to the quotas, the state was ignoring their citizenship rights: "Are we not, too, citizens of Pakistan, who live here and want our voices to be heard?" For her, the reservation of seats for women was an instance of secularizing power determined to impose its own ideas about self-representation and autonomy on women. From a liberal perspective it would appear that, in their understanding of Muslim women's agency, Jamaat women consider the ability to reject rights to be a prerequisite of citizenship rights. Their equality seems to be hinged on eliminating an imbalance that was likely to be created if one group of women was accorded the rights that were unacceptable to others. Even from an Islamic or nonsecular analysis, their demands make sense if it was accepted that the rights of the most morally authentic Muslim women should be salient even if it means denying them to those judged less pious or sinful. This can occur only in the unlikely event that Pakistan's Islamists succeed in erasing hundreds of years of Islamic traditions in South Asia that tend to blur the boundaries of sinful/pious or *kufr/zuhd*.

Engendering Localized Islamism

The religious agency of Jamaat women in Pakistan, for example, their decisions around bodily comportment and veiling, cannot be seen to emanate from a transcendental Islamic tradition in which the geography of the gendered body exists in distinction from individual destiny and collective history. Drawing on the insights of Jalal (2001), we can identify a conflict in Jamaat women's discourses between the Islamic concept of nationality or *asabiyyat* emanating from the sentiment of membership in a universalized religious community of the Muslim ummah and the territorial materiality of the Pakistani nation-state. This territorial and ideational space was created, as Jalal points out, through the flawed project of nationalism defined not by Islamists, but by the liberal/secular Muslim League, which led the struggle for Pakistan. Jalal states that the principal contradiction that badgers Pakistan's quest for an identity is that it can "neither be wholly Islamic nor completely national since the imperatives of citizenship in a territorial nation-state cannot be squared with the supra-territorial notion of a Muslim *ummah*" (Jalal 2001). Continuing with Jalal's arguments about the nation-state in Pakistan, I argue that the politico-religious project of the Jamaat disallows the possibility of accepting some of the contractual principles of modern citizenship related to the nation-state. This is most evident in the Jamaat's inability or unwillingness to accept, even in principle, the equal rights of non-Muslim citizens in Pakistan.[24]

Furthermore, I propose that in situating contemporary Islamists such as the Jamaat-e-Islami women within Islamic traditions we pay attention to the ascendance and decline of discursive regimes that signal the state of relations of power and oppositions to these at a particular moment. It is likely that the historically situated modes of participation, distinctive inflections of meaning, and locally constructed judgments may qualitatively alter both the nature of belonging as well as the nature of the tradition itself. In an indispensable study of the role of traditional ulema—who may not all be collapsed under the category of Islamists—Muhammed Qasim Zaman suggests that we may speak about a variety of Islamic discursive traditions without constructing relativist notions such as multiple Islams. Zaman has productively built on Asad's argument of an Islamic discursive tradition to look at Islam in general but also particular aspects of the Islamic discursive tradition, such as Shariah (Zaman 2002). Zaman's reconceptualization is particularly useful because, in addition to the history of discursive practices, it also enables us to look at the ruptures in that history, "especially the enormous rupture posed by the challenge of Western modernity" (Zaman 2002, 6). As Zaman observes, and as I have argued in this chapter, the encounter with modernity ruptured Islam's history in South Asia in a manner that allowed the modernists to

---

24. This is, of course, not to imply that Pakistan's liberal/secular leaders, parties, or governments have ever taken seriously the fundamental rights of religious minorities or their integration into the nation-state. The marginalized status of these groups is well-known.

look at Islam in a fundamentally different way than the traditional ulema have done. Modernist Muslims, such as Maududi, by severing their ties with classical Islam in South Asia, constructed community in ways that were meant to prepare Muslims for challenging Western colonialism and Hindu nationalism. In so doing they also deprived their followers of the rich and wide-ranging discourses developed in the region by classical and medieval exegesis, debates, and pre-modern theological explanations. As Zaman points out, this is true even in cases where older commentaries and study circles are retained, since orientation of contemporary Islamist women and men is different from that of classical Muslim communities in South Asia:

> For if the goal is, for example, to study the Qur'an not in the light of the agreements and disagreements but as if the book had been revealed to us, as if it had come for our own generation . . . and as if the Prophet had died only recently after bringing this Book to us, then such formal continuities as those constituted by the commentary of the study circle can barely conceal the reality of the fundamental rupture with the past. (Zaman 2002, 10)

While Islamist movements everywhere share some common features, such as the invoking of a common religious tradition, these do not transcend the particulars of historical and geopolitical contexts—that is, the social, cultural, and political milieu, the nation-state, the historical continuities, and the ruptures of that history. Jamaat women are not simply religious subjects seeking to survive in a modern world that has been imposed on them; rather, their religious activism is expressed through the manner in which they embrace both Islam and modernization.

When Jamaat women seek to work through the nation-state, liberal/secular feminists may accuse them of being adjuncts to male political power or of using religion for political purposes. We may as well understand that the modern and the religious are not necessarily mutually exclusive but may be entangled spheres of life for Muslims, including those termed "Islamists," who inhabit the time-space of the nation-state. This does not necessarily contradict propositions (e.g., Asad 2003; Mahmood 2005) that community may be voluntarily created in and through the practices of moral discrimination and virtue acquisition. However, it also underscores the likelihood that such practices may retrospectively promote and make hegemonic a particular conceptualization of community. This process, in turn, may fashion new forms of the individual-community relationship that may appear oppressive (for feminists, other women, non-Muslim citizens, minority sects, gays, the transgendered, and the rural and urban poor) when fused with the inherently violent practices of state formation or the brutality of community construction.

Therefore, Jamaat women's attempts to construct a "healthy" and "moral" society are experienced by many women and men in Pakistan as a hegemonic impulse to impose morality rather than the reciprocal and voluntary process of virtue cultivation that has been noted by scholars such as Mahmood and Deeb for women's politics in some other contexts.

7

Conclusion

*Gendered Selves, Modernist Trajectories,
and Community Building*

Aashiq ham az islam kharab ast o ham az kufr
(The lover cares not for Islam or kufr)
Parwana chirage haram o dayr na danad....
(Like the moth uncaring of the flame in temple or mosque....)
—**Azad,** *Sarmad the Martyr*

In this book I have attempted to bring under intellectual and political scrutiny the possibilities and limitations of the Islamist project for women in contemporary Pakistan. First, I have argued that Jamaat women's productive use of their social class and cultural location enables them to challenge the dominance of liberal/secular social and political groups and to claim the leadership of working-class rural and urban women. Second, I have also argued that Jamaat women's modernist project, while liberatory for some women in specific class, cultural, and spatial locations, is likely to be forbidding for many other gendered citizen-subjects because of the discriminatory tendencies that are integral to the construction of Islamist subjects in Pakistan. Indeed I have argued that the Jamaat's conceptualizing of Islam is an interruption rather than a progression in the customary and traditional modes of understanding Islam in South Asia.

By these two arguments, I have attempted to shift the focus of feminist theory away from the secular-versus-religious or the modernity-versus-tradition framework that continues to underpin what constitutes Islamic-religious or liberal-secular discourse in Pakistan. In addition

I have emphasized the possibilities that might inhere in traditions of Islamic cultural piety developed in the South Asian context. Rather than constructing a feminist argument by undermining local cultural practices as necessarily oppressive in contrast to a transcendent and liberating "Islamic" identity—as Muslim feminists sometimes feel obliged to do—I have argued for bringing together the best traditions of Islam and the best traditions of regional cultures in the interest of an emancipatory political discourse that could form the basis of self and community construction.

Islamism on the Streets and at the Polls

In rendering a feminist reading of women leaders of the Jamaat-e-Islami I have emphasized that we must simultaneously understand Jamaat women's self-definition as religious or pious and grasp the specificity of their claims to act as modern subjects formed through the processes of postcolonial modernity in South Asia. Through their successful reconceptualization of Muslim women's identity, their challenging of developmental secularism, and their appropriation of modern education, employment, and mobility, Jamaat women are seeking to shift the discourse on Islam, gender, and modernity in Pakistan. This brings them closer to dislodging the position that was traditionally occupied by secular progressive forces in Pakistan.

Meanwhile, a number of changes in local, national, and global politics have played a part in unsettling traditional social and political relations in Pakistan. These include Pakistan's wholehearted adoption of neoliberal doctrines for social and human development; the global power of gender and development discourses; the increasing disillusionment of people with the leadership claims of the traditional national elite; dismay over state policies toward the US-led "war on terror" and its expansion into Pakistan; and the virtual normalization of violence in the form of suicide bombings, cross border attacks from US forces in Afghanistan, and the subsuming of notions of citizenship and human rights in the relentless pursuit of "terrorists" and "militants" by national and foreign security agencies inside the country. All these have put a strain on conventional understandings of secular/religious, democratic/authoritarian, war/survival in Pakistan.

Indeed the relationship between Islamism and politics, rather than uniform or settled in Pakistan, continues to shift, change, and reformulate into unpredictable admixtures. A seeming shift in the relationship of Islamism and politics was momentarily experienced in the wake of Pakistan's general elections in February 2008. While elections are by no means an exhaustive indication of public opinion, in the present global conjuncture they are seen as a litmus test of democracy and strongly prescribed for third-world nations by universalist policymakers. As I have noted in this book, general elections in 2002 brought a taste of mainstream power to members of Pakistan's politico-religious parties, including large numbers of women. Their success was attributed to, alongside political maneuvering by the military leadership, increasing religious extremism in the country and the rising resentment over US-Pakistan crackdown on Islamist militants in the northwestern regions of Pakistan. In contrast the national elections held in February 2008 marked the crushing defeat of all political parties associated with Islam. Although the Jamaat-e-Islami boycotted the 2008 elections to protest issues of the eligibility of President Pervez Musharraf and the restoration of the judiciary, its erstwhile partners in the religiously defined coalition of parties, the Muttahida Majlis-e-Amal (MMA), lost almost all their seats to self-styled liberal/secular democratic forces.[1] The results of these elections appeared to testify to a continuing preference on the part of the people (that is, those who voted), to be represented by forces other than those who have traditionally monopolized the right to speak for "Islam." Indeed, many local and international observers read these elections as a vote for democracy, even secularism, since they brought into power parties that were traditionally associated with

1. For an account of the struggle by Pakistani lawyers for the restoration of the chief justice that eventually hastened the political fall of General Musharraf and elections of 2008, see Naqvi 2010. The latest general elections in Pakistan in May 2013 have resulted in the defeat once again of the secular/liberal parties such as the Pakistan People's Party and the Awami National Party. The defeat is attributed to worsening economic and social conditions in Pakistan and has brought to power groups that are more socially conservative but supposedly more financially capable.

liberalism and/or secularism—the Pakistan People's Party, the Awami National Party, and the Muttahida Qaumi Movement.[2]

The use of religious discourses and symbols to win voters is a long-standing feature of politics in Pakistan and is not confined to religious parties alone (Richter 1986; Weiss 1986).[3] Religious identity and symbols are exploited by various groups who draw on the underlying sympathy and public appeal of Islam for the people of Pakistan. Though all groups have used Islam for their political purposes, it is interesting that the mainstream political parties and the military have tended to abandon the authority over Islam and definitions of "Islamic" to the almost sole jurisdiction of the politico-religious groups, in the process marginalizing even the more tolerant and progressive Islamic scholars and ulema.

Many scholars have discussed aspects of the Pakistan military's deep-rooted involvement in politics and its manipulation of religious groups within a complex strategy according to which the military nurtures the religious groups to undermine traditional political parties (Rashid 2012; Zaidi 2005; Siddiqa 2007). Parties such as the Jamaat are also defeated in the electoral process since their role in the so-called military-mullah alliance exposes them to the vulnerabilities of manipulation by powerful interests and affects their credibility as moral actors. The Jamaat-e-Islami is also disadvantaged in electoral politics by its traditional policy of not allying itself with linguistic or ethnic sentiments, unlike traditional political parties and some religious parties. Thus it cannot use some of the tactics common to electoral politics in South Asia such as the creation of "vote banks" (blocs of loyal voters) through the use of force, and favor and loyalties over groups such as tenant farmers, peasants, and ethnic or kinship groups. Since neither political parties nor voters rely primarily on political ideologies or principles for voting decisions, electoral outcomes in Pakistan politics are determined more by the social, economic, and cultural situation of the candidate and voters than by a party's political manifesto.

2. For example, see Robinson 2008.

3. For a recent discussion, see Puri 2010; Haque 1983; and Afzal 1998.

In addition to these conditions, we cannot minimize the role of affective and emotional factors such as outrage, anger, and disgust in shaping popular political actions at particular moments, because of which people's spontaneous protests may not necessarily reflect their long-term political aspirations.[4] It is therefore not difficult to speculate that many Pakistanis, even though they may not support the doctrinaire and legalistic version of Islam promoted by the Jamaat, might respond to the party's call to action when an issue is framed in religious terms. Some spectacular examples of this have been witnessed in the form of protests against US military actions in Afghanistan and Iraq (since 2001), violent demonstrations against the publication of blasphemous cartoons of the Prophet Muhammad in Denmark (2005), and the campaign against attempts to modify the Blasphemy Law in Pakistan (2011). People may support a political action when emotions or beliefs are stirred without extending such support to the political manifesto and the longer-term vision of the Jamaat-e-Islami. On the whole, popular attitude toward the Jamaat-e-Islami is captured in the colloquial epithet "Jamaatia," which is a derisive reference to the limited imagination, narrow-mindedness, and indoctrination that ordinary Muslims have tended to associate with representatives of the Jamaat-e-Islami in Pakistan (Mateen 2010). The continued devotion to the Sufi shrines and the spectacular participation at *urs* (celebration of a Sufi saint) in the face of numerous suicide bombings and sabotage; the spontaneous street displays of dancing and music at Pakistan's victory in the Cricket World Cup semifinals (2011) and recurring festivities at Valentine's Day, New Year's Eve, and Basant (spring); the increasing crowds of women, *niqabi* and non-*niqabi*, at fashion and beauty events, and so on, seem to suggest that many people are not willing to submit to the prescriptions of the Jamaat-e-Islami or other Islamist groups in their daily lives. Regardless of the ability of the politico-religious parties to bring out large-scale protests

4. Although the mixture of emotions and politics is a feature of most societies, for some discussions on the role of emotions in South Asian politics, see "'Outraged Communities': Comparative Perspectives on the Politicization of Emotions." Special issue of the *South Asia Multidisciplinary Academic Journal* [online], no. 2 (2008).

and marches against the "enemies of Islam," local or external, elections continue to suggest that the majority of voters in Pakistan vote on the basis of linguistic or ethnic affiliation and practical interest.

Following the approbatory response of politico-religious groups and the ambivalent reaction of the general public to the brutal assassinations of the Punjab province governor Salman Taseer and the Minister of Minority Affairs Shaheed Bhatti in early 2011, many liberal Pakistanis began to express concerns about a growing climate of intolerance and bigotry in Pakistan. It is difficult to evaluate whether the numbers of people that protested with the politico-religious groups, for example, during the campaign to support the controversial Blasphemy Law, represent a small but visibly active fraction of a larger, more moderate public or whether, as some analysts warn, they signal a more extremist and radical transformation of what was considered to be the moderate but silent majority in Pakistan.

We may contend that the defeat of Islamic parties in provincial and national elections, as in February 2008, marks a frustration of ordinary Pakistanis, if not with the *religious* impulse of Islamist movements then certainly against their *hegemonic* impulse. However, it is also evident that the growing extremism of the past three years, due in large part to frustration with the Pakistani military and, therefore, the government's pro-American policies in Afghanistan, has produced a radicalization of religious politics in general. In response to the reportedly growing influence of the Pakistani Taliban in many areas of the country, politico-religious parties such as the Jamaat seem to be rescinding their moderate positions for fear that the economically pressed, politically disillusioned, and emotionally beaten people of Pakistan would be drawn more than ever toward extremist Muslim groups than toward the politico-religious forces. The Jamaat-e-Islami under its new amir appointed in 2010, Munawwar Hussein, has already adopted more aggressive politics, such as launching a "go-America-go" campaign and vocally protesting the US drone surveillance aircraft attacks in Pakistan as well as opposing the Pakistan army's antiterrorism operations in Federally Administered Tribal Areas (FATA). In this hardening of its political stance, the Jamaat-e-Islami may be responding to the danger of being undermined not only by the "secular" or liberal forces but more so by the extremist Islamic groups that politico-religious parties have, at least discursively, helped produce.

Gendered Islamism and Its Futures

While it is not the objective of this book to project the outcomes of political struggles, whether religious or secular, one can tentatively propose that gendered Islamism, in this case practiced by Jamaat-e-Islami women, has multiple paths open to it given the conjuncture of Pakistani politics in the early twenty-first century. If the women activists of the Jamaat-e-Islami respond to the increasing extremism in Pakistan by enjoining the leadership to liberalize their party's position toward women and religious minority citizens, as evident in the moderate Islamist parties in Turkey and other societies, the movement may widen its appeal among Pakistani women. They will be enabled in such a project both by the increasingly evident disappointments of decades of "progressive politics" and increasingly mired understandings of what constitutes such politics in Pakistan. Add to this the ongoing undermining of Islam and Muslims in Western societies, the emergence of people's revolutions against dictatorial "secular" governments in the Arab world, and the enhanced academic and philosophical understandings of the limitations of postcolonial modernity in both Western and non-Western contexts. All these have the potential to shape Islamist politics in an ecumenical direction. Conversely, if the Jamaat women leaders continue to embrace the currently dominant trend of narrow, bigoted, and exclusionary politics, they will contribute to further divergence and antagonism within women's politics and cultural identities. Like the secular modern, the Islamist modern in its gendered form is a contested space subject to multiply located challenges and negotiations by individuals and communities with the inevitability of modifications and variations.

Religious-Cultural Politics of Community in South Asia

I would like, in conclusion, to dwell on an event in our history that may also serve to boost the argument for a project of social integration beyond

hegemonic projects of Eurocentric universalism and deracinated Islamism. I turn to a moment of "failure" in South Asian political history when
religion as politics became an organizing point and a possible basis for
community, although tentative, fragile, and short lived. Through a situated reading of the religious politics of the Khilafat Movement (1919–24),
we might imagine other postsecular bases for community that contain
the potential to steer us through the thickets of race, class, caste, religion,
and sect while drawing us closer to some of the collectivist impulses of
cultural-pious subjectivity in South Asia.

The Khilafat Movement refers to the mobilizing of Indian Muslims
after World War I, when the Ottoman caliphate was internally and exter-
nally beleaguered. The Turkish caliph became the symbol of an endangered
Islam among Muslims in South Asia, who had witnessed the destruction
of the Mughal Empire by European colonizers. Between 1919 and 1924,
the Jamiat-e-Ulama-e-Hind launched the Khilafat Movement, with the
explicitly religious objective of protesting the dissolution of the Ottoman
Empire and the holy places of Islam by Britain and its allies during World
War I. The Muslim leaders of this movement won the support of Mahatma
Gandhi, who had recently returned to India from South Africa and had
acquired a reputation due to the success of his nonviolent, noncooperation
strategy in several local agitations.

The Khilafat Movement drew support from a broad group of Muslims
including ulema, modern educated Muslims, women, poets, and ordinary
people, as well as Gandhi and his supporters among the Hindu masses
(Minault 1982). The movement has been represented as an anticolonial
struggle by most Muslim historians, in Muslim popular culture in South
Asia, and by some Western writers. However, its admixture of politics and
religion elicited disapproval from secular nationalist leaders, including
the leaders of the Indian National Congress, the Muslim nationalist leader
Mohammed Ali Jinnah, and the great Bengali poet Rabindranath Tagore,
who sought to build Hindu-Muslim cooperation on nonreligious grounds
(Bose and Jalal 1997).

As it emerged, the success of Muslim-Hindu unity achieved by the
Khilafatists did not abide and the movement of 1919 to 1924 was followed by violent clashes between the two communities. This has made the

Khilafat Movement and the Gandhian agitation a controversial moment in South Asian history. However, Bose and Jalal argue that such a rendering of the struggle should not diminish its significance as a moment of harmony between Hindus and Muslims in South Asia: "It may be tempting to see this as the logical conclusion to the dangerous blending of religion and politics by Gandhi and his Khilafat allies. But then religious differences between the communities had generally been less of a barrier to forming a common front against the British than a politics of nationalism devoid of the spirit of accommodation" (Bose and Jalal 1997, 142). Bose and Jalal declare the Khalifat Movement to be a remarkable event in Indian history since "it was a courageous display of unity among Hindus, Muslims and Sikhs" (137).

In an authoritative, rational-secular reading, Hamza Alavi rejects the possibility that the Khilafat Movement of 1919–24 was an anticolonial movement of Muslims of India and argues that the statements of its leaders should not be taken literally. He laments what he considers an uncritical glorifying of the movement by Islamic ideologists, Indian nationalists, and communists, as well as some Western scholars. Alavi therefore seeks to demonstrate what he considers to be paradoxes and contradictions behind the statements of the leaders of the Khilafat Movement (Alavi 1997).

Alavi's main criticism of the movement is that it legitimized the intrusion of religion into politics and brought the Muslim ulema into the center of the modern political arena. Alavi considers this the first moment in Indian history that clergy gained such an important place in political life in South Asia (Alavi 1997, 14). Alavi offers other arguments for devaluing the Khilafat Movement. He emphasizes its neglect of the rising tide of modern Turkish nationalism, which necessitated the destruction of the Khilafat and thus proclaims it reactionary. Another reason for his criticism is his strictly class-based analysis of the movement, which reflects a conceptualization of political interests as being strictly divided along class lines.

Thus for Alavi, the emotive tenor of the speeches of Muslim leaders, such as Maulana Abul Kalam Azad, was extravagant and unfounded rhetoric that swayed his "half-educated and ill-informed audiences," who were unable to grasp and were, in any case, uninterested in the truth of what was said (Alavi 1997, 6–7). Alavi's critique of the Khalifat Movement may be considered a secular-political analysis whose main irritation is that the movement was able to mislead ordinary Muslims toward religious and communalist notions of politics rather than secular modern ones (ibid.).

On the other hand, a groundbreaking study by Gail Minault offers a different reading of the Khilafat Movement that rejects the dichotomy of religion versus secular, elite versus non-elite, and Hindu versus Muslim to offer a nuanced account of individuals, inclinations, motivations, language, texture, and tenor (Minault 1982). Her reading, engaging the actions of individual Muslims and the diverse motivations of Muslim leaders within India, is persuasive in light of postcolonial and poststructuralist attempts to disrupt homogenizing tendencies in European history that reduced Muslims to a monolithic category. Minault's study underscores some of the insights that I have engaged in this book about the complex relationship between affective dimensions of Islam and Muslim identity and the rationalist disciplinary tendencies of contemporary Islamism in Pakistan, between religion as politics and the politics of religion, between community and communality.

One aspect of Minault's study that is of particular interest in this respect is that, contrary to accounts of the Khilafat Movement that emphasize its pan-Islamic dimensions, Minault enables us to understand the important connection between Islamic religious and cultural identity and nationalism in India. Minault rejects historical accounts that emphasize pan-Islamism by focusing on the efforts of a small group of Indian Muslim leaders or assuming a monolithic response among Indian Muslims to the fate of the caliphate. While acknowledging the existence of Islamic brotherly feelings in the movement, she argues that this should not subsume the anxieties evident among Indian Muslims related to their own context, nor ignore the diverse motivations of a variety of individual actors.

For Minault, the Khilafat Movement was primarily a campaign by a particular group of Indian Muslim leaders to unite their community politically by means of religious and cultural symbols meaningful to all strata of that community. As such, it can be viewed as a quest for "pan-Indian Islam" (Minault 1982, 2). Rather than overridingly pan-Islamist in its impetus and, thus, tangential to Indian nationalism, the Khilafat

Movement is seen by Minault to have been an attempt to forge a pan-Indian Muslim constituency through the use of pan-Islamic symbols. Minault has studied the individual actors, the diverse motivations of actors, as well as their modes of mobilizing people. By examining the statements, writings, and speeches of the different Khilafat leaders, Minault delineates the belief among Muslim leaders that by uniting the Muslims of India they could build up a position of strength from which to bargain with the British government and Hindus in the Indian National Congress.

Rather than disparaging the writings of the various Khilafat leaders as emotional artistry aimed at deluding ignorant publics, Minault analyzes and illustrates the power of oratory and poetry in the mobilizing efforts of Muslim leaders. Most important, Minault categorically demonstrates the importance of affective attachments, moral sentiments, and religious feelings related to Indian elite and folk understandings and practices of Islam in building the movement. She reads the Khilafat Movement through more than its concluding moments—that is, the eruption of Hindu-Muslim violence; she examines the various elements, time periods, personalities, and modes of communication to present a multidimensional and rich account of the struggle as a political event whose underlying ethos may nevertheless be understood as religious.

The Maulana and the Mahatma

Minault's account has acquired increased importance from a recently translated set of letters between one of the main initiators of the Khilafat Movement, Maulana Abdul Bari of Firangi Mahal, who founded the Jamiat-e-Ulema-e-Hind, and Mahatma Gandhi. These letters provide important correctives to existing accounts of the Hindu-Muslim alliance and offer further insights into the sentiments and the motivations of the leaders (Jamal 2011). Some of the motivations on the part of Gandhi and Abdul Bari are illuminated by their correspondence in both English and Urdu, a language with which Gandhi was just beginning to gain familiarity. In an examination of this correspondence, Jamal argues that the Khilafat Movement needs to be considered as political and anticolonial, but that its motivations were not simply driven by political expediency.

He emphasizes the moral ethical imperative that emerges in the arguments within the letters and memoirs of the two leaders, particularly as each faced the barrage of criticism from their respective communities. One noteworthy moment in this correspondence occurs after the Khilafat Movement ended in bloody rioting among Hindus and Muslims. The leaders called a conference to discuss both their response to peace celebrations marking the conclusion of World War I and the pressing issue of the Hindu demand for cow protection from the Muslims. Gandhi suggested that the two questions not be mixed up, but rather treated on their own moral and ethical merit. Jamal cites him thus:

> Before the conference I contended that, if the Khilafat question had a just and legitimate basis, as I believe it had, and if the Government had really committed a gross injustice, the Hindus were bound to stand by the Mussalmans in their demand for the redress of the Khilafat wrong. It would ill become them to bring in the cow question in this connection, or to use the occasion to make terms with the Mussalmans, just as it would ill become the Mussalmans to offer to stop cow-slaughter as a price for the Hindus' support on the Khilafat question. (Gandhi, cited in Jamal 2011, 11–12)

Gandhi seems to be making an extraordinary effort here to emphasize the possibility of building cooperation between Hindus and Muslims that may not be reduced to political expediency. In calling for the Hindus and Muslims to support each other's struggles against injustice he is evidently making a point beyond the need to unite in the face of British colonialism. Gandhi emphasizes that Hindus may mobilize against the harm inflicted on the sentiments of the Muslims by the dissolution of the Khilafat. A similar argument for intercommunal harmony built on moral-ethical considerations is echoed in his call to the Muslims to refrain from cow slaughter.

> But it would be another matter and quite graceful, and reflect great credit on them, if the Mussalmans of their own free will stopped cow-slaughter out of regard for the religious sentiments of the Hindus, and from a sense of duty towards them as neighbors and children of the

same soil. To take up such an independent attitude was, I contended, their duty, and would enhance the dignity of their conduct. But if the Mussalmans considered it as their neighborly duty to stop cow-slaughter, they should do so regardless of whether the Hindus helped them in the Khilafat or not. (Gandhi, cited in Jamal 2011, 13–14)

Gandhi's argument was accepted by the Muslim leaders and the question of cow protection was not discussed at this conference. However, Gandhi notes in his letter that despite his counsel, "Maulana Abdul Bari Saheb said 'No matter whether the Hindus help us or not, the Mussalmans ought, as the countrymen of the Hindus, out of regard for the latter's susceptibilities, to give up cow-slaughter.' And at one time it almost looked as if they would really put an end to it" (Jamal 2011, 13).

Putting aside the question of sincerity of the sentiments attributed to the Khilafat leaders, we may appreciate the merit of such sentiments in an argument about community construction. Thus constructed, the argument for community harmony or coalition building dismantles the limitations of rights discourse, especially the notion of competing rights that marks dominant political discourse of both liberal/secular and Islamist groups in Pakistan. It opens other avenues for community building that uphold ethics, morality, and piety beyond the narrow conceptions of these terms by both contemporary liberal nationalist and Islamist nationalist discourses. Thus while historians may conclude that the Khilafat Movement was a political failure and a national disappointment, an engagement with the arguments of its leading personalities, the nature of the religious sentiments exerted, and the basis for accommodation may indicate directions for building different notions of self and community in South Asia than are being privileged at the present moment.

South Asian Muslim Feminism

The Khalifat Movement also deserves further feminist attention than it has received thus far, as a key event for the public participation of Muslim women, especially those who negotiated rather than abandoned their religious-cultural identities to establish their mark in anticolonial

nationalist politics that cannot be termed "Islamist." While the participation of women in the Pakistan movement tends to be framed within a
modernist discourse of Muslim women's rights, a postcolonial and poststructuralist engagement with political involvement of women such as Bi
Amma and Nishat-un-Nisa Begum, who were pious, but in a markedly
different way from contemporary Islamist women, may bring illuminat-
ing insights. Nevertheless, the Khilafat Movement did launch and intensify debates among Indian Muslims about women's public participation.[5]

The Khilafat Movement may be understood as a locally situated example that may not be replicated. Its wider implications lie in its insistence
on rejecting the idea of characterizing intercommunity relationships in
South Asia through the colonial terms of majority-minority (Tejani 2008).
Shabnum Tejani considers the Khilafat era to be significant for later formulations of nationalism in India since the participating groups "sought
to forge a nationalism that was built by its communities, where each, whatever its relative size, was a necessary part" (Tejani 2008, 146). By attempting to redefine Hindus and Muslims as partners in an independent Indian
nation, the Khilafat Movement offered the possibility of imagining what
Tejani has eloquently described as "a foundation for nationalism that was
not determined by Western models of democracy" (143). While such a discursive moment might appear beyond our grasp, given the divisive conditions of Pakistan in the second decade of the twenty-first century, it could
serve as a guide for progressive politics that may disrupt or even transcend
the discursively constructed notions of secular and religious for the purpose of reconceptualizing "the Muslim secular" in South Asia outside of
colonial frameworks of liberal democracy. As Tejani has argued, a formulation of the nation could be envisaged where culturally/religiously diverse
groups are integral units of a collectivity without being posited against
each other as majority and minority. While it would be untenable and

5. Abida Bano Begum, popularly known as Bi Amma, was the mother of Maulana Mohammed Ali and Maulana Shaukat Ali; Nishat-un-Nisa Begum was the wife of
Maulana Hasrat Mohani. All these men were key leaders of the Khilafat Movement. For a
discussion of South Asian Muslim women's political participation in the early twentieth
century, see Minault 1982 and Willmer 1996.

flawed to suggest that the failure of the secularizing project in Pakistan, if ever such a project was intended by the elite leadership, is the cause of the emergence of Jamaat women, it is not too far-fetched to propose that Jamaat women's successful mobilization of a modern Muslim women's identity marks the limitations of the secular as an unambiguous political project in Pakistan. The trajectory of religiously identified Jamaat women, which I map in this book, may also be read, to some extent, as the trajectory of the failures of the modernizing elite who, in their search for a transcendent zone of the secular, jettisoned their legitimacy to speak for Islam and in so doing relinquished the authority to represent the humanist and emancipatory aspects of Muslim subjectivity.

Appendix

Glossary

Bibliography

Index

APPENDIX

An Islamic Charter of Women's Rights

The Women's Rights Charter, in its English-language version, states:

"We have strong intentions and great ambitions to create an atmosphere in Pakistan where in every home, women will have their due respect in every position, as a wife, as a mother, as a sister and as daughter. This commission has such a charter for women's economic, social and political rights which can make us a bright example for the whole world." (Pamphlet published by the Women's Commission, Jamaat-e-Islami Women's Wing, Karachi, n.d.)

The charter divides women's rights into four types: economic, social, political, and legal:

Women's Economic Rights:

- Provider/guardian of every woman would be made responsible for her economic necessities.
- Bait-ul-Maal, a system of providence of government.
- Assurance of *mehr* (dowry money) to be paid by husband in accordance with his status.
- Woman's right of inheritance according to Shariah.
- Cottage industries for women compelled to work.
- Provision of suitable accommodation and workplace environment.
- Separate transportation for women.

Women's Social Rights:

- Education in worldly and religious science.
- Allocation of funds for women's education.
- Ban on gender-mixed education and establishment of women's universities in all the provinces.
- Women-only institutes for vocational and professional education.
- Women's health centers in cities and villages.
- Effective steps to eliminate customs which exploit women and deprive them of their rights as mother, daughter, sister, and wife.
- Training for women in first aid and rifle shooting within the Islamic limits.

Women's Political Rights:

- Right of casting vote independently.
- Improvement in process of political representation.
- Party making for women for social reformation and protection of their rights.

Women's Legal Rights:

- Instant and severe punishments of sexual harassment and violence against women.
- Steps to prevent threats, mental torture, and physical violence against women from spouse and his family and easing of process of Khulaa (divorce) in situations where compromise is impossible.
- Rehabilitation centers and shelters for abducted, blackmailed, and exploited women in society.
- Examining problems related to enforcement of Hudood Ordinance and legal changes in the light of Quran and Sunnah.
- Prohibition of "vulgar and shameful representation" of women for the sake of recreation or marketing of a product.

The charter calls for the establishment of Idara-e-Mohtasib (institute of accountability) for women:

"This institution shall work to stop excesses inflicted on women on every level and to provide them instant legal relief. It will ensure effective implementation of laws."

Glossary

Ahl-e-Hadith: A politico-religious party in Pakistan that believes in deriving all guidance from the Quran and Hadith and rejects any other theological tradition.

Al-Huda: An Islamic school for women set up by Dr. Farhat Hashmi in Islamabad in 1994.

amir: A chief/leader.

Aurat Foundation: Aurat Publication and Information Service set up in the mid-1980s with the stated goal of boosting women's economic and political status in Pakistan.

ayahs: Nannies.

Barelvi: A movement of Sunni Islam that originated in India in the nineteenth century. It differs sharply from Deobandi, Wahabi, and Ahl al-Hadith in incorporating many traditional practices and folk rituals associated with Sufism.

burqa: An outer garment worn by women in Pakistan that covers the entire body except the face/eyes.

chadar: A shawl covering the body and sometimes drawn over the head or face.

chardewari: Literally, "four walls"; refers to seclusion.

Congress Party: A major political party in India that led the anticolonial nationalist movement against the British in the early twentieth century.

dars: Religious lessons or discussions.

dawah or *dawat:* Invitation to Islam.

Delhi-Punjabi Saudagran: Members of trading and business communities who are believed to have migrated from Punjab to Delhi in the Moghul era and back to Pakistan at or after partition.

Deoband: A movement in Sunni Islam that began at Darul Uloom Deoband in Deoband, India, in the nineteenth century. Deobandi adherents are associated with a puritanical approach to Islam and staunch opposition to many practices of intercessionary and mystical Islam common in the Indian subcontinent.

din: Way of life or religion. Also translated as "faith."

Diyat (and Qisas) Ordinance: Under the Qisas and Diyat law a victim or his or her heir has the right to determine whether to exact retribution (qisas) or compensation (diyat) or to pardon the accused.

fiqh: Islamic jurisprudence.

Firangi Mahal: the name given to a prominent lineage of ulemas in India derived from the locality of Lucknow, which they had inhabited since the end of the seventeenth century. The Firangi Mahalis maintained a classical version of Sharia-Sufi Islam, and were eventually undermined by the twin forces of colonialism and Islamic modernism.

Hadith: Oral traditions of the Prophet Muhammad collected after his death.

hal: State or condition. In Sufism it refers to a spiritual state.

harem: A sanctified place, such as a sanctuary or tomb or the women's quarters, in which men's entry was prohibited; because of colonial travel literature the harem or women's quarter became portrayed as a zone of eroticism and desire.

hijab: Veil or headscarf worn by a Muslim woman.

hisba: Accountability; censorship; supervision.

Hisba Act/Hasba Act: A 2005 bill proposed by the Jamaat-led provincial government in Khyber Pakhtunkhwa (formerly the North-West Frontier Province) to regulate morality and religious practices.

Hudood Ordinances: Part of a state-imposed Islamization program, enacted in 1979 under the government of Zia ul-Haq. This refers to a set of five criminal laws covering rape, adultery, theft, robbery, and the prohibition of narcotics and alcohol. The laws were partially amended in 2006 by the Women's Protection Bill.

ijma: scholarly consensus.

ijtama-e-Arkan: The congregation of members.

ijtama-e-Karkunan: The congregation of workers.

ijtihad: Deductive or analogical reasoning; independent investigation of religious sources.

iman: Belief.

Islami Jamiat-e-Talibat: The women student's equivalent of the Islami Jamiat-e-Tulba.

Islami Jamiat-e-Tulba: Jamaat-affiliated Islamic organization of male students, which has been the training ground for many of the party's leaders.

Islami nizam: Islamic order in the nation-state.

Islamism: An ideology related to contemporary movements that seek to implement Islamic practices/traditions by harnessing the powers of the modern nation-state.

Islamization: In Pakistan a movement by the state to bring about social, legal, and political changes in the name of implementing the Shariah, undertaken most vigorously by military dictator General Zia ul-Haq (1977–88).

jagirdar: feudal lord or landowner.

jahez: trousseau given to the bride at the time of marriage.

Jamaat-e-Islami: Literally, "Party of Islam." Created in 1941 by Abul Ala Maududi; gained popularity after 1977.

Jamaat-ud-Dawah: An extremist group that also operates under the name Falahi Insaf (Social Justice) and is thought, by the UN, to be related to the terrorist group Lashkar-e-Tayyeba.

Jamiat-e-Ulama-e-Hind: Organization of Indian Scholars.

jihad: moral struggle or effort that may take internal or external forms, as in a holy war.

kafir: Unbeliever.

kaifiyat: A term used to describe a particular state of spiritual ecstasy.

kalima: Literally, "the word." A declaration of Islamic faith, an affirmation that "There is no God but God, and Muhammad is His messenger."

khanqah: Sanctuary built around the tomb of a Sufi saint, used for both lodging and spiritual retreat.

Khawateen Mahaz-e-Amal: Women's Action Forum.

Al-Khidmat Trust: A nongovernmental organization that supports the ideology of the Jamaat-e-Islami.

Khilafat Movement (1919–24): A movement launched in India at the end of the First World War to protest the dissolution of the Ottoman Empire.

kufr: Disbelief/heresy.

ladiniat: Literally, "without religion" or "antireligion," but Maulana Maududi uses it as a translation for the term "secularism."

madressa: Arabic word for school. In Pakistan it connotes a religious school.

Majlis-e-Shura: Consultative council.

maulana: Title used for a religious scholar, usually a religious scholar with formal training.

mazhab: Religion/religious identity.

mohajirs or *muhajirs:* A term used to describe mostly Urdu-speaking Muslims who migrated from India to Pakistan after independence in 1947.

mohtasib: State official who ensures the implementation of the laws of the land and of morality when the legal system is inadequate. This office was created by the Hisba/Hasba Bill.

momin: Believer.

mudarrisa: female teacher.

mufti: An Islamic scholar who can issue a fatwa.

mullah or *maulvi:* Popular title in Pakistan for a Muslim educated in Islam, but not always formally. Often used in a derogatory sense to indicate a minor religious leader.

Muttahida Majlis Amal (MMA): A coalition of religious political parties in Pakistan formed prior to the elections of 2002.

Muttahida Qaumi Movement (MQM): Karachi-based political party originally organized on the basis of muhajir as an ethnic and political identity.

Muslim League: A political party of Muslims in British India that became the main force for the establishment of Pakistan as a homeland for the Muslims of South Asia.

naib: Appointee.

naib amir: Vice president.

nazim/nazima: Executive members who are elected by party members.

niqab: Hijab that covers the face except for the eyes.

pir: A term used to refer to a Sufi saint in South Asia.

purdah: Maududi defined "purdah" not only as the veiling but also the sequestering of Muslim women in the home and exclusion from the public sphere of male activities.

Quran: The Holy Book of Muslims, said to be the word of Allah.

rukn: A clerk.

Sajada-Nasheen: Descendant of a pir who bears the main responsibility for the shrine and its related rituals.

salafis: Those who seek to live in the manner of the first four generations of Muslims.

shalwar-kamiz: A Pakistani outfit of trouser and tunic worn by both men and women.

Shariah: Islamic law as set out by the Quran and the Sunnah. It deals with everything from politics and economics to family law.

shirk: Idolatry.

sufism: Islamic mysticism.

Sunnah: The teachings and practices of Prophet Muhammad, including the Hadith. The Sunnah and the Quran are the basis of Shariah law.

sura: Verse of the Quran.

swara: A traditional practice of marrying women to the Quran in order to deny their inheritance.

tabligh: Proselytizing.

tafsir: Interpretation of the Quran.

takfir: Expulsion from the faith; apostasy.

ulema: Islamic scholars.

ummah: The global Muslim community.

urs: Literally, "wedding"; the term used in South Asia for the celebration of the death anniversary of a Sufi saint/pir.

Wahabism: A highly conservative branch of Sunni Islam and a form of Salafism. Created in the eighteenth century by Mohammad ibn Abd al-Wahab in Saudi Arabia.

wazu: Ritual purification (usually before prayer).

zina: Adultery and fornication.

Bibliography

Abdul Qadir, B. 2005. "Despair and Hopelessness Forbidden, Tread the Future with Caution: Maryam Jameelah (Interview with *Young Muslim Digest*)." *Young Muslim Digest* (online). www.youngmuslimdigest.com.

Abu-Lughod, Lila. 1998. "Introduction: Feminist Longings and Postcolonial Conditions." In *Remaking Women: Feminism and Modernity in the Middle East*, edited by Lila Abu-Lughod, 3–31. Princeton: Princeton Univ. Press.

Afshar, Haleh. 1998. *Islam and Feminisms: An Iranian Case Study*. London: Macmillan.

Afzal, M. Rafique. 1998. *Political Parties in Pakistan, 1958–1969*. Vol. 2. Islamabad: National Institute of Historical and Cultural Research.

Ahmad, Eqbal. 2000. *Confronting Empire: Interviews with David Barsamian*. London: Pluto Press.

Ahmad, Irfan. 2008. "Cracks in the 'Mightiest Fortress': Jamaat-e-Islami's Changing Discourse on Women." Special Double Issue 2–3. *Modern Asian Studies* 42 (March): 549–75.

Ahmad, Khurshid. 2000. "Islamic Approach to Development." In *Political Development: An Islamic Perspective*, edited by Z. Kausar, 3–25. Selangor, Malaysia: The Other Press and Research Centre, International Islamic University.

———. 2002. "Muslim Ummah at the Threshold of the Twenty-first Century." *Tarjuman-ul-Quran* (online).

Ahmad, Sadaf. 2009. *Transforming Faith: The Story of Al-Huda and Islamic Revivalism among Urban Pakistani Women*. Syracuse: Syracuse Univ. Press.

Ahmed, Farukh, ed. 1999. *Daur-e-Hazir ki Mohsina: Apa Hameeda Begum*. Lahore: Hira.

Ahmed, Ishtiaq. 2002. "Globalisation and Human Rights in Pakistan." *International Journal of Punjab Studies* 9, no. 1: 57–89.

Ahmed, Leila. 1992. *Women and Gender in Islam: Historical Roots of a Modern Debate*. New Haven: Yale Univ. Press.

Ahmed, Qazi Husain. 2002. *Pakistan: Hal Aur Mustaqbil: Dauran-e-Asiri Likhay Gaye Mazamin*. Lahore: Qaumi Press.

Alam, Muzaffar. 2004. *The Languages of Political Islam: India, 1200–1800*. Chicago: The Univ. of Chicago Press.

Alavi, Hamza. 1986. "Ethnicity, Muslim Society, and the Pakistan Ideology." In Weiss, *Islamic Reassertion in Pakistan*, 21–47.

———. 1997. "Ironies of History: Contradictions of the Khilafat Movement." *Contemporary Studies of South Asia, Africa, and the Middle East* 17, no. 1 (1997): 1–16.

Anderson, Benedict. 1991. *Imagined Communities: Reflections on the Origin and Spread of Nationalism*. London: Verso.

Asad, Talal. 1986. "The Idea of an Anthropology of Islam." *Occasional Paper Series*, 1–23. Washington, DC: Center for Contemporary Arab Studies.

———. 2003. *Formations of the Secular: Christianity, Islam, Modernity*. Stanford: Stanford Univ. Press.

Asghar Khan, Omar. 1985. "Political and Economic Aspects of Islamization." In *Islam, Politics, and the State: The Pakistan Experience*, edited by M. Asghar Khan, 127–63. London: Zed Books.

———. 2001. "Critical Engagements: NGOs and the State." In Weiss and Gilani, *Power and Civil Society in Pakistan*, 275–300.

Asian Development Bank. 2009. "Overview of Civil Society Organizations: Pakistan (Report)." ADB's NGO and Civil Society Center. http://www.adb.org/sites/default/files/pub/2009/CSB-PAK.pdf.

Ayoob, Mohammed. 2008. *The Many Faces of Political Islam: Religion and Politics in the Muslim World*. Ann Arbor: Univ. of Michigan Press.

Azad, Maulana Abul Kalam Muhiyuddin Ahmed. 2006. *Sarmad the Martyr*. London: Epicflo.com. [Mahmood Jamal translation of *Hayat-i-Sarmad* (Lucknow: Tanvir, 1910).]

Badran, Margot. 1999. "Toward Islamic Feminisms: A Look at the Middle East." In *Hermeneutics and Honor: Negotiating Female "Public" Space in Islamic(ate) Societies*, edited by Asma Afsaruddin, 159–88. Cambridge: Harvard Univ. Press.

———. 2002. "Islamic Feminism: What's in a Name?" *Al-Ahram Weekly* (Cairo), no. 569, January, 17–23.

Baker, Deborah. 2011. *The Convert: A Tale of Exile and Extremism*. Minneapolis: Graywolf Press.

Bano, Nayyer. 1999. "Apa Hameeda Begum in My View." In Ahmed, *Daur-e-Hazir ki Mohsina*, 7–10.

Bari, Farzana, and Saba Gul Khattak. 2001. "Power Configurations in Public and Private Arenas: The Women's Movement's Response." In Weiss and Gilani, *Power and Civil Society in Pakistan*, 218–47.

Barlas, Asma. 2002. *Believing Women in Islam: Unreading Patriarchal Interpretations of the Qur'an*. Austin: University of Texas Press.

Baykan, Aysegul. 1990. "Politics, Women, and Postmodernity: Women between Fundamentalism and Modernity." In *Theories of Modernity and Postmodernity*, edited by Bryan S. Turner, 137–46. London: Sage.

Bilgrami, Akeel. 1994 "Two Concepts of Secularism: Reason, Modernity, and Archimedean Ideal." *Economics and Political Weekly* 29, no. 28: 1749–61.

Blood, Peter. [1994] 1996. *Pakistan: A Country Study*. 6th ed. Washington: GOP Library of Congress.

Bose, Sugata, and Ayesha Jalal. 1997. *Modern South Asia: History, Culture, Political Economy*. London: Routledge.

Brown, Wendy. 2005. "Subjects of Tolerance: Why We Are Civilized and They Are Barbarians." Seminar on Gender and Global Locations of Liberalism, Columbia University. www.iserp.columbia.edu/downloads/brown.pdf.

Chatterjee, Partha. 1993. *The Nation and Its Fragments: Colonial and Postcolonial Histories*. Princeton: Princeton Univ. Press.

———. 2004. *The Politics of the Governed: Reflections on Popular Politics in Most of the World*. New York: Columbia Univ. Press.

Chittick, William C. 1989. *The Sufi Path of Knowledge: Ibn al-'Arabi's Metaphysics of Imagination*. Albany: State Univ. of New York Press.

———. 2000. *Sufism: A Short Introduction*. Oxford: Oneworld.

Choudhury, Golam Wahed. 1988. *Pakistan: Transition from Military to Civilian Rule*. Essex, UK: Scorpion.

———. 1995. *Constitutional Development in Pakistan*. New Delhi: Concept.

CIA. 2012. *CIA: The World Factbook, Pakistan*. Washington: US Government Central Intelligence Agency.

Cook, Michael. 2000. *Commanding Right and Forbidding Wrong in Islamic Thought*. Cambridge: Cambridge Univ. Press.

Dean, Mitchell. 1999. *Governmentality: Power and Rule in Modern Society*. London: Sage.

Deeb, Lara. 2006. *An Enchanted Modern: Gender and Public Piety in Shi'i Lebanon*. Princeton: Princeton Univ. Press.

Dehlvi, Sadia. 2009. *Sufism: The Heart of Islam*. India: Harper Collins.

Doxlowski, Gregory C. 1999. "Devotional Islam and Politics in British India: Ahmad Riza Khan Barelwi and His Movement, 1870–1920." *The Journal of the American Oriental Society* 119, no. 4: 707–9.

Ernst, Carl W., and Bruce B. Lawrence. 2002. *Sufi Martyrs of Love: Chishti Sufism in South Asia and Beyond*. New York: Palgrave Macmillan.

Escobar, Arturo. 1995. "Introduction: Development and the Anthropology of Modernity." In *Encountering Development: The Making and Unmaking of the Third World*, edited by Arturo Escobar, 3–20. Princeton: Princeton Univ. Press.

Esposito, John L. 2003. "Introduction: Modernizing Islam and Re-Islamization in Global Perspective." In Esposito and Burgat, *Modernizing Islam*, 1–14.

Esposito, John L., ed. 2003. *Oxford Dictionary of Islam*. Oxford Reference Online: Oxford Univ. Press. http://www.oxfordreference.com.

Esposito, John L., and Francois Burgat. 2003. *Modernizing Islam: Religion in the Public Sphere in Europe and the Middle East*. London: Hurst.

Esposito, John L., and John Obert Voll. 2001. "Maryam Jameelah: A Voice of Conservative Islam." In *Makers of Contemporary Islam*, edited by John L. Esposito and John Obert Voll, 54–67. New York: Oxford Univ. Press.

Ezzat, Heba Raouf. 2002. "Rethinking Secularism . . . Rethinking Feminism," January 7, http://www.islamonline.net/english/Contemporary/2002/06/Article 4.shtml.

Faiz, Ahmed Faiz. 1986. "Dua" (Prayer). In *Nuskhahay Wafa: Sar-e-wadi-e Sina* [Urdu]. Delhi: Educational Publishing House.

Farooq, Asad. 2011. "Proposing Amends in Blasphemy Laws Fatwa Demands Death for Sherry." *Daily Times online*, January 9. http://www.dailytimes.com.pk.

Foucault, Michel. 1982. "The Subject and Power." *Critical Inquiry* 8: 777–95.

———. 1991. "Politics and the Study of Discourse." In *The Foucault Effect: Studies in Governmentality*, edited by Graham Burchell, Colin Gordon, and Peter Miller, 53–104. Chicago: The Univ. of Chicago Press.

Gardezi, Fauzia. 1997. "Nationalism and State Formation: Women's Struggle and Islamization in Pakistan." In Hussain, Mumtaz, and Saigol, *Engendering the Nation-State*, 79–110.

Ghamdi, Javed Ahmed. 2011. *Ghamdi* [Weekly televised program]. Produced by Shabbir Ahmed Waghra and Saleem Safi. Broadcast March 10. Pakistan: GeoTV.

Ghaus-Pasha, Aisha, and Muhammad Asif Iqbal. 2003. "Defining the Nonprofit Sector: Pakistan." Working Papers of the Johns Hopkins Comparative

Nonprofit Sector Project, No. 42. Baltimore: The Johns Hopkins Center for Civil Society Studies.

Ghaus-Pasha, Aisha, Hafiz A. Pasha, and Muhammad Asif. 2002. "Nonprofit Sector in Pakistan: Government Policy and Future Issues." Working Paper of SPDC, No. 2. Karachi: Social Policy and Development Center.

Gilani, Syed Asad. 1999. "The Contribution of Hameeda in the Islamic Movement." In Ahmed, *Daur-e-Hazir ki Mohsina*, 31–35.

Gole, Nilufer. 1997. *The Forbidden Modern: Civilization and Veiling.* Ann Arbor: Univ. of Michigan Press.

Gordon, Colin. 1991. "Government Rationality: An Introduction." In Burchell, Gordon, and Miller, *Foucault Effect*, 1–51.

Grare, Frederic. 2001. *Political Islam in the Indian Subcontinent: The Jamaat-e-Islami.* New Delhi: Manohar.

Grewal, Inderpal. 1988. "On the New Global Feminism and the Family of Nations: Dilemmas of Transnational Feminist Practice." In *Talking Visions*, edited by Ella Shohat, 501–30. Cambridge: MIT Press.

———. 1996. *Home and Harem: Nation, Gender, Empire, and the Cultures of Travel.* Durham: Duke Univ. Press.

———. 1999. "Women's Rights as Human Rights: Feminist Practices, Global Feminism, and Human Rights Regimes in Transnationality." *Citizenship Studies* 3, no. 3: 337–54.

———. 2005. *Transnational America: Feminisms, Diasporas, Neoliberalisms.* Durham: Duke Univ. Press.

Grewal, Inderpal, and Caren Kaplan. 1994. "Introduction: Transnational Feminist Practices and Questions of Postmodernity." In *Scattered Hegemonies: Postmodernity and Transnational Feminist Practices*, edited by Inderpal Grewal and Caren Kaplan, 1–33. Minneapolis: Univ. of Minnesota Press.

———. 2000. "Postcolonial Studies and Transnational Feminist Practices." *Jouvert: A Journal of Postcolonial Studies* 5, no. 1: http://english.chass.ncsu.edu/jouvert/index.htm.

Guha, Ranajit, ed. 1982. *Subaltern Studies No. 1: Writings on South Asian History and Society.* Delhi: Oxford Univ. Press.

Haddad, Yvonne Yazbeck. 1998. "Islam and Gender: Dilemmas in the Changing Arab World." In Haddad and Esposito, *Islam, Gender, and Social Change*, 3–29.

Haddad, Yvonne Yazbeck, and John L. Esposito, eds. 1998. *Islam, Gender, and Social Change.* Oxford: Oxford Univ. Press.

Hall, Stuart. 1996. "The West and the Rest: Discourse and Power." In *Modernity: An Introduction to Modern Societies*, edited by Stuart Hall, David Held, Don Hubert, and Kenneth Thompson, 184–224. Malden, MA: Blackwell.

Haq, Farhat. 1996. "Women, Islam, and the State in Pakistan." *The Muslim World* 86, no. 2: 158–75.

———. 2009. "Mothers of Lashkar-e-Taiba." *Economic and Political Weekly* 44, no. 18: 17–20.

Haqqani, Hussain. 2005. *Pakistan: Between Mosque and Military*. Washington, DC: Carnegie Endowment for International Peace.

Haque, Ziaul. 1983. "Pakistan and Islamic Ideology." In *Pakistan: The Roots of Dictatorship: The Political Economy of a Praetorian State*, edited by Hassan Gardezi and Jamil Rashid, 367–82. London: Zed Press.

Harding, Sandra, and Kathryn Norberg. 2005. "New Feminist Approaches to Social Science Methodologies: An Introduction." *Signs: Journal of Women in Culture and Society* 30, no. 4: 2009–15.

Hasan, Naheed, and Zafar Junejo. 1999. *The State of the Citizen Sector in Pakistan*. Karachi: NGO Resource Center.

Hasan, Riffat. 2002. "My Struggle to Help Muslim Women Regain Their God-Given Rights," *Dawn.com* [online], November 7. http://www.dawn.com /weekly/review/archive.

Hatem, Mervat F. 1998. "Secularist and Islamist Discourses on Modernity in Egypt and the Evolution of the Postcolonial Nation-State." In Haddad and Esposito, *Islam, Gender, and Social Change*, 85–99.

Hoodbhoy, Pervez. 2009. "The Saudi-isation of Pakistan." *Newsline* [online], January 3.

Hussain, Neelam. 1997. "The Narrative Appropriation of Saima: Coercion and Consent in Muslim Pakistan." In Hussain, Mumtaz, and Saigol, *Engendering the Nation-State*, 1:199–242.

Hussain, Neelam, Samiya Mumtaz, and Rubina Saigol, eds. *Engendering the Nation-State*. Vol. 1. Lahore: Simorgh Women's Resource and Publication Centre.

Ikramullah, Shaista Suhrawardy. 1963. *From Purdah to Parliament*. London: Cresset.

Iqtidar, Humeira. 2011. *Secularizing Islamists? Jama'at-e-Islami and Jama'at-ud-Da'wa in Urban Pakistan*. Chicago: The Univ. of Chicago Press.

Islahi, Mohammad Yusuf. 1969. *Etiquettes of Living*. New Delhi: Markazi Maktaba Jamaat-e-Islami.

Jahangir, Asma, and Hina Jilani. 1990. *The Hudood Ordinances: A Divine Sanction?* Lahore: Rhotas Books.

Jalal, Ayesha. 2001. *Religion as Difference, Religion as Faith: Paradoxes of Muslim Identity.* Monograph Series of the Council of Social Sciences, Pakistan. Islamabad: COSS.

———. 2002. "The Religious and Secular in Precolonial South Asia." *Daily Times Pakistan,* April 21.

———. 2007. "Striking a Just Balance: Maulana Azad as a Theorist of Transnational Jihad." *Modern Intellectual History* 4, no. 1: 95–107.

———. 2008. *Partisans of Allah: Jihad in South Asia.* Cambridge: Harvard Univ. Press.

Jamal, Amina. 2002. "Entangled Modernities: Feminism, Islamization and Citizenship in a Transnational Locale." PhD diss. University of Toronto.

———. 2005. "Feminist 'Selves' and Feminism's 'Others': Feminist Representations of Jamaat-e-Islami Women in Pakistan." *Feminist Review* 81: 52–73.

Jamal, Mahmood. 2011. *Gandhi's Urdu Letters: The Maulana and the Mahatma* [eBook]. London: Ideaindia.com.

Jameelah, Maryam. 1976a. *Islam and the Muslim Woman Today.* Lahore: Mohammed Yusuf Khan and Sons.

———. 1976b. *Why I Embraced Islam.* Lahore: Mohammed Yusuf Khan and Sons.

Japan International Cooperation Agency (JICA). 1999. "Country WID Profile (Pakistan)." Tokyo: Planning Department.

Jung, Anees. 1987. *Unveiling India: A Woman's Journey.* Delhi: Penguin Books.

Kandiyoti, Deniz. 1994. "Identity and Its Discontents: Women and the Nation." In *Colonial Discourse and Postcolonial Theory,* edited by Patrick Williams and Laura Carisman, 376–91. New York: Columbia Univ. Press.

———. 1996. "Islam and Feminism: A Misplaced Polarity." *Women against Fundamentalism* 8: 10–13.

Keddie, Nikki E. 1998. "The New Religious Politics: Where, When, and Why Do 'Fundamentalisms' Appear?" *Society for Comparative Study of Society and History* 40, no. 4: 696–723.

Khan, Shahnaz. 2001. "Between Here and There: Feminist Solidarity and Afghan Women." *Genders* 33: 1–26.

———. 2007. *Zina, Transnational Feminism, and the Moral Regulation of Pakistani Women.* Vancouver: Univ. of British Columbia Press.

Konchar Farr, Cecilia. 1994. "Dancing through the Doctrine." In *Religion, Feminism, and Freedom of Conscience: Mormon Humanist Discourse*, edited by George D. Smith, 141–51. Buffalo: Prometheus Books; Salt Lake City: Signature Books.

Lumbard, Joseph, E. B. 2004. "The Decline of Knowledge and the Rise of Ideology in the Modern Islamic World." In *Islam, Fundamentalism, and the Betrayal of Tradition: Essays by Western Muslim Scholars*, edited by Joseph E. B. Lumbard, 39–77. Bloomington, IN: World Wisdom.

Mack, Phyllis. 2003. "Religion, Feminism, and the Problem of Agency: Reflections on Eighteenth-Century Quakerism." *Signs: Journal of Women in Culture and Society* 29, no. 1: 149–73.

Mahmood, Saba. 2005. *Politics of Piety: The Islamic Revival and the Feminist Subject*. Princeton: Princeton Univ. Press.

Masud, Muhammad. 2009. *Islam and Modernity: Key Issues and Debates*. Edinburgh: Edinburgh Univ. Press.

Mateen, Ameer. 2010. "Special Report on the Jamaat-e-Islami, Parts 1–3." *The News*, June 1–3.

Maududi, Maulana Abu Ala. 1939. *Purdah and the Status of Women in Islam*. Lahore: Islamic Publications.

———. 1968. "Al Amr bil Marouf wa Nahin An al Munkir." *Tafhimat*, Vol. 1, 145–55. Lahore: Islamic Publishers.

Mehdi, Rubya. 1994. *The Islamization of the Law in Pakistan*. Surrey, UK: Curzon Press.

Metcalf, Barbara D. 1996. "Islam and Women: The Case of the Tablighi Jamaat." *Stanford Electronic Humanities Review* 5, no. 1.

———. 1999. "Weber and Islamic Reform." In *Max Weber and Islam*, edited by T. E. Huff and W. Schluchter, 217–29. London: Transaction.

———. 2004. "Reading and Writing about Muslim Women in British India." In Barbara Metcalf, *Islamic Contestations: Essays on Muslims in India and Pakistan*, 99–119. New Delhi: Oxford University Press.

———. 2005. "The Study of Muslims in South Asia: A Talk at the University of California Santa Barbara, December 2." At *Islam in South Asia: Some Useful Study Materials*, website maintained by Professor Frances Pritchett, http://www.columbia.edu/itc/mealac/pritchett/00islamlinks/ikram/part0_metcalfintro.html.

Minault, Gail. 1969. "Akbar and Aurangzeb—Syncretism and Separatism in Mughal India: A Re-examination." *The Muslim World* 59, no. 2: 106–26.

————. 1982. *The Khilafat Movement: Religious Symbolism and Political Mobilization in India*. New York: Columbia Univ. Press.

————. 1982. "Purdah Politics: The Role of Muslim Women in Indian Nationalism, 1911–1924." In *Separate Worlds: Studies of Purdah in South Asia*, edited by Hanna Papaneck and Gail Minault, 245–61. Delhi: Chanakya.

————. 1998. *Secluded Scholars: Women's Education and Muslim Social Reform in Colonial India*. Delhi: Oxford Univ. Press.

Moallem, Mino. 1999. "Transnationalism, Feminism, and Fundamentalism." In *Between Woman and Nation: Nationalisms, Transnational Feminisms, and the State*, edited by C. Kaplan, N. Alarcon, and M. Moallem, 320–48. Durham: Duke Univ. Press.

Mohanty, Chandra. 1988. "Under Western Eyes: Feminist Scholarship and Colonial Discourses." *Feminist Review* 30: 61–88.

Mufti, Aamir. 2000. "The Aura of Authenticity." *Social Text* 18, no. 3: 87–103.

Mukhia, Harbans. 1999. "The Celebration of Failure as Dissent in Urdu Ghazal." *Modern Asian Studies* 33, no. 4: 861–81.

Mumtaz, Khawar. 1994. "Identity Politics and Women: 'Fundamentalism' and Women in Pakistan." In *Identity Politics and Women: Cultural Reassertions and Feminisms in International Perspective*, edited by Valentine M. Moghadam, 228–42. Oxford: Westview Press.

Mumtaz, Khawar, and Farida Shaheed. 1987. *Women of Pakistan: Two Steps Forward, One Step Back?* Lahore: Vanguard Books.

————. 1991. "Historical Roots of the Women's Movement: A Period of Awakening, 1896–1947." In *Finding Our Way: Readings on Women in Pakistan*, edited by Fareeha Zafar, 3–25. Lahore: ASR.

Munir, Muhammad. 1954. *Report of the Court of Inquiry Constituted under Punjab Act II of 1954 to Enquire into the Punjab Disturbances of 1953*. Lahore: Government Printing, Punjab.

Murad, Khurram. 1999. "Revolution—Through Bullet or Ballot?" In *Jamaat-e-Islami and National and International Politics*, edited by Khalid Rehman, Muhibul Haq Sahibzada, and Mushfiq Ahmed, 43–53. Lahore: Shirkat Press.

Mushtaq, Faiza. 2008. "Al-Huda and Its Critics: Religious Education for Pakistani Women." *ISIM Review* 22: 30–31.

Nadeem, Omar. 2001. "An Alliance for the Future." In *Logon ke Sath Sath: NGO Tehreek Ka Jaiza* (Keeping step with the people: a review of the NGO movement), edited by Zahid Islam, 8–11. Lahore: Citizens Network for Good Governance.

Nadwi, Maulana Sayyed Abul Hasan Ali. 1980. *Asr-i Hazir Mai Din Ki Tahfim-o-Tashrih*. Lucknow: Dar-ul Arafat.

Najmabadi, Afsaneh. 1998. "Feminism in an Islamic Republic: Years of Hardship, Years of Growth." In Haddad and Esposito, *Islam, Gender and Social Change*, 59–84. New York: Oxford Univ. Press.

Nasr, Seyyed Hossein. 1966. *Ideals and Realities of Islam*. London: George Allen and Unwin.

Naviwala, Nadia. 2010. "Harnessing Local Capacity: U.S. Assistance and NGOs in Pakistan." Prepared for the USAID Afghanistan/Pakistan Task Force, sponsored by the Carr Center for Human Rights Policy, Kennedy School Policy Analysis, Harvard University, http://www.hks.harvard.edu/cchrp /sbhrap/forum/article_0003/HarnessingLocalCapacity.pdf.

Naqvi, Mohammed Baqir. 2010. *Pakistan at Knife's Edge*. New Delhi: Lotus Collection.

Page, David. 1982. *Prelude to Partition: The Indian Muslims and the Imperial System of Control, 1920–1932*. Delhi: Oxford Univ. Press.

Puri, Nikhil. 2010. "The Pakistani Madrassah and Terrorism: Made and Unmade Conclusions from the Literature." *Perpectives on Terrorism* 4, no. 4: 51–72.

Qadeer, Mohammad. 2006. *Pakistan: Social and Cultural Transformations in a Muslim Nation*. London: Routledge.

Qadri, Sadakat. 2012. *Heaven on Earth: A Journey through Sharia Law from the Deserts of Ancient Arabia to the Streets of the Modern Muslim World*. New York: Farrar, Straus and Giroux.

Rahman, Tariq. 2000. *Language and Politics in Pakistan*. Karachi: Oxford Univ. Press.

———. 2005. *Denizens of Alien Worlds: A Study of Education, Inequality, and Polarization in Pakistan*. Karachi: Oxford Univ. Press.

———. 2011. "Can Pakistan End Terrorism"? *The Express Tribune*, April 16.

Rashid, Ahmed. 1985. "Pakistan: The Ideological Dimension." In *Islam, Politics, and the State: The Pakistan Experience*, edited by M. Asghar Khan, 69–89. London, Zed Books.

———. 2001. *Taliban: The Story of the Afghan Warlords*. London: Pan Books.

———. 2012. *Pakistan on the Brink: The Future of America, Pakistan, and Afghanistan*. New York: Viking Penguin.

Rashid, Ahmed, and Farida Shaheed. 1993. "Pakistan: Ethno-Politics and Contending Elites." Discussion paper. Geneva: United Nations Research Institute for Social Development.

Razack, Sherene. 2005. "Geopolitics, Culture Clash, and Gender after September 11." *Social Justice* 32, no. 4: 11–31.

———. 2007. "The 'Sharia Law Debate' in Ontario: The Modernity/Premodernity Distinction in Legal Efforts to Protect Women from Culture." *Feminist Legal Studies* 15, no. 1: 3–32.

Rehman, Ibn Abdur. 2003. "Look at the Hisba Bill Now." *Dawn.com* [online], July 25, http://www.dawn.com.

Reza Nasr, Seyyed Vali. 1994. *The Vanguard of the Islamic Revolution: The Jama'at-i Islami of Pakistan.* Berkeley and Los Angeles: Univ. of California Press.

———. 1996. *Mawdudi and the Making of Islamic Revivalism.* New York: Oxford Univ. Press.

Richter, William L. 1986. "The Political Meaning of Islamization in Pakistan: Prognosis, Implications, and Questions." In *Islamic Reassertion in Pakistan: The Application of Islamic Laws in a Modern State,* edited by A. Weiss, 129–40. Syracuse: Syracuse Univ. Press.

Rinaldo, Rachel. 2008. "Muslim Women, Middle-Class Habitus, and Modernity in Indonesia." *Contemporary Islam* 2, no. 2: 23–39.

Robinson, Francis. 1986. "Islam and Muslim Society in South Asia: A Reply to Das and Minault." *Contribution to Indian Sociology* 20, no. 1: 97–104.

———. 2000. *Islam and Muslim History.* New Delhi: Oxford Univ. Press.

———. 2002. *The Ulama of Firangi Mahal and Islamic Culture in South Asia.* Karachi: Ferozesons.

Robinson, Simon. 2008. "Religion's Defeat in Pakistan's Election." *Time World* [online], February 29, http://www.time.com/time/world/article/0,8599,1718614,00.html.

Rouse, Shahnaz. 1988. "Women's Movement in Pakistan: State, Class, Gender." *Women Living under Muslim Laws Dossier* 3: 9–17.

———. 1996. "Gender, Nationalism(s), and Cultural Identity: Discursive Strategies and Exclusivities." In *Embodied Violence: Communalising Women's Sexuality in South Asia,* edited by K. Jayawardena and M. De Alwis, 42–70. New Delhi: Kali for Women.

———. 2001. "Nationalism, Gender, and Space in Pakistan: Liberation from Above or Within?" *Against the Current* 97, no. 1: http://www.solidarity-us.org/atc/97Rouse.html.

———. 2004. *Shifting Body Politics: Gender, Nation, and State in Pakistan.* New Delhi: Women Unlimited.

Saeed, Hilda, and Ayesha Khan. 2000. "Legalised Cruelty: Anti-women Laws in Pakistan." In *No Paradise Yet: The World's Women Face the New Century*, edited by Judith Mirsky and Marty Radlett, 119–36. London: The Panos Institute and Zed Books.

Said Khan, Nighat. 1994. "Reflections on the Question of Islam and Modernity." In Said Khan, Saigol, and Zia, *Locating the Self*, 77–95.

———. 2002. "The Impact of the Global Women's Movement on International Relations: Has It Happened? What Has Happened?" In *Common Grounds, Mutual Exclusions*, edited by Marianne Braig and Sonja Woelte, 35–45. London: Zed Press.

Said Khan, Nighat, Rubina Saigol, and Afiya S. Zia, eds. 1994. *Locating the Self: Perspectives on Women and Multiple Identities*. Lahore: ASR.

Said Khan, Nighat, Rubina Saigol, and Afiya S. Zia. 1994. "Introduction." In Said Khan, Saigol, and Zia, *Locating the Self*, 1–19.

Sangari, Kumkum, and Sudesh Vaid. 1990. "Recasting Women: An Introduction." In *Recasting Women: Essays in Indian Colonial History*, edited by Kumkum Sangari and Sudesh Vaid, 1–26. New Brunswick: Rutgers Univ. Press.

Sanyal, Usha. 2005. *Ahmad Riza Khan Barelwi: In the Path of the Prophet: Makers of the Muslim World*. Oxford: Oneworld.

Schimmel, Annemarie. 2003. *Islam in the Indian Subcontinent*. Lahore: Sang-e-Meel.

———. 2006. "Historical Outlines of Classical Sufism." In *Mystical Dimensions of Islam*, edited by Annemarie Schimmel. Lahore: Sang-e-Meel.

Scott, D. 1999. *Refashioning Futures: Criticism after Postcoloniality*. Princeton: Princeton Univ. Press.

Shah, Saeed. 2011. "Mainstream Pakistan Religious Organisations Applaud Killing of Salmaan Taseer." *The Guardian online*, January 5, http://www.guardian .co.uk/world/2011/jan/05/pakistan-religious-organisations-salman-taseer /print.

Shaheed, Farida. 1998. "The Other Side of the Discourse: Women's Experiences of Identity, Religion, and Activism in Pakistan." In *Appropriating Gender: Women's Activism and Politicized Religion in South Asia*, edited by P. Jeffery and A. Basu, 143–64. London: Routledge.

Shaheed, Farida, and Khawar Mumtaz. 1992. "Islamization and Women: the Experience of Pakistan." In *WLUML Bulletin: Special Bulletin of Fundamentalism and Secularism in South Asia*, 54–64. Lahore: Shirkat Gah.

Shahnawaz, Jahan Ara. 1971. *Father and Daughter: A Political Biography*. Lahore: Nigarishat.

Shakir, Beulah. 1997. "The State and the Minorities of Pakistan." In Hussain, Mumtaz, and Saigol, *Engendering the Nation-State*, 1:260–66.

Shaukat Ali, Parveen. 1997. *Politics of Conviction: The Life and Times of Muhammed Zia ul Haq*. London: The London Centre for Pakistan Studies.

Shehabuddin, Elora. 2008. *Reshaping the Holy: Democracy, Development, and Muslim Women in Bangladesh*. New York: Columbia Univ. Press.

Siddiqa, Ayesha. 2007. *Military Inc.: Inside Pakistan's Military Economy*. London: Pluto Books.

Sinha, Mrinalini. 1999. "The Lineage of the 'Indian' Modern: Rhetoric, Agency, and the Sarda Act in Late Colonial India." In *Gender, Sexuality, and Colonial Modernities*, edited by Antoinette Burton, 207–21. London: Routledge.

Smith, Wilfred Cantwell. 1957. *Islam in Modern History*. New York: The New American Library.

Spivak, Gayatri Chakravorty. 1988. "Can the Subaltern Speak?" In *Marxism and the Interpretation of Culture*, edited by Cary Nelson and Lawrence Grossberg, 271–313. Urbana: Univ. of Illinois Press.

———. 1993. "French Feminism Revisited." In Spivak, *Outside in the Teaching Machine*, 158–92. London: Routledge.

———. 1996. "Diasporas Old and New: Women in the Transnational World." *Textual Practice* 10, no. 2: 245–69.

———. 2004. "Terror: A Speech after 9-11." *Boundary* 2, no. 2: 81–111.

———. 2005. "Use and Abuse of Human Rights." *Boundary 2* 32, no. 1: 131–89.

Stivens, Maila. 2000. "Becoming Modern in Malaysia: Women at the End of the Twentieth Century." In *Women in Asia: Tradition, Modernity, and Globalisation*, edited by Louise Edwards and Mina Roces, 16–38. Ann Arbor: Univ. of Michigan Press.

Strong-Boag, Veronica, ed. 1998. *Painting the Maple: Essays on Race, Gender, and the Construction of Canada*. Vancouver, BC: Univ. of British Columbia Press.

Tejani, Shabnum. 2008. *Indian Secularism: A Social and Intellectual History, 1890–1950*. Bloomington: Indiana Univ. Press.

Tucker, Vincent. 1999. "The Myth of Development: A Critique of a Eurocentric Discourse." In *Critical Development Theory: Contributions to a New Paradigm*, edited by R. Munck and D. O'Hearn, 1–26. London: Zed Books.

UNDP. 2005. *Political and Legislative Participation of Women in Pakistan: Issues and Perspectives*. Islamabad: United Nations Development Programme in Pakistan.

Utvik, Bjorn Olav. 2003. "The Modernizing Force of Islam." In Esposito and Burgat, *Modernizing Islam*, 43–67.

Warraich, Sohail Akbar. 2005. "'Honour Killings' and the Law in Pakistan." In *Honor: Crimes, Paradigms, and Violence against Women*, edited by Lynn Welchman and Sara Hossain, 78–110. London: Zed Books.

Waseem, Mohammad. 2006. *Democratization in Pakistan: A Study of the 2002 Elections*. Lahore: Oxford Univ. Press.

Weiss, Anita M. 1986. "The Historical Debate on Islam and the State in South Asia." In Weiss, *Islamic Reassertion in Pakistan*, 1–20.

———, ed. 1986. *Islamic Reassertion in Pakistan: The Application of Islamic Laws in a Modern State*. Syracuse: Syracuse Univ. Press.

———. 1998. "The Slow Yet Steady Path to Women's Empowerment in Pakistan." In Haddad and Esposito, *Islam, Gender, and Social Change*, 124–43.

Weiss, Anita M., and S. Zulfiqar Gilani, eds. 2001. *Power and Civil Society in Pakistan*. Karachi: Oxford Univ. Press.

Willmer, David. 1996. "Women as Participants in the Pakistan Movement: Modernization and the Promise of a Moral State." *Modern Asian Studies* 30, no. 3: 573–90.

Zaheer, Sajjad. 2007. *The Light: A History of the Movement for Progressive Literature in the Indo-Pakistan Subcontinent: A Translation of Roshnai*. Translated by Amina Azfar. Karachi: Oxford Univ. Press.

Zaidi, S. Akbar. 2005. "State, Military, and Social Transition: Improbable Future of Democracy in Pakistan." *Economic and Political Weekly* 3: 5173–81.

Zaman, Muhammad Q. 2002. *The Ulama in Contemporary Islam: Custodians of Change*. Princeton: Princeton Univ. Press.

Zia, Afiya S. 2009. "The Reinvention of Feminism in Pakistan." *Feminist Review* 91: 29–46.

Zia ul-Haq, Mohammad. 1979. "Interview to Nelson News, Weekend Television, London." In *President of Pakistan, Gen. Mohammad Zia ul Haq: Interviews to Foreign Media*, Vol. 2, *January–December*, Directorate of Films and Publications, Ministry of Information and Broadcasting. Islamabad: Government of Pakistan.

Zubair, Umm. 1999. "Some Facets of the Personality of Hameeda Begum." In Ahmed, *Daur-e-Hazir ki Mohsina*, 15–30.

Index

Abdul Bari, Maulana, 260–62

Abu Hanifa, 235

activism, 137; discourse and, 140; importance of, 151; as jihad, 97

Adab-e-Zindagi (Etiquettes of Living) (Islahi), 127–32

adultery (*zina*), 64, 107–8

Afghanistan, 4, 25, 28, 242, 251, 254–55

Afghan War, 146–47, 152, 181

Afroze, Rehana, 171

Afshar, Haleh, 48–49, 53

agency: context of, 68; of Jamaat-e-Islami women, 54–56, 68; political, 47; religious, 14, 53–54, 56, 210, 214; secular, 5, 214

Ahmad, Khurshid, 189–93, 189n10

Ahmad, Qazi Hussain, 18, 89, 170

Ahmad, Sadaf, 58–59

Ahmed, Farukh, 118–19

Alavi, Hamza, 27, 258

Allahabadi, Akbar, 223

alterity, 2

Amin, Qassim, 125

amr bil maruf (to enjoin good and forbid evil): Hanafi view of, 235–37; Hanbali theology and, 230–32; Maududi's view of, 232–35; moral citizens and, 208–9, 211–12, 214, 229–38, 243; as religious duty and doctrine, 229–37

Anderson, Benedict, 72

Arab Gulf: Arabization and, 154–57, 175; Pakistan and, 101–2, 102n12, 146, 154–57; purdah and, 156–57, 157n12; women, 101–2, 156–57

Arabization: of middle class, 154–57; Saudi Arabia influencing, 155–57; women's rights as human rights and, 175

Asad, Allama Muhammad, 122

Asad, Talal, 5, 6n7, 8n10, 11, 217

assemblies, gendering, 15–18

Aurat Foundation, 15, 105, 185, 188

Awami National Party, 26, 252, 252n1

Ayesha: development and, 186–89, 193–94, 197–99, 204; in Karachi, 197–99; moral citizens and, 239–42, 244–46; new modernity and, 163; politics of morality and, 133–35; Women's Commission and, 163, 197–99, 204

Azad, Maulana Abul Kalam, 219–20, 220n9, 258

Badran, Margot, 49–51

baithak (temporary schools), 129–30

Bangladesh, 92–93, 93n10

Bano, Nayyar, 116–17

Barelvi, Ahmed Reza, 3

Barelvi Islam, 2–3, 3n4

Barlas, Asma, 51–52

Begum, Hameeda: *Daur-e-Hazir ki Mohsina* about, 115–16; *dawat* and, 116, 119–20; "God's Kingdom on Earth," 119; Maududi and, 116, 132; middle class and, 118; politics of morality and, 115–21, 132–34; writing and, 116–18

benefactress of the present era, A (*Daur-e-Hazir ki Mohsina*), 115–16

Bengal, 72

Bhutto, Zulfiqar Ali, 179–80

Blasphemy Law, 172n1, 254–55

burqa: alterity signified by, 2; encouraged, 202; purdah and, 1–2, 1n1

catachresis, 138

CBOs (community-based organizations), 182

CEDAW (Convention to Eliminate All Forms of Discrimination Against Women), 15, 172, 245

Chatterjee, Partha, 72–76, 76n2, 143–44, 164

citizenship: contractual principles of, 247; gendered discourse of, 145–48; postcolonial, 74; secular, 79. *See also* moral citizens

civil society, 174–75, 183

civil war, in Pakistan, 92–93

class: engendering, 27–28; English and, 31–32; in Karachi, 24–27; in Lahore, 24–26; modernity signifiers specific to, 166–67; in postcolonial state, 164–69; professional, 85; research sites, 23–26; salariat, 27; Urdu and, 31–32; veiling and, 58; Westernized elite, 31. *See also* middle class

classical Islam, 248

clerical authority, 208n1

Commanding Right and Forbidding Wrong in Islamic Thought (Cook), 229–33

communality, 221–24

communal politics, 142

communal separatism, in India, 142

communism, 146

community: construction, 45, 208–9, 214, 248–64; Islamism and, 81, 221–24; in motion, 103, 161; Quran and, 208; religious-cultural politics of, 256–60. *See also* self/community notions

community-based organizations (CBOs), 182

Companies Act, 183

consultative council (Majlis-e-Shura), 21–22, 147

Convention to Eliminate All Forms of Discrimination Against Women (CEDAW), 15, 172, 245

Cook, Michael, 229–33, 235–36

cow protection, 261–62

Das, Veena, 33

Daur-e-Hazir ki Mohsina (A benefactress of the present era), 115–16

dawat (invitation), 90, 94, 116, 119–20, 148

decolonization, 13

Delhi-Punjabi Saudagran, 127–28

democracy: modernity and, 75–76; religion and, 102–3; secular and, 11

Deobandi, 3, 6

development: Khurshid Ahmad on, 189–93, 189n10; Ayesha and, 186–89, 193–94, 197–99, 204; din implemented in, 193–95; discourses of, 178, 186–95; elite and, 190–91; Farida and, 206–7; GAD and, 174, 174n3, 189–93, 206; gender and, 170–207; Islamizing, 204–7; Jamaat-e-Islami women and, 170–207; middle class and, 173, 176, 184, 186, 188, 197, 200, 203, 205–7; narrative of, 48; neoliberalism in, 179–80; of NGO sector, 177–86; objections to, 172–73; Pakistan's policy, 179–83, 251; Samina and, 185–86; urban, 44; violence against women and, 188–89; WID and, 174, 174n3, 180–81, 185, 189–93, 206; Women's Commission and, 193–204

din (faith): compulsion in, 243; development and, 193–95; implementing, 193–95, 209; Maududi and, 159n14, 160, 160n16, 195, 226

discourse: of citizenship, 145–48; discriminatory, 211, 213; of gender and development, 178, 186–95; Islamist, 167; self-formation and activism through, 140

discriminatory discourse, 211, 213

dissent, 80–81, 80n5

East Pakistan. *See* Bangladesh

economy, women and, 198–99

education, 152–54, 166, 203, 206. *See also* schools

Egypt, 55–56, 80, 125

elections: boycotted, 23; Islamism and, 251–56; Jamaat-e-Islami and, 16–17; partyless, 182; of 2002, 15–17, 252; of 2008, 252, 252n1

electoral politics, Jamaat-e-Islami women and, 85–88, 151–52

elite, 4, 7, 38; construction of, 165; development and, 190–91; religious, 177; secular modernizing, 14n14, 79, 79n4, 166–67; Westernized, 31–32

elitism, 8n9, 12n12

emancipation, 8, 23–24

emotional factors, in politics, 254

employment, of women, 204, 206

empty time, 73; prayer time and, 73–74; summer time, 109–10

English: class and, 31–32; medium, 1, 1n2; purdah narratives in, 1

enjoin good and forbid evil, to. *See amr bil maruf*

equality, 200, 205, 246–47

escape-from-Islam narratives, 1–2, 1n3

ethnicity, in Karachi and Lahore, 24–26

Etiquettes of Living (Adab-e-Zindagi) (Islahi), 127–32

Ezzat, Heba Raouf, 52, 56

faith, 33–39, 121–27. *See also* din

Faiz, Ahmed Faiz, 80–81, 80n5

family, reformulations of, 227–29

Farida: development and, 206–7; new modernity and, 163–64; public-religious spaces and, 94–99, 105; purdah and, 97

Fatima, 103–4, 158–59, 161–62

feminism: approaches of, 44; contextually specific accounts of, 214; fundamentalism entangled with, 7–11, 67, 113–14, 167; hegemonic forms of, 46–47; Islamism and, 11–12; Islamization and, 64–68; Jamaat-e-Islami women and, 2, 43, 46–49, 52–64, 67–69, 125–26, 133, 137, 185–87, 205–6, 248, 251; post-Islamic, 46–69; poststructuralist, 46, 54; skepticism about, 52–53; South Asian Muslim, 262–64; transnational, 42–44; WAF and, 11, 64–67, 105, 171. *See also* Islamic feminism; secular feminism

"Feminist Movement and the Muslim Woman, The" (Jameelah), 125–26

feminists: feudalism and, 198; label of, 51–52; postcolonial, 191–92
feudalism, 197–99
Firangi Mahal, 33, 260
folk Islam, 33
Foucault, Michel, 29, 54, 71, 73, 139–41, 215n7
freedom, historical understandings of, 219
fundamentalism, 7–11, 67, 113–14, 167

GAD. See Gender and Development
Gandhi, Mahatma, 257–58, 260–62
gender: development and, 170–207; discourse of, 178, 186–95; equality, 200, 205, 246; gap, 193; importance of, 196; in modern Islamic nation, 141–43; in postcolonial state, 164–69; reformulations of, 227–29; research sites, 23–26
Gender and Development (GAD), 174, 174n3, 189–93, 206
gendered assemblies, 15–18
gendered Islamism, 256
gendered modern, 138–39, 141
gendered politics, 153, 184
Ghamdi, Jawed Ahmed, 233–34
global modernization theory, 8
"God's Kingdom on Earth" (Begum), 119
governmentality, 71–73, 140, 214–15
government discipline, for moral citizens, 209–10, 237
Government of India Act of 1919, 142
Grewal, Inderpal, 139
gunahgaar (sinful) subjectivity, 4n5

Hadia: on Jamaat-e-Islami women's roles, 23; public-religious spaces and, 88, 91–94, 99, 106, 108–9; on women's rights, 194
Hadith, 50–51, 129, 210
Hanafi Islam, 211, 211n4, 233, 235–37
Hanbali theology, 230–32
harem narratives, 1n3
hari (landless peasant), 197–98
Hasba Act. See Hisba Act
Hashmi, Farhat, 58–59, 63–64
Hassan, Riffat, 50–51
hijab, 1, 57, 155–57
Hinduism: Islam and, 3, 27, 34, 40, 78–79, 83, 92, 121, 142–43, 212, 222–23, 227, 248, 257–63; Khilafat Movement and, 257–61; nationalism and, 248
Hisba Act, 214, 237–43
HRCP (Human Rights Commission of Pakistan), 108, 171, 238–39
Al Huda school, 58–60, 62–64
Hudood Ordinance: challenges to, 11, 64, 107, 184; negative impact of, 64–65, 64n4, 67, 107–8, 171, 181, 201; of Zia ul Haq, 65, 181
humanist subjectivity, 10
humanist traditions, of Islam, 212
human rights, 67–68, 175–76
Human Rights Commission of Pakistan (HRCP), 108, 171, 238–39
Hussein, Munawwar, 255

Ibn Arabi, Muhiuddin, 5n6
Ibn Hanbal, 230–31
Ibn Taymiyya, 6n7, 231–32
identity: in India, 222; Islamic, 7–8, 215–19, 223–24; knowledge/power related to, 139–41; Maududi and, 223–24; of Pakistan, 79, 246–47; in theory/politics/Islamic identities, 215–19
Iffat magazine, 117–18

Ijtama-e-Arkan, 21
Ijtama-e-Karkunaan, 21
imagined communities, 73
Imamate, 208n1
imperialism, Maududi on, 144–45
India: Azad and, 220n9; communal separatism in, 142; cow protection in, 261–62; Gandhi and, 257–58, 260–62; Khilafat Movement in, 257–63; middle class in, 143; nationalism in, 142, 248, 259; partition of, 7n8, 27, 79, 99; reformers in, 224–28, 233; social identities in, 222
interlocutors, participants as, 28–32, 38
internal conversion, 159, 159n14
International Institute of Islamic Education for Women, 58
International Women's Day, 171, 185n9
interviewees, participants as, 28–32, 38
intolerance, 255
invitation (*dawat*), 90, 94, 116, 119–20, 148
Iqbal, Allama, 36–37, 36n28, 70, 88
Islahi, Mohammed Yusuf, 127–32
Islam: Barelvi, 2–3, 3n4; classical, 248; communism and, 146; defending, 221; dichotomies in, 10, 33; difference and, 224–27; as discursive tradition, 5, 247; in escape-from-Islam narratives, 1–2, 1n3; folk, 33; Hanafi, 211, 211n4, 233, 235–37; Hinduism and, 3, 27, 34, 40, 78–79, 83, 92, 121, 142–43, 212, 222–23, 227, 248, 257–63; historical formation of, 6; humanist traditions of, 212; identity in, 7–8, 215–19, 223–24; Khilafat Movement and, 257–63; in modern Islamic nation, 141–43; modernity and, 34–35, 141–45, 162, 227–28; mysticism in, 2, 4–6, 36n28, 80–81,

225, 227; negotiations of faith in, 33–39; in Pakistan, 3, 57–64, 70–72, 76–82; Pietist, 160; political, 13, 41, 56, 218; in postcolonial state, 164–69; poststructuralism and, 46; power of, 72; production and, 192–93; reform, 224–28, 232–33; scriptural, 33; secularism and, 10; Shia, 208–9, 208n1, 230; social system of, 83–84, 187; Sufi, 2, 6, 224, 227, 236, 254; in theory/politics/Islamic identities, 215–19. *See also* Jamaat-e-Islami; South Asian Islam; Sunni Islam
Islam and the Muslim Woman Today (Jameelah), 124
Islamic feminism: defined, 48–50; newly emerging subjects in, 46–69; in Pakistan, 57–64; Quran and, 50–51, 55; secular feminism and, 48–53; beyond tolerance, 53–56; *Zanan* and, 49
Islamism: common features of, 248; communality and, 221–24; community and, 81, 221–24; contemporary expression of, 10; contextually specific accounts of, 214; elections and, 251–56; feminism and, 11–12; gendered, 256; Hanbali theology and, 230; hegemonic impulse of, 255; inegalitarian impulses of, 217; of Jamaat-e-Islami, 212, 250, 256; localized, engendering, 246–49; middle class and, 84–85, 150; modernism and, 34, 162; moral citizens and, 212, 217–18, 246–49; negative representations of, 32; neoliberalism and, 148–50; religious construction of, 71; religious nationalism as, 24; secular-progressive opposed to, 79; self/community notions and, 221–24; on streets, 251–56; women's movements and, 113, 113n1

Islamist, 6–7, 167, 226

Islamization, 103, 107, 139, 169;
feminism and, 64–68; of gender
and development, 204–7; gendered
discourse of citizenship and, 145–48;
high era of, 96; insufficient, 171; new
modernity and, 145–48; of transnationality, 68–69, 150, 150n7, 175; Zia
ul Haq and, 11, 145–47, 146n5, 152,
175, 177–78, 181

JAC (Joint Action Committee for
People's Rights), 171, 237–38

jahez (trousseau), 128

Jamaat-e-Islami (Party of Islam):
Bangladesh and, 92–93, 93n10;
Blasphemy Laws supported by,
172n1; changes in, 17–18, 114–15,
150–52; continuities in, 114–15;
distinctiveness of, 20; elections and,
16–17; Hisba Act and, 214, 237–43;
historical formation of Islam and,
6; Al Huda compared with, 62–64;
ideology of, 3; Islamism of, 212,
250, 256; Lahore as home of, 26; as
male-led movement, 113; Maududi
and, 3, 11, 34–35, 39–41, 55, 62,
91–92, 113, 142–43, 159–60, 168, 195,
202–3, 211, 214, 223, 245; membership, 4; misperceptions about, 96–97;
organizational structure of, 20–21;
origin of, 3–4, 92; political project
of, 81–82, 84–85; popular attitude
toward, 254; in professional classes,
85; recruitment structure of, 150;
Reza Nasr and, 39–42, 142–44,
152, 159, 223–26; vanguard of new
modernity and, 39–42; violence and,

234–35; voting in, 22; Zia ul Haq
and, 146–47

Jamaat-e-Islami women: achievements
of, 105–6; agency of, 54–56, 68;
education of, 152–54, 166; electoral
politics and, 85–88, 151–52; engagement with, 12–14; feminism and, 2,
43, 46–49, 52–64, 67–69, 125–26, 133,
137, 185–87, 205–6, 248, 251; gender,
development, and, 170–207; gendered
selves and, 248–64; Hisba Act and,
237–43; human rights and, 67–68;
making of, 43–44; moral citizens
and, 208–49; negotiations of faith
and, 33–39; as outsiders, 75; politics
of morality and, 113–35; positioning
of, 53, 114, 151, 177; postcolonial citizenship of, 74; public-political and,
78, 82–85; public-religious spaces
and, 44, 70–112; purdah and, 82–85;
role of, 23, 85–87; self-construction
of, 137, 140, 145, 214, 251; September
11, 2001, and, 74–75, 189; skepticism
of, 30–31; subjectivity of, 56, 140;
urban development project of, 44; as
vanguard of new modernity, 39–42,
45, 136–69; veiling and, 60–61,
147, 156–58; woman question and,
170–207; women's groups of, 184–85;
Women's Wing of, 6, 12, 19–23, 60,
86–87, 97, 101, 103, 105, 116–17, 121,
131–32, 184–86

Jamaatia, 254

Jamaat-ud-Dawah, 59–61

Jameelah, Maryam: conversion of, 122–
23; "The Feminist Movement and
the Muslim Woman," 125–26; *Islam
and the Muslim Woman Today*, 124;
Maududi and, 121–24, 121n3, 126,

148, 163; in Pakistan, 121–25; politics
of morality and, 121–27, 133–34;
"Why I Embraced Islam," 123
Jamiat-e-Talibat, 153
Jamiat-e-Tulba, 152–53
jihad, 97, 146
Jinnah, Mohammed Ali, 72, 78–79,
141–42, 257
Joint Action Committee for People's
Rights (JAC), 171, 237–38

kafalat (security, responsibility), 187, 193
kafir (unbeliever), 172n1
Kaplan, Caren, 139
Karachi: Ayesha in, 197–99; City Council, 94–95, 98–99, 104, 127, 158; class
in, 24–27; Delhi-Punjabi Saudagran
in, 127–28; ethnicity in, 24–26; *kutchi
abadi* of, 127–30; population, 25n22;
tensions in, 100; University, 96, 153;
urban development project in, 44
Khan, Mohammed Yusuf, 122
Khilafat Movement, 257–63
Khyber Pakhtunkhwa (KPK) Province,
214, 237–38
knowledge: of the heart, 5n6; identity
related to, 139–41; types of, 218
KPK Province (Khyber Pakhtunkhwa
Province), 214, 237–38
kutchi abadi (shantytowns), 127–30

Lahore: ethnicity and class in, 24–26; as
Jamaat-e-Islami home, 26; population, 25n22; Sadia in, 199–204
landless peasant (*hari*), 197–98
Larkana, 197–98
law of *Diyat* and *Qisas*, 201

liberalism, 54, 217, 221
Lip Service Muslims, 84
localized Islamism, engendering,
246–49
lower middle class, 38, 58, 64, 150, 156,
188

Mack, Phyllis, 54
Mahmood, Saba, 6n7, 54–56
Majida, 127–29, 131
Majlis-e-Shura (consultative council),
21–22, 147
Mansurah, 26
Manto, Sadat Hasan, 117
Maria, 94–99, 106, 158
Maududi, Maulana Abul Ala: *amr bil
maruf* and, 232–35; Bangladesh and,
93n10; Begum and, 116, 132; community construction and, 248; din
and, 159n14, 160, 160n16, 195, 226;
on imperialism, 144–45; internal
conversion and, 159, 159n14; Islamic
social system and, 187; Jamaat-e-
Islami and, 3, 11, 34–35, 39–41, 55,
62, 91–92, 113, 142–43, 159–60,
168, 195, 202–3, 211, 214, 223, 245;
Jameelah and, 121–24, 121n3, 126,
148, 163; modernity and, 233; Muslim identity and, 223–24; mysticism
and, 227; public-religious spaces and,
81–85, 89–92, 131; on purdah, 81–84,
113, 131–32; on religious authority, 209; Reza Nasr on, 159, 223–24,
226; Samina and, 89–90; secularism
translated by, 138; *Tafhim ul Quran*,
55, 55n2, 90, 127, 129, 232; *Tarjuman-
ul-Quran* and, 116
medium, 1, 1n2, 197

Mian Tufail Mohammed, 120–21
middle class, 68, 147; Arabization of,
154–57; Begum and, 118; development and, 173, 176, 184, 186, 188,
197, 200, 203, 205–7; education of,
152; Islamism and, 84–85, 150; lower,
38, 58, 64, 150, 156, 188; modernity
and, 143–44; nationalism and, 85;
politics of piety and, 63; research
sites and, 23–24; subjectivity, in
India, 143; upper, 38–39, 58, 64, 66;
veiling and, 58
military: frustration with, 255; politics
and, 17n15, 253; rule, 180
Minault, Gail, 259–60
Ministry of Women Development,
Social Welfare, and Special Education (MOWD), 181
MMA. See Muttahida Majlis-e-Amal
modern: community construction and,
248; defined, 137–38; gendered,
138–39, 141; Islamic nation, gender
in, 141–43; mysticism undermined
by, 225; state power, 71; women,
construct of, 146
modernity: class-specific signifiers of,
166–67; critiques of, 138; defined,
137–38; democracy and, 75–76;
fundamentalism and, 7–8; gendered
subject's location in, 2; Islam and,
34–35, 141–45, 162, 227–28; Maududi
and, 233; middle class and, 143–44;
new engagement with, 44; politics
of, 162; religion and, 47–48, 223–24;
rupture caused by, 247–48; secularism and, 13, 72, 79, 79n4, 168–69,
217–18; time-space of, 73; trajectories
of, 248–64
modernization: catalysts of, 13; elitism and, 8n9, 12n12; in global

modernization theory, 8; secularizing
elite and, 14n14, 79, 79n4, 166–67;
woman question and, 173–74; women
in politics and, 15
modesty, 14
mohajirs, 24–25, 99, 158, 197
Mohanty, Chandra, 30, 47
Mohtasib, 239–41, 243
moral citizens: amr bil maruf and,
208–9, 211–12, 214, 229–38, 243;
Ayesha and, 239–42, 244–46; contestations of secular and religious
and, 239–46; creation of, 208–49;
government discipline for, 209–10,
237; Islamic South Asia and, 212–15;
Islamism and, 212, 217–18, 246–49;
Jamaat-e-Islami women and,
208–49; Quran and, 208–11, 232–34;
Reza Nasr and, 225–26; self/commu-
nity notions and, 219–29; Shahida
and, 239–43, 245; Sunni Islam and,
208–9, 208n1, 211–12, 211n4; theory/
politics/Islamic identities and,
215–19
morality, politics of: Adab-e-Zindagi
and, 127–32; Ayesha and, 133–35;
Begum and, 115–21, 132–34;
Jamaat-e-Islami women and, 113–35;
Jameelah and, 121–27, 133–34;
Majida and, 127–29, 131; overview
of, 113–14; publicity and, 134–35;
Tayyeba and, 129–31
MOWD (Ministry of Women Development, Social Welfare, and Special
Education), 181
MQM (Muttahida Qaumi Movement),
19, 26, 99
muhajirs, 24–25, 99, 158, 197
Muhammad the Prophet, 119, 124,
208n1, 209; message of, 90–91; as

perfect human being, 228; Usman
and, 241n20
Mumtaz, Khawar, 57–58, 66
Musharraf, Pervez, 23, 151, 180, 185n9;
Hisba Bill and, 238; public-religious
spaces and, 86, 89; U.S. and, 17, 28
Muslim Family Laws Ordinance of 1961,
107–8
Muslim League, 92, 141, 198, 246
Muslims: in Bengal, 72; Lip Service, 84;
secular, 217, 263; self/community
notions among, 219–29; South Asian
Muslim feminism and, 262–64;
subjectivity of, 5, 6n7, 47, 84–85, 210,
218, 225, 228, 264
Muslim woman question. See woman
question
Muttahida Majlis-e-Amal (MMA),
16–17, 104, 168, 202, 237–38, 252
Muttahida Qaumi Movement (MQM),
19, 26, 99
mysticism: dissent and, 80–81; in
Islam, 2, 4–6, 36n28, 80–81, 225,
227; Maududi and, 227; modernism
undermining, 225

Najmabadi, Afsaneh, 48–49, 53
nationalism, 11, 86, 99, 114, 246; Indian,
142, 248, 259; middle class and, 85;
religious, as Islamism, 24; secular
and, 78, 143–44
Nazima, 21–23
Nazimabad, 98, 158
neoliberalism: adoption of, 251; in
development, 179–80; Islamism and,
148–50
new modernity: Arabization of middle
classes and, 154–57; Ayesha and,
163; changes in Jamaat-e-Islami and,

150–52; cultural intersections of
local, national, and global in, 152–54;
engendering, 144–45; Farida and,
163–64; Fatima and, 158–59, 161–62;
gender in modern Islamic nation
and, 141–43; Islamism, neoliberalism, and, 148–50; Islamization and,
145–48; Jamaat-e-Islami women
as vanguard of, 39–42, 45, 136–69;
Maria and, 158
New Year's Eve, 242, 242n22, 254
NGO. See nongovernment organization
NGO Resource Center (NGORC),
179–83, 179n5
Nisar, Atiya, 170, 198–99
nongovernment organization (NGO),
9, 52–53, 96, 105, 148; NGORC and,
179–83, 179n5; objections to, 172;
policymaking by, 183; sector, development of, 177–86; transnational
relations and, 181–82
nontransmitted knowledge, 5n6
North-West Frontier Province (NWFP),
214, 237–38

Objectives Resolution, 102
Oriental Occidentals, 84
Ottoman Empire, 257

Pakistan: Arab Gulf and, 101–2, 102n12,
146, 154–57; bodily issues in, 131;
civil society in, 174–75, 183; civil war,
92–93; class engendered in, 27–28;
creation of, 7n8, 141–42; development
policy of, 179–83, 251; feminism and
fundamentalism entangled in, 7–11,
67, 113–14, 167; HRCP in, 108, 171,
238–39; Islamic feminism in, 57–64;

Pakistan (*cont.*)

Islam in, 3, 57–64, 70–72, 76–82; Jameelah in, 121–25; national identity of, 79, 246–47; partition and, 7n8, 27, 79, 99; political changes in, 251; research sites in, 23–26; rights agreements signed by, 172; secular feminism in, 57–64, 67; secularism in, 69, 71–72, 77–80, 79n4, 176, 210–11, 218, 220–22, 252, 264; social integration in, 148–50; woman question in, 151, 170–207; women's movement in, 11–12, 64, 66–67, 113, 184. *See also* Jamaat-e-Islami; Karachi; Lahore

Pakistan Muslim League, 20, 26

Pakistan People's Party (PPP), 19–20, 26, 93, 198, 252, 252n1

participants, 28–32

partition, 7n8, 27, 79, 99

Party of Islam. *See* Jamaat-e-Islami

Pathans, 25

personal sphere, 210, 210n3

Pietist Islam, 160

piety: historical understandings of, 219, 251; movement, 55; politics of, 62–63

pious subjectivity, 6n7

poetic dissent, 81

political agency, 47

"Political and Legislative Participation of Women in Pakistan: Issues and Perspectives" (UNDP), 15–16, 19–20

political Islam, 13, 41, 56, 218

political organizing, 136

political society, 72, 75–76

politico-religious movements, 139–40

politics: changes in, 251; communal, 142; cultural, 136–69, 256–60; electoral, 85–88, 151–52; emotional factors in, 254; gendering of, 153, 184; of governed, 73; military and, 17n15, 253; of

modernity, 162; of piety, 62–63; progressive, 256; in public-political, 78, 82–85; religion as component of, 70, 89–92, 112, 253, 258–59; religious-cultural, of community, 256–60; as religious vocation, 88–103, 110–11; secularism and, 71; in theory/politics/Islamic identities, 215–19; Urdu as language of, 88; women in, 8–9, 15–23, 70, 85–103, 110–12. *See also* morality, politics of

postcolonial citizenship, 74

postcolonial feminists, 191–92

postcolonialism, 46

poststructuralist feminism, 46, 54

power: identity related to, 139–41; of modern state, 71; of religion, 72

PPP. *See* Pakistan People's Party

private sphere, 210, 210n3, 236, 241–44

production, Islamic framework of, 192–93

professional classes, Jamaat-e-Islami in, 85

progressive politics, 256

Progressive Writers Movement, 117, 117n2

publicity, 134–35

public-political space, 78, 82–85

public-religious spaces: electoral politics and, 85–88; Farida and, 94–99, 105; Fatima and, 103–4; Hadia and, 88, 91–94, 99, 106, 108–9; Jamaat-e-Islami women and, 44, 70–112; Maria and, 94–99, 106; Maudedi and, 81–85, 89–92, 131; Musharraf and, 86, 89; politics as religious vocation in, 88–103, 110–11; purdah and, 82–85; Razia and, 100–101, 103; Samina and, 70, 74–75, 87–91, 94, 103–6, 112; summer time and,

109–10; women's sense of solidarity and, 103–9

public sphere, 210, 210n3, 241–44

purdah: Amin against, 125; Arab Gulf and, 156–57, 157n12; burqa and, 1–2, 1n1; as choice, 202; defined, 1n1, 83; descriptions and, 158n13; Farida and, 97; Jamaat-e-Islami women and, 82–85; Maududi on, 81–84, 113, 131–32; narratives, 1–2; in parliament, 8; public-religious spaces and, 82–85; Quran and, 82–83

Purdah and the Status of Women in Islam (Maududi), 81–84, 132

Al Qaeda, 74–75

Quran: community and, 208; gender equality in, 200; Islamic feminism and, 50–51, 55; moral citizens and, 208–11, 232–34; purdah and, 82–83; study of, 158; Tayyeba and, 130–31; veiling and, 82–83, 202; Waliullah and, 225

Qutb, Sayyed, 187, 232

Rahman, Tariq, 32

rape (*zina*), 64, 107–8

Razack, Sherene, 138

Razia, 100–101, 103

reflexivity, 29

Rehman, I. A., 239–40, 242, 244

religion: *amr bil maruf* as doctrine of, 229–37; and agency, 14, 53–54, 56, 210, 214; authority, 208–9, 208n2; compulsion in, 211, 236, 243; contestations of, 239–46; democracy and, 102–3; elite, 177; Islamism constructed in, 71; meaning of, 136, 138; modernity and, 47–48, 223–24; and

nationalism, 24; as political component, 70, 89–92, 112, 253, 258–59; power of, 72; secularism defining, 71–72; symbols, 253; vocation, politics as, 88–103, 110–11; Women's Commission and, 195–204

religious-cultural politics, 256–60

research: participants, 28–32; reflexivity in, 29; sites, 23–26

responsibility: domestic, 97–98, 111–12, 124–26, 200–201; *kafalat*, 187, 193

Reza Nasr, Seyyed Vali: Jamaat-e-Islami and, 39–42, 142–44, 152, 159, 223–26; on Maududi, 159, 223–24, 226; moral citizens and, 225–26

Sadia, 199–204

Said, Edward, 47

Said Khan, Nighat, 177–78, 185n9

salariat, 27

Samina: development and, 185–86; Maududi and, 89–90; public-religious spaces and, 70, 74–75, 87–91, 94, 103–6, 112; Al Qaeda and, 74–75; on tolerance, 167–68

Saudi Arabia: Arabization influenced by, 155–57; Ibn Taymiyya and, 231–32; Razia and, 100–101; Tayyeba and, 130–31; violence against women in, 194; Wahabism in, 3n4, 4

schools: *baithak*, 129–30; Al Huda, 58–60, 62–64; Karachi University, 96, 153; medium of, 1, 1n2; of Sunni Islam jurisprudence, 211, 211n4

scriptural Islam, 33

secular feminism: Islamic feminism and, 48–53; Jamaat-e-Islami women and, 2, 43, 205–6, 248; in Pakistan, 57–64, 67 secularism: and agency, 5, 214; and citizenship, 79; construction of, 71; contestations of, 239–46; defined, 14n14; democracy and, 11; and elites, 14n14, 79, 79n4, 166–67; Islam and, 10; limitations of, 14, 264; Maududi translating, 138; modernity and, 13, 72, 79, 79n4, 168–69, 217–18; and Muslims, 217, 263; nationalism and, 78, 143–44; negative connotations of, 139, 139n3; in Pakistan, 69, 71–72, 77–80, 79n4, 176, 210–11, 218, 220–22, 252, 264; politics and, 71; problematized, 8n10; religion defined by, 71–72; undermined, 9, 11

secular progressives, 79, 165

security (*kafalat*), 187

self/community notions: in construction of Islam and difference, 224–27; in gender and family reformulations, 227–29; Islamism, communality, and, 221–24; moral citizens and, 219–29; among South Asian Muslims, 219–29

September 11, 2001, 74–75, 189

Shaheed, Farida, 57–58, 66

Shahida, 189, 239–43, 245

shantytowns (*kutchi abadi*), 127–30

Shariah, 50–51, 126, 131, 195, 237–38

Sharif, Nawaz, 26, 238

Sharif, Shahbaz, 26

Shia Islam, 208–9, 208n1, 230

Sindh, 197–98

sinful (*gunahgaar*) subjectivity, 4n5

sisterhood, 74–75, 105–9

Smith, W. C., 40

social integration, 148–50

social organizing, 136

social system, Islamic, 83–84, 187

social workers, 182

sociological inquiry, 42–44

solidarity, women's sense of, 103–9

South Asian Islam: characteristics of, 220; classical, 248; feminism in, 262–64; moral citizens and, 212–15; religious-cultural politics of community and, 256–60; self/community notions in, 219–29; tradition in, 80, 251; understanding of, 10; women's movements and, 113

Spivak, Gayatri C., 30, 77, 138, 228

state power, 71

subaltern, 76, 77n3

subject formation, 139, 221

subjectivity: *gunahgaar*, 4n5; humanist, 10; of Jamaat-e-Islami women, 56, 140; middle-class, in India, 143; Muslim, 5, 6n7, 47, 84–85, 210, 218, 225, 228, 264; pious, 6n7

Sufi Islam, 2, 6, 224, 227, 236, 254

summer time, 109–10

Sunni Islam, 192, 230–31; described, 2–3; moral citizens and, 208–9, 208n1, 211–12, 211n4; reformers, 224; schools of jurisprudence, 211, 211n4

Suraiya, 153

Tablighi Jamaat, 60, 62, 86, 150

Tafhim ul Quran (Maududi), 55, 55n2, 90, 127, 129, 232

Tagore, Rabindranath, 257

Taliban, 102, 244, 255

Tarjuman-ul-Quran, 116, 189

Taseer, Salman, 138n3, 172n1, 255

Tayyeba, 129–31

Tejani, Shabnum, 263

temporary schools (*baithak*), 129–30

theory/politics/Islamic identities, 215–19

tolerance, 53–56, 167–68, 255

tradition, 80, 157, 218–19, 251

training, 161
transnationality: of feminist inquiry, 42–44; Islamizing, 68–69, 150, 150n7, 175; NGOs and, 181–82; of women's rights as human rights framework, 175–76
transnational public sphere, 44–45
trousseau (*jahez*), 128
Trust for Voluntary Organizations, 181–82
2002 elections, 15–17, 252
2008 elections, 252, 252n1

ulema, 34, 82, 208, 233, 247, 258
unbeliever (*kafir*), 172n1
UNDP. *See* United Nations Development Programme
United Nations Decade for Women, 180, 180n7
United Nations Development Programme (UNDP), 15–16, 19–20, 186
United States (US), 17, 28, 251–52, 254–55
upper middle class, 38–39, 58, 64, 66
urban development project, 44
urbanization, research sites and, 23–26
Urdu, 25, 128, 166; class and, 31–32; as language of politics, 88; medium, 1, 1n2, 197; purdah narratives in, 2
US *See* United States
Usman, Hazrath, 241, 241n20

Valentine's Day, 242, 242n22, 254
veiling: appeal of, 57–58, 156–57; as choice, 202; class and, 58; contemporary emergence of, 9n11; emancipation and, 8; hijab, 1, 57, 155–57; Jamaat-e-Islami women and, 60–61,

147, 156–58; middle class and, 58; mobility and, 14; Quran and, 82–83, 202; reasons for, 2. *See also* burqa
violence: Jamaat-e-Islami and, 234–35; against women, 188–89, 193–94, 201; Women's Commission and, 193
virtue cultivation, 249
voting, in Jamaat-e-Islami, 22

WAF. *See* Women's Action Forum
Wahabism, 3–4, 3n4, 6, 61, 227, 232
Waliullah, Shah, 224–25
war on terror, 17, 28, 189, 251–52, 254
Westernized elite classes, 31–32
Western progressives, 177
"Why I Embraced Islam" (Jameelah), 123
WID. *See* Women in Development
woman question: Jamaat-e-Islami women and, 170–207; modernization and, 173–74; in Pakistan, 151, 170–207
women: Arab Gulf, 101–2, 156–57; in assemblies, 15–18; autonomy of, 245–46; CEDAW and, 15, 172, 245; disunity of, 118–19; domestic responsibilities of, 97–98, 111–12, 124–26, 200–201; economy and, 198–99; emancipation of, 8, 23–24; employment of, 204, 206; International Women's Day and, 171, 185n9; Jamaat-e-Islami groups of, 184–85; modern, construct of, 146; perils of representing, 28; in politics, 8–9, 15–23, 70, 85–103, 110–12; religious, agency of, 53–54; rights of, 175–76, 194; shifting space of, 177–86; solidarity of, 103–9; status of, 186–87; as symbol, 86; UN Decade for, 180,

women (*cont.*)
180n7; violence against, 188–89,
193–94, 201. *See also* Jamaat-e-Islami
women
Women in Development (WID): critique
of, 189–93; development and, 174,
174n3, 180–81, 185, 189–93, 206
Women's Action Forum (WAF), 11,
64–67, 105, 171
Women's Commission, 239, 241n21;
Ayesha and, 163, 197–99, 204;
development and, 193–204; establishment of, 196; religion and, 195–204;
Sadia and, 199–204; violence against
women and, 193
women's movement: emergence of, 184;
Islamism and, 113, 113n1; in Pakistan, 11–12, 64, 66–67, 113, 184; sisterhood distinguished from, 74–75;
South Asian Islam and, 113

women's rights as human rights, 175–76
women's wings: of Jamaat-e-Islami, 6,
12, 19–23, 60, 86–87, 97, 101, 103, 105,
116–17, 121, 131–32, 184–86; of political parties, 18–23
writing, 116–18

Zainab, 153
Zaman, Muhammed Qasim, 247–48
Zanan, 49, 51, 55
Zia, Shehla, 15
Zia ul Haq, General Mohammed, 4, 89,
180; Hudood Ordinance of, 64–65,
181; Islamization and, 11, 145–47,
146n5, 152, 175, 177–78, 181; Jamaat-
e-Islami and, 146–47; partyless elections of, 182
zina (adultery and rape), 64, 107–8
Zubair, Umm, 117, 119–20